Before Porn Was Legal

Before Porn Was Legal

THE EROTICA EMPIRE OF BEATE UHSE

Elizabeth Heineman

University of Chicago Press

Chicago and London

Elizabeth Heineman is associate professor in the Department of History and in the Department of Gender, Women's, and Sexuality Studies at the University of Iowa. She is the author of *What Difference Does a Husband Make? Women and Marital Status in Nazi and Postwar Germany* and editor of *Sexual Violence in Conflict Zones: From the Ancient World to the Era of Human Rights.*

The University of Chicago Press, Chicago 60637
The University of Chicago Press, Ltd., London
© 2011 by The University of Chicago
All rights reserved. Published 2011
Printed in the United States of America

20 19 18 17 16 15 14 13 12 11   1 2 3 4 5

ISBN-13: 978-0-226-32521-7 (cloth)
ISBN-10: 0-226-32521-0 (cloth)

Much of chapter 3 appeared as "The Economic Miracle in the Bedroom: Big Business and Sexual Consumer Culture in Reconstruction West Germany," *Journal of Modern History* 78, no. 4 (2006): 846–77. Much of chapter 4 appeared as "'The History of Morals in the Federal Republic': Advertising, PR, and the Beate Uhse Myth," in *Selling Modernity: Advertising in Twentieth-Century Germany*, ed. Pamela E. Swett, S. Jonathan Wiesen, and Jonathan R. Zatlin (Durham, NC: Duke University Press, 2007), 202–29.

Library of Congress Cataloging-in-Publication Data

Heineman, Elizabeth D., 1962–
  Before porn was legal : the erotica empire of Beate Uhse / Elizabeth Heineman.
    p. cm.
  Includes bibliographical references and index.
  ISBN-13: 978-0-226-32521-7 (cloth : alk. paper)
  ISBN-10: 0-226-32521-0 (cloth : alk. paper) 1. Uhse, Beate, 1919–2001. 2. Beate Uhse A.G. 3. Businesswomen—Germany—Biography. 4. Sex-oriented businesses—Germany—History—20th century. 5. Women-owned business enterprises—Germany—History—20th century. 6. Pornography—Germany—History—20th century. I. Title.
  HQ18.32.U47H45 2011
  306.77092—dc22
  [B]
                         2010030713

♾ The paper used in this publication meets the minimum requirements of the American National Standard for Information Sciences—Permanence of Paper for Printed Library Materials, ANSI Z39.48-1992.

Contents

Acknowledgments

I accumulated many debts in the writing of this book. Let me first acknowledge the financial ones. The following agencies helped to fund my research: the National Endowment for the Humanities (FA-36988-02), the German Academic Exchange Service, the Howard Foundation, the State of Iowa Arts and Humanities Initiative, Faculty Scholar and Dean's Scholar awards from the University of Iowa, the College of Liberal Arts and Sciences at the University of Iowa, and International Programs at the University of Iowa.

Many archivists, librarians, and scholars helped me to work through vast quantities of paper in state, church, university, and private archives and libraries. I would like to thank Anja Adelt, Ursula Brendt, Gerhard Fürmetz, Erwin J. Haeberle, Friederike Johann, Susanne Krejsa, Nadine Müller, Volkmar Sigusch, and Rainer Stahlschmidt. I had the extraordinary fortune to gain access to internal records of many erotica firms as well as the industry's interest group during the course of this research. For their willingness to share industry papers with me, I thank Jörg Dagies, Irmgard Hill, Uwe Kaltenberg, Gesa Münzmaier, Claus Richter, Dirk Rotermund, Ulrich Rotermund, Gerhard Schmitz, Jörg Schröder, Lore Schumacher, and Jürgen Weber. Many individuals shared private papers or erotica libraries with me but preferred to remain anonymous. I thank them for their generosity.

One side product of this project was the creation of the Beate-Uhse Archive and a library of sexual science at the Forschungsstelle für Zeitgeschichte in Hamburg (FZH). Irmgard Hill and Ulrich Rotermund generously donated papers from Beate Uhse (the firm) and Beate Rotermund (the person), and Jörg Dagies contributed the valuable sexological library of the Walter Schäfer Gruppe. The director and deputy director of the FZH, Axel Schildt and Dorothee Wierling, committed resources to the processing and storage of the new collections. Librarian Karl-Otto Schütt processed the new library acquisitions, and Linde Apel arranged for the transcription and storage of interviews. My deepest thanks go to archivist Angelika Voß-Louis, who processed and cataloged the voluminous collection from Beate Uhse.

Justin Bartsch and Christine Brandenburger provided research assistance at early stages of this project. Javier Samper Vendrell helped to edit a portion of the manuscript, and Amy Braun meticulously examined the galley proofs. I am especially grateful to Matthew Conn for his careful reading of the final manuscript and his work on the index.

Many scholars offered encouragement, provided feedback on drafts, shared tips and sources, or organized conference panels or lectures that allowed me to share preliminary findings. These included Doris Bergen, Frank Biess, Belinda Davis, Glenn Ehrstine, Jennifer Evans, Peter Fritzsche, Michael Geyer, Dagmar Herzog, Paul Jaskot, Ralph Jessen, Paul Lerner, Josie McClellan, Sonja Michel, Maria Mitchell, Robert Moeller, Thomas Pegelow, Sven Reichardt, Bernhard Rieger, Julia Roos, Johanna Schoen, Detlef Siegfried, Julia Sneeringer, Pamela Swett, Annette Timm, Richard Wetzell, Dorothee Wierling, Jonathan Wiesen, and Jonathan Zatlin. I am sure there are others who deserve similar thanks; with a project of such duration, it becomes difficult to keep track. I thank anyone whom I inadvertently omitted from this list.

Despite the passage of time since graduate school, I continue to discover ever more ways I profited from the wisdom and engagement of my mentors, Konrad Jarausch, Gerhard Weinberg, and Judith Bennett. In more recent years, I have benefited from my humane and intellectually lively colleagues in the Department of History and the Department of Gender, Women's, and Sexuality Studies at the University of Iowa. I thank Douglas Mitchell of the University of Chicago Press for his commitment to this project and Kathy Gohl and Carol Saller for their careful editorial work.

In a household in which the personal, the political, the professional, and the scholarly mingle in impenetrable ways, first Johanna Schoen and then Glenn Ehrstine were partners in every sense of the word, and I thank them both. Members of the extended Schoen family welcomed me into their homes and made my research trips personally as well as intellectually rewarding, and my own family of origin politely declined to remind me just how long I've been working on this book. When I informed my son Josh that this book would appear in print in the imminent future, he declared that he couldn't remember a time when Beate Uhse had not been part of his life. It must be a strange thing to grow up as the child of sexuality studies scholars. I only hope he has learned as much from me as I have from him.

Prelude   *The Beate Uhse Myth*

To begin, a brief biography of the most famous German to remain unknown to Americans: Beate Uhse.

Beate Köstlin was born in 1921 to a lawyer and one of Germany's first female physicians. After the birth of the second child, the family decamped from Berlin to an East Prussian estate. Here Beate grew up as an athletic, outdoorsy child. The Köstlins provided their children with a progressive upbringing, including encouragement for daughters as well as sons to chart their own life courses, an open education in sexual matters, and, in Beate's case, a stint at a Waldorf boarding school. After a year as an au pair in England, Beate, long fascinated by flight, decided to get her pilot's license. She was the only young woman in her class of sixty.

When the Second World War began, all licensed pilots were inducted into the Luftwaffe. Women did not fly combat missions, but Beate flew test flights and ferried planes to the front. She married her flight instructor, Klaus Uhse, had a child, and became a widow when Klaus died in a flight accident. With the Soviets surrounding Berlin in April 1945, Uhse commandeered a rickety plane, loaded the baby and nanny on board, and flew west. She crash-landed in the sandy dunes of Schleswig-Holstein, Germany's northernmost province.

After a stint in a prisoner-of-war camp (she was released because of the baby), she turned, like so many others, to the black market to survive. Here she specialized, initially, in children's toys. Soon, however, she learned of an even greater need: contraception. In those desperate years right after the war, pregnancy could be a catastrophe. Beate penned a brochure explaining the rhythm method. Grateful customers snapped up the brochure and asked for other items, like condoms and books on sexuality. Banned, as all Germans were, from flying, Beate Uhse had found her second calling.

Piece by piece, Uhse built the world's largest erotica empire. In the 1950s, she struggled against a hostile legal environment to build a substantial mail-order business and, in the process, educated a profoundly ignorant population about sex. In the 1960s, Uhse opened the world's first aboveground bricks-and-mortar erotica shops and became a highly visible spokesperson for sexual enlightenment. With the legalization of pornography in 1975 she became Germany's largest pornographer. As night follows day, she became, in the 1980s, a target of the feminist antipornography movement. The morning after the Berlin Wall opened in 1989, Uhse had busses on site to distribute catalogs to enthusiastic East Germans, and her business quickly expanded eastward. In the 1990s, Uhse pioneered web-based pornography, and hers became the first erotica firm in the world to be traded publicly on the stock exchange.

Beate Uhse's life, in short, is a tour through Germany's twentieth century. In the words of her biographer, Uta van Steen, "It never fails to astonish, how closely her own life mirrors the history of her country."[1] Along the way, she had a media-worthy personal life: a second marriage to a man who brought two children into the family (they had one more together) and an acrimonious divorce from him twenty-odd years later; a long-term relationship with an African American man who was a generation her junior; the integration of her sons into her business and subsequent division of the firm in a manner perceived to reflect family tensions; and a continued athleticism and business innovation as an older woman.[2]

For Germans, the name Beate Uhse was synonymous with sex. (The public continued to think of her as Beate Uhse, the name of the firm, although after her second marriage her legal name was Beate Rotermund. This book refers to the firm as Beate Uhse and the person as Beate Rotermund.) In 1972, a survey commissioned by the company found that she enjoyed an 87 percent name recognition among West Germans.[3] By 1984, the figure had risen to an astounding 94 percent, making Rotermund by far West Germany's best-known personality.[4] Nor did East Germans require any introduction before rushing to her shops with the opening of the border. Upon her death in 2001, the tabloid *Berliner Zeitung* declared: "Her success story—it is the history of sexual morals in the Federal Republic."[5]

The subject of this book is the history of sexual morals in the Federal Republic, as revealed by that aspect of sexuality in which Beate Rotermund made her name: commerce. It is the story of Beate Uhse, its competitors, its customers, its detractors and defenders, and the state's efforts to control the industry it dominated. Although this story takes place in West Germany, it has worldwide significance: already in the early 1950s, one of Beate Uhse's West German competitors claimed, plausibly, to be the world's largest erotica firm. Rotermund died in 2001, but her firm remains the industry giant to this day. And although Americans still don't know her name, the commercialized sexual world she helped to create—including, for example, soft porn on television—is one of the biggest culture shocks that American visitors to Germany experience.

1 Introduction

Sex, Consumption, and German History

Beate Rotermund's biography is fascinating by any measure. But the story of Beate Uhse is important because it tells of social, legal, and cultural change so profound that it created a world that would have been unrecognizable just a generation earlier. And while many such momentous changes have occurred because of radical political or economic upheaval or a particularly devastating war, this one occurred in a period notable for its peace, political stability, and economic growth. Furthermore, at the center of this history was not political organization or economic change but rather sex.

The era of West Germany's economic miracle—roughly 1948 to 1973—constitutes the core of this study. In the early postwar period, Germans were too poor, and the economy too uncertain, for the erotica industry to flourish, despite the collapse of Nazi censorship. By contrast, in the early years of the Federal Republic, economic expansion created consumer demand and encouraged aggressive business practices.[1] Increasingly integrated markets enabled West German firms to dominate international trade, even as liberal legislation permitted smaller states like Denmark and Sweden to play a major role in shaping the industry. By the time of the recession of the 1970s, the consumerist landscape had been permanently altered. Furthermore, West Germany joined other Western states in liberalizing its sexual-criminal code in the late 1960s and early 1970s. Among other things, West Germany eliminated "obscene texts and images" as a legal category and substituted "pornography," which, as of January 1, 1975, was regulated rather than banned.

Changes in the sexual environment made the world of 1975 unrecognizable from the perspective of 1950, but those changes were embedded in political, economic, social, and cultural developments, both domestic and international. And they were embedded in individual life histories, like that of Beate Rotermund. This introduction outlines the ways that the "history of sexual morals in the Federal Republic" reveals these other stories.

Learning Liberalism through Sexuality

After the Second World War, a population that had deeply internalized Nazi norms transformed itself, in a single generation, into one of the most reliably liberal societies in the world. To be sure, under its first chancellor, Konrad Adenauer, West Germany embraced an authoritarian political style and upheld sharp social hierarchies. Yet in the 1950s, West Germans became acquainted with parliamentary rules of play, party politics, and pluralism—all in a context of increasing wealth and stability, unlike their experience in the Weimar Republic (1919–33). Social and cultural changes brought popular internalization of liberal values in the 1960s and 1970s. Historian Ulrich Herbert has called this "liberalization as a learning process."[2]

At both the political and the popular level, sexuality was a site for learning liberalism, not a matter to be reformed once liberalism was learned. In the eighteenth century, practitioners of civil society understood male virility as the basis of married men's authority in the household; this authority underpinned their claims of autonomy against the claims of the absolutist state. The bourgeois sexual-moral order thus underlay the very notion of liberal citizenship. With the transition from absolutism to liberalism, the state became the guarantor rather than the repressor of civil society. Upholding the sexual-moral order that justified liberalism became a state function, even though, after a few radical experiments, secular law regarding such matters as homosexuality, adultery, divorce, and contraception differed little from church law. Yet liberalism's language of equality before the law complicated matters: why should women, homosexuals, and men too poor to support their own households be lesser citizens? The tension between the state's role in upholding a sexual-moral order giving married men a monopoly on full citizenship, on the one hand, and liberalism's claims of equality, on the other, has not been fully resolved to this day.[3]

In the nineteenth century, the enfranchisement of unpropertied men awarded active citizenship to masses of people who did not adhere to bourgeois notions of propriety. Protesting the legal double standard for men and women, feminists gained increased rights for women and, in the early twentieth century, the vote in many places. At the same time, industrialization and urbanization created new sexualized spaces and mass markets. Moral purity activists battled what they saw as the corruptions of liberalism, where the enfranchisement of women and working-class men, socialized by tawdry consumer culture, was liberalism's logical and dangerous consequence. The Papal Encyclical of 1864 denounced liberalism as incompatible with Catholicism, and Protestants also numbered among antiliberal moral purity activists. In the context of this "moral panic," Western states across the political spectrum tightened their obscenity legislation. The United States, with the world's most liberal political structures at the time, in 1873 adopted the Comstock Act, which barred the dissemination of "obscenity" through the mails, effectively banning contraception. In 1871, a newly unified Germany, dominated by illiberal Prussia, adopted Prussian legislation on matters ranging from same-sex acts to prostitution, overturning more liberal standards in states such as Baden. In 1900, Germany adopted the Lex Heinze, which among other things banned the dissemination of obscene texts and images.

The political crises of the twentieth century, however, changed the equation. Although Christian conservatives—by the 1920s worried not only about liberalism but also about communism—exhibited sympathies to fascism between the wars, World War II led them to see "godless" communism and fascism as twin dangers. Where conservatives had previously seen liberalism as threatening the sexual-moral order, they now considered a sexual-moral order necessary to defend liberalism against Communism or Nazism.[4] So, for example, West German conservatives secured the passage of the Law on the Dissemination of Youth-Endangering Texts and Images in 1953. Conservatives hoped this law would help youth to gain a firm moral sensibility that would protect them from the temptations of political radicalism. Those who considered civil liberties central to liberalism also compared a liberal sexual culture favorably to the situation under Communism, but on different terms, contrasting their society's relative openness with East Germany's intolerance of a sexualized youth culture.[5] In West Germany, the term *Rechtsgut*, or "object of the law," encapsulated the liberal notion that the proper concern of the law was to protect individuals and the community from harm, not to preserve a moral order.[6] Still, liberals took for granted that a well-functioning society required some sort of sexual-moral order.[7] Those who would liberalize the law did not want the state dictating morality; they presumed that a mature citizenry would regulate itself.

After World War II, liberals and conservatives differed culturally on what range of behaviors constituted a healthy sexual-moral order, and they differed politically on the proper role of the state in shaping that sexuality. They wrestled, however, with the exact same questions: how to balance liberalism's reliance on a sexual-moral order, on the one hand, and its promise of individual freedom, on the other. Major legislation typically brought party-line votes, with the Christian Democratic Union (CDU) and Christian Social Union (CSU) backing preservation of the sexual-moral order and the Social Democratic Party (SPD) and Free Democratic Party (FDP) prioritizing civil liberties, but members of all parties struggled with the balance between the two. For that reason, this book distinguishes between "liberal" and "conservative" voices in each debate, regardless of protagonists' party affiliation.

Sexual consumer goods or erotica held a unique place in this debate. If the state wished to uphold the sexual-moral order by regulating not only behavior but also commerce, then economic liberalism—the freedom of the marketplace from state interference—was at issue. Furthermore, unlike disapproved forms of sexual behavior, such as homosexuality or premarital sex, erotica employed media and so evoked such liberal principles as freedom of the press. Finally, although erotica was often associated with illicit activity, it could also serve married couples, people educating themselves for marriage, scholars, and connoisseurs of art and literature. Some objects served medical functions. Until the "porn wave," contraceptives and informational texts were the backbone of the industry. Whether erotica strengthened or disrupted the sexual-moral order was thus open to question.

With the "porn wave" that started in 1969, arousing texts, images, and films replaced contraceptives and informative books as the lynchpin of the industry. With this shift, solitary pleasure-seekers became a more important constituency. Masturbation occupied an awkward place in the catalog of dubious sexual behaviors, since it had been identified as a major problem not by the church but rather by Enlightenment thinkers.[8] Masturbation threatened the rational subject because of its solipsistic nature, its prioritization of fantasy over reason, and the fact that, as a purely internal and secret act, it was subject to no inherent constraints. With the rise of psychology in the twentieth century, adult masturbation came to be seen as a sign of arrested development: a failure of the path that should transform the egoistical, sensual infant into a civilized adult. In both the classical Enlightenment and the modern psychological iteration of the problem, masturbation indicated that one was unfit for civil society. A society of masturbators threatened the liberal order.

Even aside from political formation, masturbation posed a different question. Opponents to church-based restrictions on nonprocreative sex might argue that other types of sexual relations—premarital, marital with contraceptives, homosexual—served to strengthen human bonds, a worthy goal in its own right. But what social goal did masturbation serve?

While members of government and civil society debated the (de)regulation of homosexuality, divorce, and abortion, they were silent on masturbation. There was no need to debate its decriminalization, since it was not illegal. Masturbation was, however, a central subtext of debates about arousing texts and images, whose legal status *was* at issue. The same question that applied to other sexual activities might be applied to masturbation: whom did it harm?

As activists and legislators sorted out the relationship between liberalism and sexuality, ordinary West Germans tried to create good lives for themselves, in part by establishing satisfying sexual partnerships. During and immediately after World War II, sex outside traditional restraints had flourished, but often in contexts of suffering or violence. Most West Germans dreamt of a return to "normalcy," even if they had never experienced what they considered normal: a married couple living together; the husband earning enough to provide a few extras; the wife caring for just the right number of offspring; children untraumatized by war, bereavement, or hunger. This private vision of "normalcy" coincided with theories of the "traditional" family as a bulwark against totalitarianism, and it helps to explain the power of ideologies of domesticity across the West.[9]

Yet wedding bells or reunification after wartime separation did not always lead couples to live happily ever after. Ensconced in their conjugal homes, couples faced problems that neither state nor church cared to address. Economic need led most to want to limit the size of their families. A poor sex education, shame, and sexual traumas of recent years made unsatisfying or even abhorrent sex a point of tension for many couples.

Furthermore, the fact that so few Germans had ever experienced "normalcy" had a flip side: Germans *had* lived through many other things. Memories of emotionally laden experiences during the Nazi years left a yearning for something more than security—at least, once security was assured, and as long as it was not endangered in the search for "something more."[10] Associated with stability, the family was a safe place in which to seek intensely felt experience—unlike the mass political movements in which so many Germans had earlier sought "something more" and which still constituted a frightening counterexample to the East. With fewer married mothers working for pay than ever before, an ideology of masculinity serving the family rather than the nation, and the domestication of leisure, more time with children was one way of intensifying family experience.[11] Deeper bonds with one's spouse was another. For established couples, a more powerful erotic bond offered intensely felt experience in a stable setting. At a time when nearly all political parties intoned women's equality while insisting on distinct roles for men and women, concern for erotic pleasure made men and women equally important, even as it permitted—even celebrated—biological difference and distinct functions. The "privatization of emotion" promised to quell some of the dangers of public emotion.

Neither state nor church offered any help to people who were sexually alive but unwed. There were gay men and lesbians, straight lovers who could not marry, and "surplus" women left by male deaths in the war. There were young people who wanted to learn about sex even if they did not want to have it yet, or who desired sex although they were not ready for marriage. These young people, with their enforced sexual ignorance, became West Germany's married couples. Even if church and state approved of marital sexuality, a wedding ceremony did not magically transform sexually ignorant single people into knowledgeable and confident spouses.

For married couples and single people alike, sex was usually about personal happiness, not the health of the state or God's plan. This prioritization of the individual ran counter to authoritative structures, and it was part of the process by which West Germans began to internalize liberal values.

The history of emotion is thus closely tied to the history of liberalism. Germans had recently emerged from an emotionally illiberal regime. The Nazis had choreographed public displays of emotion while penalizing deviant expressions of emotion, whether utterances of opposition to the regime, sympathy toward a member of a group deemed outside the national community, or "defeatist" words about the war. Expressions of certain political sentiments were risky after 1945, but the Federal Republic had few state-imposed strictures against expressions of emotion.

Still, in both regimes, emotional suffering might coincide with the imposition of state penalties. In Nazi Germany, the goal of safety for oneself and one's family might conflict with the goal of remaining true to deeply held political, religious, or ethical convictions. In the Federal Republic, the goal of retaining a secure place among family and friends might conflict with the goal of fulfilling erotic and emotional longing for someone of the same sex. The Jehovah's Witness who followed her conscience in Nazi Germany, like the gay man who followed his erotic desires in the Federal Republic, risked state-imposed penalties.

Yet even when state-imposed penalties did not come to pass, emotional suffering—the inner torment individuals experience when two or more high-priority personal goals are irreconcilable—could be crushing.[12] Consider the Jehovah's Witness who survived the Third Reich by renouncing her faith, the gay man in either regime who remained celibate out of fear of arrest, or the war widow who cohabitated with her lover because marriage would terminate her widow's pension, only to be snubbed by her neighbors. Importantly, the scenarios continue within marriage: the couple who wanted to limit the size of their family but equally wanted to remain faithful to the dictates of the Catholic Church; the woman who loved her husband but abhorred sex.

A liberal political regime could reduce emotional suffering, but more was required to achieve "emotional liberty": individual sovereignty over core internal values and goals.[13] Assuming contraceptives were legal and available, could a couple *emotionally* permit the goal of achieving economic stability to take priority over the goal of following Church dictates? Could a teenaged girl *emotionally* permit her desire for her lover to trump her need for her parents' approval?

The social setting played a great role in determining the answer to such questions. Did Catholics overwhelmingly follow Church rules regarding contraception, or did a large number observe these dictates in their breach? Just how strong were community strictures against sexually active teenaged girls, and did easily available subcultures exist in which the rules were more relaxed? And let us examine that assumption about the availability of contraceptives: even if their sale was legal, did obtaining them require that one submit to social censure or overcome high barriers of internal shame, or did the market regime and the transmission of sexual attitudes create an environment in which not only the legal but also the social and emotional barriers to purchasing contraceptives were lowered?

In other words, emotional liberty required not just the political institutions of liberalism but also a population that has internalized notions of pluralism among self-determining individuals.[14] To "learn liberalism" was thus to learn not only new rules of political interaction, but also new rules of social interaction.

The marketplace played a significant role in changing the rules of social interaction. As economic recovery shifted to the beginnings of affluence in the late 1950s, the expression of personal tastes in home furnishings and fashion marked a growing expectation of autonomy among consumers.[15] So did the expression of personal desires and tastes in sexual consumer goods— but here, consumers' most intimate relationships were at stake. Increased consumer opportunity combined with the desire for satisfying personal relationships to make sexual consumption a key site for West Germans to "learn liberalism."

How were couples to achieve erotic pleasure? Pregnancy had profound consequences, and an unhappy sex life could turn the best of friends into divorcing spouses. Thus joint discussion of such wares as contraceptives, marriage manuals, and remedies for sexual dysfunction was critical.[16] Yet shame and poor sex education complicated couples' communication, while state regulation and social convention gave men privileged access to goods. In postwar West Germany, however, the rise of big mail-order companies facilitated sexually integrated consumption. This was not just a matter of access to goods: such consumption also improved consumer education, eased communication between partners, and gave women a greater voice in family decision making.

A generation after the Second World War, the tension regarding the place of a sexual-moral order in political liberalism found resolution in much of the Western world, on paper at least. Between the late 1960s and early 1970s, state after state decriminalized homosexuality and adultery, legalized pornography and abortion, and loosened myriad other restrictions on consensual adult sexual expression. West Germany reformed its sexual-criminal code in two installments in 1969 and 1973. The break was not complete, as continuing battles over abortion and homosexuality made clear. With social sanctions still in place after legal reform, not only was emotional liberty incomplete but political liberty remained at risk. Yet the premise had shifted. It was no longer the liberal state's job to uphold a sexual-moral order. Rather, the state was to guarantee citizens' freedoms, imposing limits only when the exercise of those freedoms harmed others. Proponents of renewed restrictions subsequently may have been motivated by their understanding of morality, but their public arguments usually employed claims of harm: women or children harmed by pornography, fetuses harmed by abortion, and so on.

All liberal states shared this struggle over the relationship between sexuality and liberalism. Still, the fact that they resolved it at practically the same moment is remarkable, considering national differences in the history of liberalism and its alternatives. Not only did Germany's history of liberalism differ from that of Great Britain, Denmark, or the United States, but Germany's unique experience with the *anti*liberal alternatives of Nazism and Communism touched every aspect of German life.

The relationship between sexuality and the state was at issue in antiliberal ideologies, just as it was in liberalism. While denizens of liberal states struggled with two possibilities (was the liberal state to protect a sexual-moral order, or was it to protect individual freedoms?), West Germans had to mull over these alternatives and two more as well: Nazism's vision of sexuality, and Communism's. The fact that neither Nazism nor Communism had a single, unified vision of sexuality (just as liberalism lacked a single, unified vision) further complicated matters. With liberalism, Nazism, and Communism in competition for much of the early and mid-twentieth century, divergent philosophies about the relationship between state and sexuality carried special weight in Germany.

Postfascist, Postwar, Post-Weimar, Post-Wilhelmine

What did this history mean for West Germans, for whom fascism was a near memory and communism a near threat, but only liberalism a present-day lived experience? Dagmar Herzog posits a close relationship between West Germans' discourses of sexuality, on the one hand, and memories of the Nazi past on the other.[17] Postwar Germans fighting to restore a conservative sexuality regarded fascism as permissive; those promoting liberalization painted fascism as sexually repressive. Both sides, in other words, claimed they were fighting fascism through their sexual agendas. Thus memories of fascism drove postwar sexual history, and claims about sexual history drove postwar political battles that, on the surface, had little to do with sexuality.

This interpretation raises an interesting puzzle. The overall contours of sexuality in twentieth-century Germany resembled those of other Western societies: a loosening of mores in the interwar years that intensified with the disruptions of the Second World War, a postwar effort to reverse this trend leading to the conservative 1950s, sexual liberalization in the 1960s, feminism and gay rights activism in the 1970s, a high level of commodification by the 1980s, and postmodern forms of sexuality such as queer and virtual sexuality in the 1990s. When postwar West Germans talked about sexuality, they told a distinctly German story. But when they lived sexuality, they differed little from other Westerners.[18]

There are two possible explanations for this fact. One is that Germans with a "public" interest in sexuality—those who legislated it, published on it, taught or preached about it—gravitated to the most extreme negative example: Nazism. The stakes were especially high for them, since they wanted to influence societywide sexual mores and behavior. Those who lacked this public interest—who mainly sought private happiness—had less need to focus on a dramatic morality tale. And so "ordinary people" could "permit" their sexuality to be steered by variables other than responses to the Nazi past: how religious they were, how integrated into a society of mass consumption, and so on. In this explanation, there is a gap between elite discourse and the behavior of "ordinary people."

A second explanation is that the gap is more apparent than real: that the Nazi past played a role for those with a "public" and those with only a "private" interest in sexuality, but that in both cases the Nazi past was only one of several pasts, and both groups also frequently interpreted the present "on its own terms." Historians, however, are sensibly concerned with the depth of Nazism's impact on German society and so have paid particular attention to the aftermath of Nazism in their postwar histories. In this explanation, there is a gap between the concerns of postwar Germans and those of historians.

Both explanations contain an element of truth. To account for both German specificity and its part in a larger, international story, this book points out four ways in which West Germans defined their situation against their past. West Germany was at once postfascist, postwar, post-Weimar, and post-Wilhelmine.

The simultaneously seductive and repulsive memories of Nazi-era sexuality were evident in the postwar years. Nazi-era marriage manuals remained best sellers in the early 1950s, for example, even as revived Weimar-era classics were advertised as "Banned by the Nazis!"[19] When Rotermund became a celebrity in the 1960s, her history as a Luftwaffe pilot—a sort of Aryan super-woman: athletic, daring, and sexual—contributed to the public's fascination with her. Later, that same history gave sexual revolutionaries and feminists a convenient way to link commercialized sexuality and West Germany's incomplete reckoning with the Nazi past.[20]

Yet postwar societies that did not share Germany's political history shared many of the traumas of the immediate past and a role for sexuality in recovery. All combatant states experienced a postwar marriage and baby boom. Phenomena such as improved housing (which permitted couples more privacy) and the playboy (mainly a fantasy, but a marketable one) were common across the Western world. Sex manuals and popular magazines educated Western populations, and films laced with erotic tension offered relief from memories of war and the discomforts of continuing shortages.[21]

If all political factions claimed Nazism as a negative example, then all could agree about the urgency of *not* replicating whatever forces had brought the Nazis to power. And so the Federal Republic was also a "post-Weimar" society.[22] For moral purity advocates, the Weimar Republic's sexual culture had been alarming, a signal of collapsing mores that, in hindsight, had helped to pave the way for Nazism. Liberals argued, to the contrary, that the illiberalism that would have suppressed Weimar sexual culture was the same illiberalism that had made Germans so vulnerable to Nazism's appeal. To the extent that Weimar's sexual culture might have signaled a desire to escape the traumas of a lost war, revolution, hyperinflation, and economic depression, however, liberalizers hoped that their second postwar era, following 1945, would provide an environment for more stable sexual relations.

For denizens of Weimar Germany, the Weimar era was most remarkable in contrast to what had preceded it: the Wilhelmine age. Yet when it came to sex, the "post-Wilhelmine" age extended well into the post–World War II years.[23] "Post-Wilhelmine" thus suggests the longer-term relaxation of sexual mores through the twentieth century, as "post-Victorian" might in Britain. As shorthand, "post-Wilhelmine" obscures the complexities of sexuality under Wilhelm II (r. 1888–1918).[24] Instead, the term refers to a time whose remembered or imagined sexual conservatism served as a foil for reformers, and a model for moral purity advocates, throughout the twentieth century.

In West German debates on sexuality, references to 1900 were as common as references to 1933, the year Hitler came to power. In 1900 the Lex Heinze, Germany's notoriously strict obscenity code, went into effect. Nearly three-quarters of a century later, liberalizers asked, incredulously, how anyone could possibly believe that West Germans should be governed by sexual laws put into place in 1900. The year 1900 was not a negative example per se, as 1933 was. References to 1900 were usually agnostic about the Wilhelmine era in its own right; they simply implied that an awful lot had changed since then and that it was a scandal that the law hadn't kept up. After two world wars, revolution, fascism, genocide, and political division, to say "1900" was to evoke a distant world. If liberalizers considered this a clear argument for reform, however, conservatives argued that this distant world had been better than what had come since. For liberals and conservatives alike, the Wilhelmine era represented "how things used to be," the starting point from which subsequent eras, for good or ill, deviated. Whether West Germans should be "post-Wilhelmine" was not a given: rather, it was a point of strenuous debate.[25]

Business and Consumption

If sexuality in the 1950s and 1960s was postfascist, postwar, post-Weimar, and post-Wilhelmine, was it anything in its own right? It was. First, after experiencing a postwar revival of religiosity, western Europeans renegotiated both personal religiosity and the authority of Christian churches in public life. The postwar churches were not unremittingly hostile to sex. Instead, they celebrated sexual pleasure within procreative and loving marriage as a foil for other sexual paths. By the 1960s, however, frustration with the churches' prohibitions on premarital sex and (for Catholics) contraception led to massive disillusionment with organized Christianity, accelerating a long decline in church attendance.[26]

Second, during the generation following the war, sexuality became inextricable from consumerism. To focus on business and consumption is to emphasize a trend of the *longue durée*, but one whose ultimate resolution seemed uncertain until the recovery from World War II was well under way.[27]

By the twentieth century, bought objects that aroused the consumer or that promised to enhance sexual pleasure or health were an unavoidable part of sexual experience for Western populations. Improved control of fertility meant replacing coitus interruptus with condoms, which became reliable and affordable in the late nineteenth century, and which became familiar to a generation of men who received them courtesy of the military in the First World War.[28] With universal literacy by the end of the nineteenth century, the production of limited runs of erotic literature for a male elite turned into mass production of titillating works for both sexes. Cheap photographic reproduction made circulation of pictures of nude female bodies a rite of passage combining sex education, colonial positioning, arousal, and male bonding.[29] Between the wars, popular sexological works offered a new type of sex education.[30] In short, even leaving aside fashion and cosmetics, whose connection to sex was implied rather than explicit, material objects mediated sexual knowledge, arousal, and health for most denizens of industrialized society. The intervention of material objects into one's sexual history—as well as the struggles to obtain them, make them available, or limit their distribution— helped to define sexuality in the late modern era.

Entrepreneurs of sexual consumer goods, like their detractors, often referred to their sector as "erotica," although those who stuck to selling more "respectable" objects such as sexual-scientific books rejected this label. Erotica included any object whose function was to enhance the consumer's sex life: arousing images and texts, instructional materials, sex aids, virility formulas, lingerie, contraceptives, and more. Erotica differed from pornography, which referred only to representations of sex. Some considered nearly any text or image regarding sex to be pornography. Others differentiated between materials that concerned sex but were not arousing, those that might arouse some readers but also had qualities such as social commentary or aesthetic value, and those whose sole function was arousal—and called only the last category pornography. Sex aids, contraceptives, and lingerie were not pornography by anyone's definition, although some considered texts describing their use or images illustrating them to be pornographic.

For the most part, however, the term "pornography" was not relevant during the first two postwar decades. Instead, West Germans debated which text, image, or object was "obscene," "indecent," or "youth endangering," with the first two terms used interchangeably. Those were the legally actionable categories. "Pornography" became central only in the late 1960s. At that point, materials whose sole purpose was arousal moved from a marginal to a dominant position in the marketplace. Lawmakers eliminated the category "obscene texts and images and objects intended for obscene use" from the criminal code and introduced "pornography," which was regulated rather than banned starting in 1975. Legal debates henceforth concerned the question of which texts and images were pornographic. Other types of erotica (aids, contraceptives, lingerie) were irrelevant to this discussion. This book follows contemporary terminology. "Erotica" refers to the entire range of sexual consumer goods. "Pornography" refers to items so classified once "pornography" replaced "obscene texts and images" as the culturally and legally relevant category.

Ordinary people experienced sexual consumption as part of increased consumption more generally. In Germany, the rise of mass consumption proved a unifying phenomenon in a century of sharp political breaks.[31] The late Wilhelmine era and the middle years of the Weimar and Nazi periods offered tantalizing glimpses of mass consumption, promises that were spectacularly fulfilled during West Germany's economic miracle. In between,

1.1. Sexual consumer culture in Nazi Germany. Germans became familiar with the logo for Fromms condoms when the firm rose to market dominance during the Weimar years. This sign from the Nazi era, to be hung in a drug store window, coyly advertises "Fromms sponges," which let passersby know that condoms were available inside. *Source: 75 Jahre Fromms: Ein Condom macht Geschichte* (Zeven: MAPA, 1994).

however, were periods of dire scarcity: the second half of the First World War and early Weimar years, the Great Depression, the "rubble years" 1943–48.[32]

Sexual consumption served important functions in times of both "pain and prosperity," while also provoking anxieties about both.[33] During the Weimar era, daring cabarets were a marker of urban modernism; abortifacients, contraceptives, and erotic literature could be had from peddlers and mail-order firms; vending machines sold condoms in barracks, men's restrooms, barbershops, and pubs. Decency advocates abhorred this sexual marketplace, and the Nazis came to power partly on a promise to "clean up the streets." Once in power, the Nazi regime attacked products contrary to its racial utopia—gay magazines, modernist literature incorporating erotic themes, contraceptives—but sexual consumption could also serve regime goals. Condoms prevented sexually transmitted diseases that caused infertility. Marriage manuals urged race consciousness in selecting a mate. Risqué books made a beloved form of entertainment a benefit of economic recovery. Even as the military distributed condoms and erotic literature to its troops, however, the war reduced supplies to civilians, and the defeat brought catastrophic shortages to all. After the war, renewed access to condoms helped to mark the end of shortages posing existential threats. Marriage manuals aided couples laboring under economic and personal strains. Small luxuries, like lingerie, could symbolize the transition to plenty. Eventually, pornography appeared as a marker of simultaneous consumer and sexual excess.[34]

The erotica industry underwent its greatest expansion during the society of affluence that emerged in the West after the Second World War. During the economic miracle, West Germans described themselves as progressing through consecutive "waves" of consumption: the food wave, the clothing wave, the housing wave, the car wave. In the mid-1960s they discovered a sex wave.[35] With increased prosperity, consumers sought to satisfy desires ranging from knowledge about sex to heightened sexual experiences. Entrepreneurs worked both to satisfy those desires and to stimulate greater demand.

The latter task included not only marketing attractive products but also creating an unintimidating social and legal environment for potential customers. The sexual consumer goods industry thus both responded to and shaped consumer tastes, social mores, and legal frameworks.

This commercial sex wave had a greater impact than the sexual revolution of the late 1960s. Rhetoric linking sexual and political liberation attracted much media attention but directly touched only a small part of the population. The same was true of experiments in living one's radical sexual politics, such as communes whose house rules forbade exclusive relationships.[36]

To be sure, the lines between "sex wave" and "sexual revolution" were not hard and fast, yet terminology reflected important national differences. U.S. Americans spoke of "sexual revolution" in the early 1960s to describe the sexualized commercial environment, even before the onset of experiments in cohabitation among middle-class youth or radical theorizing about sexuality and politics.[37] West Germans, by contrast, had a distinct name for this earliest stage, with commerce at its heart: the sex wave.[38] With the "rubble years" a living memory, West Germans found a label that gave equal measure to the sexual and commercial aspects of what they observed around them. For U.S. Americans, consumer culture may no longer have warranted special note: only the sexual aspect was surprising.

How did consumers interpret their consumption? Sexual consumption was invested with broad symbolic meaning. For some it reflected the moral downfall of the West; others felt it signaled liberation from repressive church-based mores. But the meanings of sexual consumer goods also emerged from their routinized functions in everyday life.[39]

"Routine" included acquiring goods in the first place. Aside from legal barriers, consumers faced practical challenges. Were goods affordable? Was it convenient to purchase them? Could consumers educate themselves about available products? With whom could they discuss potential purchases? Were outlets equally accessible for male and female, married and single, rural and urban customers? Did consumers risk being cheated in an illicit marketplace? Did the manner of packaging, advertisement, and distribution erect cultural barriers against potential customers?

West German entrepreneurs pioneered solutions to these challenges of consumption. Before the Second World War, the distribution of erotica across the industrialized world was largely specialized: pharmacies sold condoms, peddlers sold erotic literature, and so on.[40] Two decades before any other state, however, West Germany had large firms employing aboveboard business practices that offered a comprehensive array of sexual consumer goods by mail order. By the early 1950s, single West German firms sold contraceptives, erotic literature, birds-and-bees books for children, solid manuals and titillating exposés for adults, advice books concerning matters of the heart, devices for calculating fertile days, nude photo series, services for developing home photos, lingerie, aphrodisiacs, genital prosthetics, breast enhancers, mechanical sex aids, chemical remedies, and gag items. Like the shift from corner markets to self-service grocery stores, comprehensive mail order brought a simultaneous explosion of product choice and increased consumer autonomy. West German erotica firms brought together "racier" and more "legitimate" goods (explicit photos on the one hand, marriage manuals on the other), items suggesting rational calculation and irrational desire (contraceptives and arousing texts), objects associated with female and male consumers (lingerie and virility formulas). Furthermore, well before the sexual and feminist revolutions, West German firms developed methods of marketing and languages of sex that lowered cultural barriers to sexual consumption, for example by moving consumption from sexually segregated to heterosocial spaces.

West Germany's unique marketplace built on Germany's longer history as a pioneer in sexual science, an industrial and commercial giant, and, putting the two together, a major producer of condoms and sexual literature since the late nineteenth century. These two categories of goods constituted the backbone of the industry in the first two postwar decades, when West Germany alone had large comprehensive erotica firms. Both the dominant goods and the means of marketing them made this an unusually "couples-friendly" marketplace, and erotica firms emphasized that they helped to create and preserve happy marriages. Condoms aided couples who needed to control their fertility while their resources were scarce, and sexual-scientific works helped to correct the ignorance that interfered with sexual pleasure and thus caused marital strife. By permitting couples to shop in the privacy of their homes, mail order helped to remove the stigma of the back alley from sexual consumption, and it eased sensitive discussions between partners who felt awkward speaking of sex.

Erotica firms' emphasis on marital compatibility may seem like a recipe for marginalizing other sexual actors. If experience in this marketplace was part of "learning liberalism," then the result would be a further entrenchment of the equation of liberalism with married heteronormativity. But the matter was more complicated than that. On the one hand, major distributors such as Beate Uhse were strictly heterosexist in their language and offerings. An alternative marketplace in gay publications existed in the 1950s, only to be shut down by the end of the decade.[41] Big firms' avoidance of gay publications was largely practical. Gay male sex was illegal, so materials that might be interpreted as fostering such sex were automatically guilty of abetting indecency and endangering youth. By contrast, entrepreneurs could argue that their straight-oriented goods aided marital sex, which was not only legal but encouraged. However gladly they might have sold gay-oriented products had it been less risky, erotica firms' stress on marital compatibility marginalized those who sought their happiness elsewhere.

On the other hand, even as entrepreneurs used the language of marriage to lower legal and cultural barriers to consumption, they were happy to sell to people in all sexual situations. Single heterosexuals could obtain contraceptives, and women need not rely on men's initiative. Lesbians and gay men could buy books on homosexuality (which often constituted pleas for tolerance, albeit on the grounds that homosexuals were not to blame for their pathology) and images that could be viewed with a homoerotic gaze. In both cases, mail order protected customers from the gossip that might follow purchases at the local pharmacy or bookstore.

Perhaps more important, in terms of structuring larger social attitudes, was the market's emphasis on self-fulfillment. When religious and state authorities granted the value of a satisfying sex life, it was as a means to other goals: population growth, the stabilization of the state through the stabilization of the family, the creation of an environment for the education of Christian children. If, however, individuals were justified in seeking better sex lives simply because it would make them happier, then there was no reason sex must be restricted to marriage or even to heterosexual pairings. By redefining the purpose of sex within marriage, sexual consumer culture elevated marital bonds while simultaneously enabling a more sympathetic hearing of claims outside marriage.

Erotica firms were thus part of a "queer history of heterosexuality" in which the dismantling of many rigid dualisms, not just homo- versus heterosexuality, characterized changes in the Western sexual-moral order. Among these dualisms have been, historically, the opposition of marital sex to nonmarital sex of all kinds, and the opposition of "natural" sexual encounters to those in which fantasy (often involving the use of arousing texts or images) was the prime element.[42] In challenging both of these supposedly firm dualisms, the erotica industry changed the sexual lives of millions of "confirmed heterosexuals." It also helped to make the opposition of hetero- versus homosexuality less tenable, simply by disrupting the notion of a single acceptable variety of sexual experience.

During these early years, when it had no parallel in the world, the reach of the West German erotica industry was tremendous. According to industry insiders, by the early 1960s half of all West German households had patronized a mail-order erotica firm at some point or other;[43] millions more had visited other outlets such as pharmacies or vending machines selling condoms. Nor was this the end of German innovation. In the early 1960s, West Germany established the first aboveground bricks-and-mortar erotica shops.

With sexual consumption, the tension between women as consuming agents and women as objects of consumption takes an extreme form. Access to contraceptives is crucial to women's control over their bodies; pictures of nude women offer those very bodies to the marketplace. Were erotica firms selling a mutually respectful erotic love that promised to put the sexes on a more equal footing, or were they selling a self-interested lust that, in an environment of male privilege, would only deepen that privilege?

What, indeed, was the relationship between lust and love? According to Christian tradition, love is one of the seven heavenly virtues; lust is one of the seven deadly sins. In the postwar years, the Christian churches took the position that sexual pleasure within marriage enhanced Christian love, but Christians had to overcome socialization based on a long history of Church denigration of sexual pleasure in any setting. And just as the churches began to reconcile lust and love, science appeared to reify the distinction between body (lust) and soul (love). While sex reformers of the interwar years (often physicians) had preached the interdependence of physical pleasure and emotional bonding in companionate marriage—a position echoed by reforming Christians of the postwar years—sexual scientists in the 1960s turned to laboratory research to measure arousal by stimuli like pornographic film, tracking such measures as heart rate and body temperature.

Reformers of the interwar and early postwar years promoted marriage manuals; sexual scientists of the 1960s measured responses to pornography. This fact underlines the questions of gender and power implicit in products with such an ambivalent relationship to lust and love. To understand the impact of the industry on the hierarchies of gender, we thus must consider the marketplace as a whole, rather than single categories of objects such as pornography or sex aids.[44] Seen in this light, the mechanics of the marketplace can be as important as specific goods. Marketing practices can locate consumption in sites of conjugal partnership or limit it to sites of illicit sex; they can make goods easily available to both sexes or only to one.

All consumer spaces were gendered.[45] Some created an environment that strongly privileged members of one sex (usually men); others created an environment that facilitated consultation between partners. Vending machines in men's restrooms were strictly off-limits to women; barbershops, which also sold condoms, effectively so. Mail-order catalogs, by contrast, circulated in the home and were thus conducive to joint shopping and discussion of sex. Bricks-and-mortar shops, while open to women, were uncomfortable places for them, and they rarely created an environment favorable to sensitive discussions between partners.

Furthermore, there could be great variation even within a single type of outlet. Beate Uhse catalogs included a photo of the founder and described her family life, creating an easy point of identification for women that other mail-order catalogs lacked. Until well after the Second World War, it was hard for a woman to ask for contraceptives at the pharmacy, but starting in the mid-1950s pharmacies began to station young women at the cash registers, which created an awkward situation for men hoping to stock up on condoms.[46] Erotica shops that placed lingerie by the entrance made it easy for women but embarrassing for men to enter; those that displayed porn by the entrance turned the tables.

West Germans' early exposure to this sexual marketplace was unique. Yet by the 1970s, the West German marketplace resembled that of other Western states—and this was a marketplace that would evoke strong feminist protest in the 1980s. Not only did the sites of consumption change, with storefronts as the public face of the industry and "mainstream" outlets increasingly carrying erotica, but so did the main products and the advertised benefits of consumption. While condoms and basic informational texts were the industry's mainstay well into the 1960s, by the mid-1970s pornography was the industry's backbone. In the 1950s and early 1960s, erotica was marketed as an aid to companionate pleasure. Pornography promised pleasure in the solo activities of voyeurism and masturbation, and it targeted men. Given this fact, it is not surprising that antiporn feminists concluded that the end result of a liberalism learned through the marketplace was simply a new variant on the privileged male sexual subject.

Geographies of Sexual Consumption

Because of their early development of comprehensive erotica firms, West Germans' experience of the sexual marketplace stood out. Nevertheless, West Germany was part of a larger, international story of sexual consumption.

By the 1970s a highly developed sexual consumer culture characterized most of the Western world. As in many aspects of consumer culture, U.S. exports, styles, and business practices influenced Germans. West German erotica entrepreneurs attended marketing seminars in the United States, and West German authors incorporated the findings of American sexual science into their sex manuals. Later, American antiporn feminists provided inspiration for West German feminist critiques of the industry. Other non-European influences were also at play, as texts and images regarding the "exotic erotic" situated European sexual consumption within a (post)colonial context.

Regional influences within Europe were also important, and one can usefully break down West Germany from a national unit into regions, each part of a sexual culture influenced by its closest neighbors. In far northern Germany, Scandinavian influence traced back to Danish control over Schleswig-Holstein and Hamburg's Altona neighborhood until Bismarck's wars of the 1860s. Beate Rotermund's postwar home of Flensburg bordered on Denmark; its population, like South Denmark's, included speakers of high German, low German, and Danish. Casually Protestant and mainly rural, Schleswig-Holstein was equally distant from the intense moral purity activism of Catholic regions and from the high modernity of Berlin. In the late 1950s, a "package from Flensburg" meant erotica from Beate Uhse. A decade later, a "package from Denmark" meant pornography from the first country to legalize it.

Baden-Württemberg, in Germany's southwest, had historic and cultural ties to France and Switzerland. Baden-Württemberg resulted from the 1952 union of Baden, whose strong liberal tradition originated in its lengthy occupation by the armies of the French Revolution, and Württemberg, whose pietistic traces could still be observed in a deep cultural conservatism. The province bordered on the long-disputed region of Alsace-Lorraine, and family histories spanning the border were common. One such family was that of Stuttgart native Walter Schäfer, founder of what, in the 1950s, was Europe's (and probably the world's) largest erotica firm, and his wife Gisela, daughter of Alsatians who had moved to Stuttgart after World War I. Frequent trips to France kept Schäfer up to date on French fashions in erotic literature.

To Baden-Württemberg's east is Bavaria. United by anti-Prussian sentiment with Austria, Bavaria also shared with its southern neighbor a strong identification with the Catholic Church. The main difference was that Bavaria's capital, Munich, was historically less cosmopolitan than Vienna, which before the Holocaust had had a higher proportion of Jews than any other European city, and where only recently had the influence of immigration from throughout the Habsburg Empire begun to wane. Vienna was also a historic center of sexual science and commerce, and Munich authorities were distressed by its postwar renaissance, as "obscene" literature flowed from Vienna into Bavaria.[47] If we accept that the Catholic Church is nonterritorial, we might include the ancient archbishopric of Cologne, on the River Rhine, in this "imagined community" defined by its deep Catholicism. This area was the heart of moral purity activism, personified by Cologne's Robert Schilling, head of the Federal Panel for Examining Youth-Endangering Texts from 1954 to 1966. What "banned in Boston" meant to the American film industry, "banned in Cologne" meant to West German erotica entrepreneurs.

None of these regional cultures remained regional, however. If Walter Schäfer sold books about Parisian nightlife, then Rotermund would have to follow suit, if she wanted to keep up. For his part, Schäfer would have to pay heed to Scandinavian styles. Both entrepreneurs had plenty of mail-order customers in Bavaria, Austria, and the Catholic Rhineland. The leaders of Cologne's moral purity activism scene became the leaders of the Federal Republic's moral purity activism scene. Furthermore, all of these entrepreneurs and activists addressed a population that had experienced tremendous geographic mobility, whether through Wehrmacht service or because they had fled the East at the end of World War II. And sexual influences crossed international borders and even oceans. Germans had absorbed the erotic energy of U.S. movies and music since the interwar period; now West Germans formed romantic alliances with British, French, and U.S. occupation soldiers.

Germany reciprocated in this international exchange of sexual influence. German sexual scientists had set international standards since the late nineteenth century, and their research was referenced by the United States Commission on Obscenity and Pornography in the late twentieth.[48] Commerce was an especially important element in Germany's clout. In the interwar period Germany exported fifty million condoms a year;[49] in the 1950s Walter Schäfer exported fully half his wares to lands as distant as Latin America and China. Once Rotermund began attracting international press coverage in the mid-1960s, she spread a powerful image of commerce in sexual wares in West Germany. The French might be especially erotic, the Americans prudish, the Scandinavians permissive, but the Germans, according to this catalog of stereotypes, were particularly adept at turning sexuality into a modern, efficient business.

Beate Uhse—and Everyone Else

No one was better at turning sexuality into a modern, efficient business than Beate Rotermund. Since the mid-1960s, Rotermund—in her public persona as Beate Uhse—has been the face of the West German erotica industry. But her celebrity extends beyond her identification with the industry. With its stations in reformist Weimar Germany, militaristic Nazi Germany, the "prudish" 1950s, the social changes of the 1960s and 1970s, and reunification, Rotermund's life is often read as a history of Germany's twentieth century.

We can thank Rotermund herself for this framing of her life story. In an industry characterized by anonymity and secrecy, Rotermund openly identified herself, her firm, and German history in product catalogs starting in the early 1950s. Soon the firm was distributing brief biographies of Rotermund to journalists, and by the mid-1960s Rotermund was a celebrity. Over time, this practice evolved into the firm's careful cultivation of the "Beate Uhse myth," a story compelling yet simple enough to become anchored in the public consciousness and take on its own legs as a marketing device.[50] Long accustomed to drawing on Rotermund's own accounts of her life, the media's countless retrospectives in the 1990s and beyond all summarized her 1989 "as-told-to" autobiography.[51] We know little about Rotermund that she did not tell us herself, and even the common framing of her history as a biography that tells the story of Germany's twentieth century is Rotermund's own.

The Beate Uhse myth eventually far exceeded its initial purpose. For the firm, the myth began as a means of establishing brand identity. For the West German public, it became a way of understanding history. With or without Beate Uhse, the interplay of sexuality, commerce, and Germany's twentieth century would have constituted a complicated web. Through her personalized marketing and, later, celebrity, however, Rotermund directed what might have been an inchoate set of associations to striking images: the female Luftwaffe veteran, the woman of the rubble, the unashamed peddler of erotica. A narrative patched together from fragmentary signals of an evolving postwar culture became a seamless story describing the Nazi past, the rubble years, the economic miracle, and sexual liberation as a natural progression.

Beate Uhse's importance for the story told in this book is thus twofold. First, Beate Uhse created a framework for West Germans, consumers of erotica or not, to interpret sexuality, history, and consumption in twentieth-century Germany. So powerful is this interpretive framework that it can distort our understanding of the "actual" histories of consumption, business, and state activity that constitute the second area in which the firm and person were important. Beate Uhse shaped West Germans' sex lives by educating and provisioning them and by helping to define the legal boundaries of sexual consumption. Even without the myth, Beate Uhse would have had a significant impact on the history of sexuality in (West) Germany. But the notion that Beate Uhse's story *is* the "history of morals in the Federal Republic" has helped to foster Germans' erroneous belief that Rotermund was the only, or at least by far the most important, erotica entrepreneur during the "pioneering" years. In fact, Rotermund had plenty of company.

In other words, the blinding light of Beate Uhse can make it hard to see the many other entrepreneurs who helped to create postwar sexual consumer culture. These include giants like Walter Schäfer, head of the world's largest erotica firm in the 1950s. They include village artisans like Alfred Weber, who developed sex aids in his workshop and sold them to people like Schäfer and Rotermund, and older family firms like Dublosan, which had contracted with the city of Berlin to maintain vending machines with condoms since the Weimar era.[52] They include medium-sized retailers like Christiane Schumacher (a pseudonym), whose response to her husband's imprisonment for disseminating obscenity was to go into business for herself; authors like Richard Wunderer, who made a small fortune authoring sex manuals under his own name and erotic fiction and pornography under pseudonyms; the Munich

'68ers who discovered that selling plaster casts of their sexual organs and films of their sexual experiments could help to keep their commune afloat; and many more.[53]

To broaden the focus beyond Rotermund is not simply to restore forgotten entrepreneurs to history. Rather, it is to gain a different understanding of the marketplace and the ways it shaped West German sexuality. If Rotermund had significant competition even in the early days, then rather than looking for an explanation of how she became a lone pioneer, we must think about the conditions that encouraged dozens of entrepreneurs to get into the business. If more customers bought from Schäfer than from Beate Uhse in the 1950s, then surely it matters that Schäfer's catalogs communicated different messages about sexuality than did Beate Uhse's. Rotermund's openness about her business, compared to some entrepreneurs' anonymity, tells us something, but so does Wunderer's middle position: to attach his name to his work in some instances but remain hidden in others.

This book aims to do justice to the Beate Uhse myth and its impact, and also to the history that the myth has helped to obscure. It does so by devoting portions to each part of the story. The first two chapters following this introduction focus on state regulation of the industry, and then the industry and its consumers, in the conservative 1950s. Here Beate Uhse appears as one firm among many. Chapter 4 examines the Beate Uhse myth from its origins within the firm until the mid-1960s, when Beate Uhse became a public figure. Chapters 5 and 6 explore the industry, its consumers, and state regulation through the "sex wave" (of the 1960s) and the "porn wave" (of the early 1970s). Finally, the Postlude follows the Beate Uhse myth from the legalization of pornography to the twenty-first century.

The Cast of Characters, and What We Know about Them

Entrepreneurs—both famous and obscure—were only part of the story. This book follows four groups: the state and its representatives, members of civil society, erotica concerns and the people behind them, and consumers.

As consumer wealth expanded and erotica firms mastered modern marketing techniques, state regulation became the main hindrance to the growth of the erotica sector. The state's control of entrepreneurs was direct, its control of consumers indirect. The law regulated the manufacture, distribution, and display of "obscene" or "youth-endangering" materials. It did not prohibit purchase or ownership, but if selling was illegal, then how were customers to buy? The industry and its consumers were effectively allies in the struggle for a more open marketplace, although consumers tried to remain anonymous whereas businesses had no choice but to confront the state directly, given how frequently they were taken to court. In some branches of the economy, consumers might look to the state as an ally against exploitative businesses, for example by requesting price controls. But consumers who felt cheated by erotica firms did not complain to the government. The consumer's biggest hurdle, like that of business, *was* the state.

Businesses and consumers, however, expressed their interests in different ways. Erotica firms addressed their desire to sell to both customers and the state. With advertising, they urged customers to buy; with legal defenses and petitions for legislative reform, they urged the state to permit them to sell. Furthermore, their importance as employers and taxpayers could turn local opinion in their favor, and their success made them interesting to the media. And business was organized: already in 1951, several firms banded together to form a trade group, which grew to represent some seventy establishments.

Consumers did not address the government. They made their desires known only to erotica firms. And unlike erotica entrepreneurs, who knew each other, consumers were isolated. They might tell relatives or close friends their favored sources for goods; they often discussed their purchases with their intimate partners. But anonymity was important to consumers, and they certainly did not organize, for example in consumer advocacy groups.

Actually, consumers did address the state. They did so not as customers, however, but rather as doctors, educators, moral purity crusaders, advocates of civil liberties, or other parties whose interest was ideological or professional, not personal. That is, they spoke as members of civil society. Moral purity associations desired a stricter regime; civil rights organizations urged liberalization. Youth advocates pressed for whatever they felt was in the best interests of youth. Physicians weighed in with their opinion of what would improve individual and public health.

What do we know about our various players? In the case of the state and civil society, quite a lot. In regulating the industry, the state produced mountains of papers: parliamentary debates regarding legal reform, court cases, ministerial records regarding the regulation of certain goods, and so on. The news media reported on state proceedings, while members of civil society published their own reports and programs for reform and kept internal records regarding their activities.

Businesses, for their part, kept records on product development, marketing strategies, legal problems, sales, and more. Businesses are often reluctant to open their archives, and the erotica industry is historically secretive. Nevertheless, several firms and the industry trade group opened their files to me, and the records, though incomplete, were a gold mine. This book is, to my knowledge, the first history of sexuality based on corporate records from comprehensive erotica firms anywhere in the world.

The Beate Uhse myth, however, creates challenges for researching the industry. Rotermund enjoyed extensive media coverage; her competitors left little trace in the media. Rotermund, determined that her publishing house have the same legitimacy as any other press, deposited all her publications at the National Library. Not all of her competitors were so conscientious. Firms that went out of business threw out their papers; Beate Uhse has papers dating back fifty-plus years, and the staff's and Rotermund's survivors' sense of the firm's historic importance led them to agree to my proposal that they deposit those papers in a public archive. Other firms permitted me to use their files on site, but none have donated them to a public archive.[54] Unless this changes, future researchers will be tempted to write about the industry using the only papers that are easily accessible—Beate Uhse's—further reinforcing the sense that Beate Uhse is the whole story. The problem persists even outside conventional locations of research. Early Beate Uhse catalogs are collectors' items, frequently sold on German eBay; the same is not true of ephemera from other firms. I located only one catalog of another firm on eBay. It was listed under the heading "Beate Uhse's Competition."

To rely only on Beate Uhse's own materials would be to reiterate the myth. Instead, this book aims to historicize it. Luckily, government agencies and moral purity associations tracking the industry in the 1950s and 1960s could not see into the future, and so they kept records on many firms. The corporate papers of other firms were available—if a little harder to locate. My interviews with CEOs, employees, and descendants of entrepreneurs revealed much about this unusual world of entrepreneurs who shared many of the concerns of the business community but were marginalized from it because their product was sexual in nature. The records of the industry trade group spoke to areas of cooperation that went unnoted in corporate records, since the latter emphasized competition.

In the end, the industry's customers remain the most mysterious. Only the most finicky record keeper, unafraid of discovery, would maintain a written account of her erotica purchases, and only an exceptional diarist would write down not only details of his sex life, but also how bought goods figured into it. In the case of business, intergenerational oral tradition made it possible to interview children or younger colleagues of deceased entrepreneurs, but there is little point in interviewing people about the finer points of their parents' sex lives. The few voices of consumers I found are precious indeed. A woman sent me the carbon copies of two letters her father sent to an erotica firm, which she had discovered upon cleaning out his attic after his death.[55] (How many customers made copies of such correspondence in the first place?) In an interview, a former employee of an erotica firm reflected on her exposure to sexual consumer goods before she took the job.[56] Court records hinted at the family conflict surrounding a mother's legal complaint against the erotica firm whose catalogs she discovered in her twenty-eight-year-old son's dresser drawer.[57] A witness suggested relationships between Nazi-era and postwar consumption when he explained, in another court case, that he was interested in nude photos "just as a soldier stationed in France, for example, had been interested in these sorts of pictures."[58] These are scraps, however, and completely inadequate for drawing larger conclusions about consumers.

Nor is there much information about consumers in governmental files or those of civic and social organizations. The firm, not the consumer, violated the law by disseminating obscene materials. At the end of the period under study, academics began to examine consumers, for example to discover the effects of pornography on the viewer. Methodologically naive by today's standards (and even today there is no consensus about how to research such subjects), these studies are most valuable for what they reveal about scholars' desire to insert research into public debate.

Entrepreneurs, by contrast, had a great interest in collecting information about consumers. And customers, by the hundreds of thousands, laid out their sexual problems in letters to erotica firms. The letters would be an unparalleled find for historians of sexuality—if they still existed. But they are gone. Once the letter was answered or the transaction completed, the firm had no need to hold on to the correspondence, which in any case might endanger the customer's confidentiality in case of a police raid.

We are left with sales figures and demographic data collected by firms engaged in market research, and with selective quotes from letters collected for the purpose of marketing. We have these only from firms large enough to devote resources to such activities and committed enough to growth to consider it worthwhile. That is, we are limited to materials from Beate Uhse, whose data on and quotes of customers may be the best information we have on erotica consumers for the 1950s and 1960s anywhere in the world.

Finally, a word about what this book does not address. In examining the marketplace in sexual consumer goods, it does not explore sexual services, such as prostitution and stripping. There was, of course, overlap: photographs of a stripper might appear in a collection of erotic images. This book examines the regulation, sale, and consumption of the photographs but not the live show. In addition, by focusing on aboveground businesses, their customers, and state efforts to regulate them, this book does not explore the world of underground trade in images and objects that were clearly illegal. Either subject—trade in sexual services, or trade in clearly illegal wares—would almost certainly reveal milieus of greater abuses and of sexually more marginalized actors than we will find in these pages.

How about the studio model, or the models in pornographic films? ("Models" was the industry term for subjects of both still and moving images.) Can this study help to untangle debates about exploitation of women versus women's agency in this aspect of the sex industry? Unfortunately, sources that would permit us to answer this question for the period before the legalization of pornography are scant. The state did not prosecute the production of "obscene" images: it was their dissemination that was illegal. Big distributors left good records; the fly-by-night photographers and underground filmmakers who supplied those distributors did not. Decency advocates and social workers worried about "endangered girls" who might fall into prostitution, but when it came to explicit photographs, the imagined victims, and thus the objects of study, were underage viewers, not models. In the absence of written records, the anthropological and journalistic methods that have proved so fruitful in investigating the production of pornography today cannot be applied retrospectively.[59]

Like all works of historical research, this one is incomplete. Yet we know enough about West Germany's erotica industry, its customers, and its regulation to know that it is a fascinating story, and one with worldwide implications. It is the story of the commercialization of intimate lives that defines sexuality today. With that in mind, let us begin.

2 The Permissive Prudish State

A Tale of Two Cities

In its October 1952 newsletter, the Cologne-based Catholic moral purity association Volkswartbund (loosely, the League of Guardians of the People, or Guardians) announced a triumph: the Bundestag had approved the Law on the Dissemination of Youth-Endangering Texts and Images (or Law on Youth-Endangering Texts).[1] The author recounted the Guardians' role in gaining the law's passage. In January 1949, the organization had prepared a draft law to protect youth from "filth and trash" in print. When the Federal Republic was founded a few months later, that draft became the basis for the bill the Ministry of the Interior presented to parliament. The Guardians' director had testified before the Bundestag Committee for Youth Welfare, and the organization had provided numerous agencies with materials discrediting claims that such writings were harmless. Yet there was still work to do. The Bundesrat had not yet passed the bill, and the Federal Panel for Examining Youth-Endangering Texts (or the Indexing Panel), which the law charged with indexing youth-endangering works, needed to get up and running. It would be important to protect the Indexing Panel from being overwhelmed as it started out, and panelists would need to be educated about what kinds of materials were morally dangerous. Luckily, years of experience had given the Guardians a clear picture of the situation. Citizens should thus send worrisome materials to the Guardians, which would examine them and forward appropriate items to the Panel.

For contemporary critics and for historians, the passage of the Law on Youth-Endangering Texts, the activities of the Indexing Panel, and the influence of the Guardians illustrate the linked prudishness and illiberalism of Adenauer's West Germany. The creation of a censoring body and the greater concern with sexual rather than with violent or racist writings were especially troubling after Nazism and two world wars.[2] And the Law on Youth-Endangering Texts was not the only sign that postwar West Germans were less tolerant of sex than they were of echoes of the Nazi past. Not only did obscenity laws from 1900 remain on the books, but even the most antiquated were occasionally enforced, creating such spectacles as the conviction of parents on charges of "procurement" for permitting a daughter's fiancé to spend the night.[3] The sodomy laws, including Nazi-era revisions criminalizing even a suspicious glance between men, were upheld by the Constitutional Court, and gay men endured raids, denunciations, and imprisonment.[4]

Ground zero of this state-sponsored sexual repression was Cologne. An ancient archbishopric, Cologne housed the Guardians, which grew out of a men's moral purity league founded in 1898 and which answered directly to that city's bishop. Cologne was also home to future chancellor Konrad Adenauer. Adenauer's Christian Democratic Union (CDU), an experiment in ecumenical Christian democracy intended to overcome some of the divisions that had helped the Nazis to power, needed to tempt Catholic votes away from their traditional political home, the Center Party. It thus appealed to culturally conservative Catholics, whose program of "re-Christianization" triumphed over a short flurry of interest in Catholic Socialism as the basis of postwar Catholic politics.[5] Conservative sexual politics also provided common ground between Catholics and Protestants, who not only had inherited centuries of mutual distrust but also differed on key political questions such as the appropriate level of state involvement in the economy.[6]

And so Cologne's conservative Catholicism strongly informed politics in the early CDU, North Rhine–Westphalia (West Germany's largest and most heavily industrialized province), and the Federal Republic. In seeking a dominant role for conservative Christianity in West German politics, Cologne had an ally in Bavaria, with Munich a second hotbed of moral purity activism. The sleepy capital of Rhineland-Palatinate, Koblenz, where future arch-conservative family minister Franz-Josef Würmeling served in the provincial government, rounded out what some moral purity activists described, in homage to Winston Churchill's "iron curtain," as the "erotica curtain."[7]

This state-sponsored sexual conservatism evidently reflected cultural mores more generally. West Germans who grew up in the 1950s recall that no one explained the "facts of life" to them, and sexual transgressions were discussed in whispers even more hushed than the fleeting references to the Jewish family that had once lived down the street.[8] Whether this climate represented continuity with Nazi sexual repression (according to sexual revolutionaries' interpretation) or a postwar rejection of the Nazis' incitement to sexual activity (as Herzog argues), the result was what sexual revolutionary Reimut Reiche termed an "erotic ice age."[9]

Children, however, are not the most reliable witnesses of their parents' sexual worlds. In fact, sexual culture in the 1950s was complex. Moral purity activists produced mountains of sex-hostile writings and helped to usher through repressive legislation, but their story cannot explain why the 1950s was the decade in which mail-order erotica became a routine part of adult West Germans' lives.[10]

Equally important as the "erotica curtain" was a city like Flensburg, in Schleswig-Holstein. By the late 1950s, word that a "package from Flensburg" had arrived earned a nudge and a wink: how many people knew of anyone in Flensburg besides Beate Uhse, who was as closely associated with her city as the Guardians were with Cologne? If North Rhine–Westphalia was a hotbed of moral purity activism, then Schleswig-Holstein was a hotbed of, well, apathy. Bordering on Denmark, which would become the first country to legalize pornography in 1967, Flensburg was as casually Protestant and borderline Scandinavian as Cologne was intensely Catholic.

As the erotica business grew in the 1950s, key figures recognized their own trio of cities that tugged at the "erotica curtain": Flensburg, Stuttgart, and Frankfurt am Main. The first two housed West Germany's major erotica firms. The third was West Germany's center of sexual science and progressive social science research. Frankfurt (in Hessen) and Stuttgart (in Baden-Württemberg) were historical centers of liberalism, and even Schleswig-Holstein's dominant CDU reflected more the irrelevance of socialism to rural life than the antimodernity of intensely Catholic regions.

The sexual consumer goods industry blossomed in the 1950s not just in spite of or as a remedy to state-backed sexual conservatism, but in large part because of state activity. During the 1950s, courts, provincial administrative bodies, and even the Indexing Panel undermined moral purity advocates' efforts to impose their vision. For every province in which Christian conservatives dominated, there was another informed by a more liberal philosophy, and West Germany's federal structure enabled the latter to frustrate the efforts of the former. The Indexing Panel proved both more moderate and less powerful than its opponents had feared. And the erotica industry created effective strategies to head off legal troubles and shape permissive interpretations of the law.

The battle over the Law on Youth-Endangering Texts and obscenity legislation might appear as one between illiberalism and liberalism, with opponents valuing freedom of expression and freedom of the press, while proponents revealed illiberal tendencies. But these battles were in fact struggles over the meaning of liberalism. Which took priority: the sexual-moral order that underpinned liberalism, or liberalism's claims of equality and civil liberties? Moral purity advocates in Weimar Germany had argued for a Schmutz and Schund Law (a Filth and Trash Law—passed in 1926, it was the predecessor to the Law on Youth-Endangering Texts) to combat the corruptions of liberalism. But proponents of the Law on Youth-Endangering Texts considered such a law necessary to defend liberalism against Communism and Nazism.[11] Rather than understanding the Law on Youth-Endangering Texts and obscenity legislation as illiberal relics, we can see them as an echo of one of liberalism's founding tenets: the necessity of a sexual-moral order. It then becomes evident that many proponents of the legislation, no less than its detractors, were "learning liberalism."[12]

In addition to struggling over the relationship between sexuality and liberalism, West Germans puzzled over the relevance of past experience for this debate. Did one need to go back to the Wilhelmine age, before the lifting of censorship in Weimar Germany, to find an acceptably "clean" consumer and media environment? Did efforts to restore a moral order after World War I contain lessons for the current postwar moral crisis? Had Nazism, despite all its crimes, at least cleaned up Weimar's "degenerate" streetscape? Or were Nazis' means of cleaning up "degeneracy" inseparable from their crimes, meaning West Germans could not have one without the other? Or had Nazi Germany not been so wholesome at all, even sexually? Was it responsible for postwar degeneracy—either by having started a disastrous war, or more deeply by scrambling the moral order at its roots? If so, was the antidote a strictly controlled sexual-moral order, or was it a liberal defense of personal freedoms, including sexual freedoms?

This chapter begins by examining Christian conservatives' success in gaining legal restrictions on the sexual consumer goods industry with the Law on Youth-Endangering Texts. Christian conservatives tarred the Nazis with accusations of sexual license. But there was no popular consensus that the Nazi era had been sexually permissive, or even that the Nazi era was the most relevant point of reference. Supporters of the legislation favorably compared the "clean" streets of the Nazi era with the "filth" that now filled newsstands, which reminded them instead of Weimar "degeneracy." Yet in seeking new legislation, decency advocates did not eye Nazi-era measures: indeed, the Nazis' creation of a central censoring agency in 1935 had consigned the Filth and Trash Law to oblivion. Instead, decency advocates recognized parallels between their own age and another postwar era, in which the upheavals of World War I and revolution had convinced Christian conservatives that only drastic measures could preserve the moral order.[13] Opponents of the new legislation did not evoke images of sexual license in Nazi Germany but rather Nazi censorship of political writings and the artistic avant-garde, including erotic materials. But they also referred to other troubled histories of censorship: the obscenity law of the Wilhelmine era, the Filth and Trash Law of the Weimar years. Perhaps most important, the debate around the Law on Youth-Endangering Texts was not just about the role of sexual morality in overcoming Germany's past. Rather, it concerned the simultaneous need for sexual morality and a liberal political order in this task.

The chapter then examines the hindrances in mobilizing the state to truly inhibit the erotica industry's growth. Outspoken Social Democrats protested restrictions, but four other factors were at least as important during this period, when the CDU/CSU had a firm grip on national governance. The first was many conservatives' commitment to civil liberties. The second was West Germany's federal structure, which gave Social Democrats significant powers at the provincial level. The third was a simple oversight: the Law on Youth-Endangering Texts neglected mail-order firms, which exploited the loophole to become the dominant players in the industry. In addition to these political/structural considerations was a cultural one. An effective battle against obscenity and youth endangerment required detailed discussion of the offending objects, but such discussions violated deeply internalized feelings of shame regarding sex. The very difficulty of speaking and writing about illicit texts, images, and objects stymied decency advocates' efforts to battle it.

Finally, the chapter turns to the erotica industry's engagement with the state. Legal troubles created insurmountable challenges for many small firms. The consequence, however, was not to suppress the industry but rather to aid its concentration in the hands of a few giants, which allowed them to more effectively confront legal challenges. And as we will see in the next chapter, mail order helped to democratize sexual consumption and sexual attitudes, reducing the hierarchies between men and women, between those using goods associated with "licit" and "illicit" sex, between country dwellers and city dwellers. This process, too, aided the learning of liberalism—this time among the industry's customers.

The Tenuous Triumph of Moral Purity Crusaders: The Law on the Dissemination of Youth-Endangering Texts and Images

By the time currency reform opened a marketplace in sexual consumer goods, the Guardians had accumulated much practice in advocating the cause of decency. Much of the organization's postwar leadership recalled the successful battle for the 1926 Filth and Trash Law. Like many cultural conservatives, they had embraced National Socialists' promises to combat Weimar-era "degeneracy" and had subsequently been distressed by the Nazis' support for nonmarital childbearing and sexual liberties for the racial elite. Still, shared nationalism and anti-Bolshevism as well as the fluid boundaries between antimodernism, anticosmopolitanism, and anti-Semitism enabled the Guardians to continue work through the Nazi years.[14]

The Guardians' facilities were destroyed in a bombing raid in 1943. When the organization began publishing its newsletter again in the spring of 1946, it cited the subsequent cessation of activities as evidence of its victimization under Nazism.[15] It castigated the Nazis for having created a morally disoriented population (illicit sexual behavior, rather than violence or racism, marking moral disorientation) and recalled visits from the Gestapo to confirm that the Nazis had felt threatened by the Guardians' supposedly loud criticism of the regime.[16] The organization also, however, criticized modernity more generally for Germany's moral downfall. It railed against those who took a "materialist" approach to combating the postwar epidemic of sexually transmitted disease (by approaching it in epidemiological rather than moral terms) and erotic entertainment, from village dances to urban cabarets.[17]

With currency reform in June 1948, racy publications suddenly seemed to hang from every newsstand. Within a couple of years, Robert Schilling, district attorney in Cologne, counted seventy-one publishing houses specializing in nudist magazines, "lifestyle reform" magazines featuring articles about sex, and dime novels with violent and sexual content.[18] Even mainstream magazines carried classified ads for contraceptives, sexual literature, and individuals seeking nonmarital, same-sex, and sadomasochistic liaisons.[19] Convinced that "sexualism," liberalism, fascism, and materialism were intertwined dangers, the Guardians quickly turned their attention to this explosion of sexual consumer culture. By 1950 at the latest, the Guardians were publishing pamphlets with alarming titles like *World Danger: Pornography!* but also such sober-sounding essays as *Erotic-Sexual Literature as the Subject of Judgments under §184 of the Criminal Code.*[20] The Guardians sent their publications to decision makers, and they were excerpted in both mass-market and professional publications.[21]

Eleven months passed between currency reform and the establishment of the West German state, so antiobscenity activists focused initially on the local scene, convincing at least two dozen cities to ban "filth and trash" from their news kiosks.[22] Only a tiny portion of kiosks were municipally owned, however. From decency activists' perspective, private kiosk owners must be hit with lawsuits under the provisions of §184 of the criminal code, which prohibited the distribution of "obscene" writings, images, and objects. Yet citizens rarely filed complaints.[23] When courts examined items, they seldom ruled them obscene, and the rare conviction came long after an item had sold out anyway.

The cities of the "erotica curtain" thus established bodies to bring more objects under official scrutiny and to move quickly to confiscation. Discussions between the Guardians and the city of Cologne resulted, by early 1950, in the establishment of a municipal office, with Robert Schilling at its head.[24] Within months Cologne had produced more confiscation orders than many comparable municipalities combined, and the city's five major suppliers to newsstands instituted a program of self-censorship.[25] Bavaria and Rhineland-Palatinate established provincial-level Indexing Panels; by fall 1952, a total of 298 confiscation orders had brought in 156,436 offending items in Bavaria.[26] The erotica industry knew that its products faced poor prospects in Cologne, Koblenz, and Munich.[27]

The products, however, continued to do well everywhere else. Few charges of indecency in print were filed, and courts threw out such charges far more often than they did complaints of other crimes.[28] Decency advocates thus hoped to revive the 1926 Filth and Trash Law, a response to the moral panic following World War I. Under that law, two national-level Indexing Panels (one for north and one for south Germany) had examined works suspected of having sexual content (filth) or lacking literary quality (trash). Although it was illegal to sell obscene works, writings indexed as "filth and trash" simply faced restrictions on their advertisement, display, and distribution to minors—but this was enough to effectively remove them from the marketplace. The establishment of the Reich Chamber of Culture in 1935 voided the 1926 law: now *all* publications went through a central censoring office. Allied censorship replaced Nazi censorship in 1945, but the Allies' aim was not to protect youth from sexual content or bad prose. Once paper became available again, there were thus no controls on materials that fell short of the legal standards of obscenity.

The Guardians recognized a familiar postwar phenomenon: juvenile delinquency in a state too weak to respond.[29] By early 1949, the Guardians and the Protestant Inner Mission produced draft laws based on the 1926 legislation. Rhineland-Palatinate passed a provincial Law for the Protection of Youth from Filth and Trash in October 1949.[30]

That same month, the CDU's parliamentary faction called for a national law. (The Federal Republic had been established in May.) Parliamentary proceedings were anything but smooth: even assigning the bill to committee was controversial.[31] After months of debate, the Committee for Youth Welfare remained deadlocked on whether the "core principles" of the bill were sound; once it emerged from this impasse, the committee required another half year to discuss specific measures before passing it on. The Bundesrat rejected the Bundestag's hard-won version, and then it rejected the version produced by the reconciliation committee. The law was finally passed on June 9, 1953—three and a half years after the government began work on it.

All of this parliamentary Sturm und Drang indicated that big issues were at stake. The project nearly collapsed under arguments about core principles. First, was the law necessary: did it address a problem so urgent as to require new legislation? Second, if so, would this solution be effective? Third, was it constitutional? Debates on two specific paragraphs also nearly derailed the bill. The first concerned publications of the naturalist (nudist) movement. The second concerned the relationship between the federation and the provinces.

Although the confessional organizations wanted a new Filth and Trash Law, the Interior Ministry quickly determined that discrimination against two literary genres, however tasteless, was unconstitutional, since freedom of the press and freedom of expression were anchored in the constitution as basic rights. And basic rights could be restricted only to protect youth. The ministry thus offered a Law on the Dissemination of Youth-Endangering Texts. Still, as late as the 1960s, many continued to refer to it as the Filth and Trash Law.[32]

The shift from "filth and trash" helped the new law to conform to West Germany's constitution, but it also signaled important developments within conservative Christianity. Since the late nineteenth century, Catholic "re-Christianizers" had battled such symptoms of modernity as secularization, materialism, and liberalism.[33] The Russian Revolution, the failed German Revolution of 1918–19, and the appeal of socialism and communism in Weimar Germany had made the threat of communism ever more pressing, and fear of the unruly masses was one element behind the 1926 law: cheap literature, decency advocates believed, led members of the lower orders to dissolute and criminal lifestyles. But interwar Catholic re-Christianizers had considered liberalism as dangerous as socialism, and this hostility to liberalism had contributed to many Christian conservatives' attraction to fascism.

After the Second World War, this group initially fell back on familiar analyses of what ailed Europe, and their recourse to the 1926 law as a model for their 1949 draft reflected this tendency. Yet Catholic re-Christianizers increasingly saw Communism as the main threat to a Christian Europe—and liberalism as the best defense against it. Conservative Protestants, for their part, had likewise favored antiliberal parties before 1933 and had likewise feared the unruly masses—thus their support of the 1926 law. But they had never been alienated from the German state as Catholics had been, and their greater representation among the bourgeoisie had left them less distressed by materialism. After the war, Protestant and Catholic moral purity activists were moving toward a common stand that liberalism was a necessary bulwark against communism.[34] What this would mean in practice, however, was a difficult question. Liberalism was to defend a Christian Europe, and so upholding liberal principles could not take priority over re-Christianization when the two were in conflict, or the means would have become the end. Yet if liberal principles were sacrificed, then Christian Europe was in danger.

The Law on Youth-Endangering Texts was a flashpoint of cultural conservatives' struggle over this conundrum. The CDU-led government, which produced the draft, insisted that the law was not censorship.[35] The state would prevent no work from being published or put on the market, and even if a work was indexed, it could still be sold. Rather, the law would control distribution and advertisement in order to uphold the constitutional obligation to protect youth—and in the CDU's view, the law erected high structural barriers to taking such action. Indeed, numerous constituents found the proposed legislation too weak, accusing the government of sacrificing the youth to the "idol of freedom of the press."[36]

The law's opponents on the political left saw the proper balance between liberal freedoms and youth protection to contain a greater emphasis on the former. But for them, too, it was a matter of balance—not an absolute priority of liberal freedoms. Even the law's opponents on the left agreed that filth and trash were reprehensible. Pointing out that truly obscene materials were already banned by the criminal code, they implicitly approved this variant of censorship.[37] Yet in comparing the minimal peril of texts and images to the dire threat posed by current living conditions, opponents of the law declared that war had proven more dangerous to young people than sex. Not infrequently, they added another hazard: the remnants of Nazi-era socialization in young people's psyches. Fascism, too, was worse than sex. But the Law on Youth-Endangering Texts, in Free Democrats' and Social Democrats' eyes, revealed that fascism had left at least as dangerous a mark on adults as it had on children: the temptation to censor. What began as an effort to protect youth could easily become censorship of political speech, art, and scholarship.[38]

The draft of the Law on Youth-Endangering Texts permitted certain agencies to submit works for indexing (in the final version: the federal Ministry of the Interior and the provincial ministries with competence over youth welfare). The works would be reviewed by an Indexing Panel whose members included (in the final version) three provincial representatives as well as affiliates of literary and publishing circles, religious and youth welfare communities, the bookselling business, and the teaching profession. If the Indexing Panel indexed the work (a two-thirds majority was necessary), then it was illegal to sell it to minors or to display or advertise it openly, and some types of retailers (newsstands, traveling peddlers, bookshops in train stations) were prohibited from carrying it at all. No work could be indexed simply because of its political, social, religious, or ideological content, and works serving art, scholarship, research, or pedagogy could not be indexed. Affected parties such as authors and publishers could appeal Panel decisions in court.

This law would be the new state's first limitation on basic rights. Evoking Nazi censorship, the Social Democratic Party (SPD) objected strongly in parliament, just as journalists and literary figures did in editorials, resolutions, and speeches.[39] Limiting basic rights was permitted only if to do so was necessary for the protection of youth, and only if to do so would indeed result in the protection of youth. Opponents argued that youth's real problem was abysmal socioeconomic conditions. A law restricting reading materials was not necessary to improve their situation, nor would it be effective in doing so, and so it was unconstitutional. The CDU/CSU granted that this law alone would not solve young people's problems but considered it an indispensable element of a solution, both necessary and effective. The Committee for Youth Welfare remained deadlocked for months on these "core principles." The Bundesrat, meanwhile, declared that the draft set too low a threshold for limiting basic rights.[40]

At the root of these debates regarding the necessity, and thus the constitutionality, of restricting the dissemination of publications was the question: Could texts and images endanger youth, and if so, which texts and images? Even youth psychologists and pedagogues who supported the law testified that it was impossible to demonstrate that texts and images caused young people to take up criminal behavior.[41] Pointing to reports of young criminals who were found to possess "trashy literature," proponents essentially argued that anecdotal evidence was good enough. If they waited until causality could be demonstrated, then the damage would already have been done.[42] The law's opponents argued that restricting basic rights required hard evidence of damage. These discussions rarely distinguished between violent and sexual literature.

Yet the question of how the potential damage of sexual images and texts compared to that of other messages commanded attention elsewhere in the debate. All agreed that the term "youth-endangering" required definition and that sex was not the only dangerous influence (although some made this issue a central argument, while others conceded it only when put on the spot). In the end, the law specified "immoral" works and works that glorified crime, war, or racial hatred. Since the latter categories required separate listing, they implicitly fell outside the category "immoral": "immoral" meant "sexual." But influences beyond sexual immorality, the law acknowledged, could endanger youth.[43]

Yet many proponents of this balanced list of dangerous materials simultaneously supported the automatic restriction of nudist publications. The notion of restricting some objects without indexing was a response to a perceived weakness of the 1926 law. Indexing took time, and so materials remained in circulation, sometimes for weeks, until the next meeting of the Panel. Decency advocates wanted a way to intervene quickly in pressing cases. The 1953 law permitted local authorities (the youth bureau, the police) to request a court order authorizing the immediate confiscation of "obviously deeply youth-endangering" items. The Panel, at its next meeting, would determine whether to index the item or to lift the restrictions. A separate provision restricted the circulation of nudist publications without any formal proceedings, or even a local decision that they were "obviously deeply youth-endangering." Lawmakers did not consider similar measures for any other category of publication. In the debate about nudist publications, the question was direct: were sexual materials necessarily and uniquely damaging to youth?

Nudism had originated as one of many "lifestyle reform" movements in pre–World War I Germany, had flourished in the Weimar era, and had persisted, with some restrictions, during the Nazi years. Naturalists argued that their nudism was not sexual, that it was those who obsessively covered up the body who imposed a necessarily sexual meaning on it.[44] Furthermore, they pointed out, the Basic Law prohibited discrimination based on a person's or group's "worldview," and naturalism was a worldview.[45]

The Bundestag deliberations, however, were not a debate between nudists and their critics. As naturalists sadly noted, not a single member of parliament belonged to their movement.[46] Opponents of the provision did not contest conservatives' complaint that many "naturalist" magazines had nothing to do with the movement and instead were purely commercial endeavors, profiting from the marketability of nude female bodies (images of men being few in these publications).[47] Nor did they challenge conservatives' contention that, however nonsexual naturalists might consider their images, a publication featuring a large number of nude photographs could be sexual for many readers. Rather, critics of the provision, including many members of the governing coalition, argued that none of these objections warranted limiting basic rights. Proponents of the restriction of naturalist publications maintained a slight majority in the Bundestag. The measure remained one of the law's most controversial features, but it remained in place until the Constitutional Court declared it unconstitutional in 1971.[48]

Federalism had proven controversial in drawing up the Basic Law. Distrustful of centralized German states, the Western Allies had demanded significant provincial authority, but federalism also had fans in Bavaria, historically wary of the economically more powerful, and largely Protestant, north. The most durable marker of Bavarian regionalism was the Christian Social Union, which worked in concert with the CDU at the national level but remained a distinctly Bavarian institution. In other words, there were schisms even within the conservative world of Christian Democracy, and the relationship between federation and province, especially regarding cultural matters, was at its core. North Rhine–Westphalia and Rhineland-Palatinate (home of Cologne and Koblenz) pushed for a national Law on Youth-Endangering Texts, convinced that interstate commerce would undercut provincial efforts. Bavaria (whose capital was Munich) and its next-door neighbor, Baden-Württemburg, challenged the federation's competency to promulgate the law.[49] Bavaria lost the fight. The law passed on June 9, 1953.

The law's passage was a victory for conservatives. It validated a variant of censorship, even if the state would not vet works before their publication or distribution.[50] It allowed authorities to confiscate "obviously deeply youth-endangering" publications without a hearing before the Panel. And it singled out a genre that could be considered sexual as necessarily and uniquely dangerous. Yet the battle had been difficult, and there were limitations. Except for nudist magazines, the mere presence of content that might be interpreted as sexual was no longer adequate to index a work, as it had been in the 1926 law. Sexual danger (like other kinds of danger) required evaluation on a case-by-case basis. Opposition to the law was a minority position in parliament, but it remained the stance of the SPD, which led several provincial governments. Even conservatives differed in their comfort with the law's attempt to regulate sexual consumer culture within a liberal framework. Radical decency advocates felt it compromised the moral order in the name of civil liberties. More moderate cultural conservatives considered some aspects of the law to violate basic rights.

Moderation and Apathy: Monitoring Youth-Endangering and Obscene Materials

Decency advocates hoped the Law on Youth-Endangering Texts would usher in an age of more stringent enforcement. Instead, after reaching a high point in 1952–53, convictions for disseminating "obscene" materials declined precipitously.[51] Some materials that might previously have gone to criminal court now went to the Indexing Panel, but that agency was less powerful and more moderate than decency advocates had hoped (and opponents had feared). Evocations of the danger of censorship continued to be as vital as reminders of a supposedly libertine Nazi regime or the sexual chaos of the immediate postwar years. Self-control on the part of the industry made official action less necessary. Self-control, however, could signal retreat, as when the film industry self-censored rather than risk state action[52]—or it could be a strategy to stretch the boundaries of what was acceptable, as when mail-order erotica firms distributed their catalogs carefully to show that they did not endanger youth.

It took over a year to develop implementation guidelines for the law, appoint an Indexing Panel and director, and review the first items.[53] In the meantime, local officials could seek confiscation of "obviously deeply youth-endangering" items. Later detractors of the law focused on the Indexing Panel, but this provision, which bypassed the Panel, was far more draconian and left much more room for arbitrary and inconsistent censorship.[54]

Local courts' rulings on obscenity had varied widely; this provision empowered those same courts to employ a lower threshold to confiscate "obviously deeply youth-endangering" materials.[55] The paragraph was intended for cases so urgent that they could not wait for the next monthly meeting of the Panel, but until the Panel took up its work, anything that required action met this definition of "urgent." By the time the first Panel convened, local authorities in activist-conservative provinces had developed the habit of petitioning the courts for all items they considered "obviously deeply youth-endangering," whether or not the manner of distribution made time of the essence.[56] This practice was an opportunity to continue to apply local standards. Liberal Hessen may have ignored naturalist magazines, but Bavarian authorities considered marriage manuals describing birth control "obviously deeply youth-endangering" and whisked them from the marketplace.[57]

The provision on "obviously deeply youth-endangering" materials drove newsstand operators to despair. Not only might valuable stock be confiscated, but retailers were criminally liable for carrying items subsequently identified as "obviously deeply youth-endangering." (They were responsible for limiting the circulation of "youth-endangering" works only after they appeared on the published index.) Every word of the phrase "obviously deeply youth-endangering" was open to interpretation, and any police officer could make the initial call.[58] Hundreds of titles, some in foreign languages, might move through a kiosk in a week. Kiosk owners could not possibly examine each of them, particularly given the time-sensitive nature of periodicals, the hectic pace of kiosk work, and the minimal level of education of many kiosk owners.[59] Yet the Constitutional Court declared in 1955 that this was indeed the expectation. Furthermore, the court said, "obvious" did not mean that the youth-endangering nature of an item was evident on first glance (for example, by looking at the cover or the table of contents). Rather, "obvious" meant the danger to youth would be clear to any sensible adult who read the whole work.[60] Newsstand owners learned to be cautious, and decency advocates credited the Law on Youth-Endangering Texts with cleaning up the kiosks.[61] Local authorities, however, and not the Indexing Panel, could take credit (or blame) for this development.

The sanitation of newsstands was counterbalanced, in part, by the law's inadvertently permissive stance on mail order and on privately owned libraries. The law prohibited newsstands, bookstores in train stations, and traveling peddlers from selling indexed works. It said nothing about mail-order sellers or private libraries, and so they could carry youth-endangering works as long as they restrained from displaying or advertising them openly.

A Bavarian report noted in 1959 that at the time the law was drafted, "the need for protection in regard to private libraries was not yet recognized."[62] A whole branch of the publishing industry produced works (nearly 3.5 million volumes annually by 1960) solely for private libraries, which charged small fees to borrow books.[63] Specializing in "trash"—westerns, gangster novels, war stories—with a smaller dose of "filth" in the form of "marriage novels," some 30,000 pay libraries loaned approximately 600 million books per year by 1955, by one estimate—compared to 15 million loans from public libraries.[64] Most were run as small side businesses (in bars, stationary stores, tobacco shops) or out of the home by people who had no idea of the law and were sometimes only marginally literate themselves. Four-fifths of the books indexed through the summer of 1958 circulated mainly or exclusively in pay libraries. From beginning to end, those charged with implementing the Law on Youth-Endangering Texts acknowledged that enforcing it in pay libraries was impossible. The end came, though, in the early 1960s, as television claimed the leisure hours of those who had formerly turned to cheap literature, and pay libraries went into decline.

The crafters of the Law on Youth-Endangering Texts were equally oblivious to mail order. Robert Schilling, however, was not. While cracking down on Cologne newsstands in 1950, he traced firms whose names arose in a year's worth of obscenity cases. In addition to seventy presses specializing in sexual works, he was astonished to discover some fifty mail-order firms for erotica. The Guardians rushed his findings into print, updating the number of firms as he discovered more (the number tripled within a year), and Schilling tried to convince decency advocates that they were missing a fast-growing danger if they persisted in focusing on newsstands.[65] The terms of the debate for the law had been set, however, and lawmakers could not be convinced to add mail order.

After the law's passage, the Ministry of the Interior tried to plug the gap by decreeing that mail-order firms fell under the same restrictions as newsstands and peddlers since the customer did not enter the store.[66] Decency advocates believed the catalogs themselves could be indexed as youth-endangering. Mail-order erotica catalogs, after all, described such items as textured condoms and penis-enlarging ointments. When the Indexing Panel had been in operation barely two months, the Guardians urged the Ministry of the Interior to submit a petition to have one of Beate Uhse's catalogs indexed. But the ministry declined: the catalogs were mailed in sealed envelopes, making it potentially difficult to demonstrate that they were accessible to youth—and if the petition failed, mail-order erotica houses would surely step up their activity.[67] Frustrated, decency advocates turned to the courts, but less than a year later, the Constitutional Court vindicated the ministry's caution, determining that such catalogs endangered youth only if the publications were likely to come into their hands. With the right distribution methods—such as those practiced by defendant Beate Uhse—young people would come across the catalogs only in extraordinary circumstances.[68] Now mail-order erotica firms could cite a Constitutional Court decision in their favor.

Mail-order firms thus had to distribute catalogs with care, but they could advertise sexual wares. If the recipient responded with an order or a request for more information, subsequent mailings to that person were not public advertising and so could include indexed works. This method was technically parallel to the bookstore offering established customers indexed works under the counter. But for mail-order firms, the "offer" took the form of mass mailings: by the mid-1950s, Beate Uhse mailed 100,000 ads per week, and its biggest rival, Gisela, advertised items like the *Kama Sutra* with mailings of millions.[69]

Mail order became *the* means of obtaining indexed sexual literature.[70] Even if a firm avoided indexed works altogether, there were enough other books to sell, never mind objects that made concerns about "filth and trash in print" seem positively quaint. Even when erotica firms distributed catalogs less carefully, indexing was of no use.[71] A firm's 1957 catalog, for example, was distributed too quickly for a confiscation order under the provisions for "obviously deeply youth-endangering" materials to have any effect, much less for the Panel to meet, and the 1958 catalog was a different work and thus not covered by an indexing of the 1957 edition.[72] The Law on Youth-Endangering Texts gave mail-order firms a near monopoly in "youth-endangering" writings, and mail order created a new sexually explicit genre—the erotica catalog—that the Law on Youth-Endangering Texts could not reach.

Thus critical categories of works never made it to the Indexing Panel, either because they were confiscated by local authorities as "obviously deeply youth-endangering," or because the law overlooked them. Nevertheless, the Indexing Panel was the federal agency associated with the Law on Youth-Endangering Texts, and both the contemporary media and historians have seen it as a symbol of the censoring, prudish mood of the 1950s.

In fact, however, the history of the Indexing Panel was ambivalent. The Guardians certainly exercised disproportionate influence. The organization exploited its connections to prod North Rhine–Westphalia to submit an extraordinary number of petitions, and it forwarded its own list of suspect items to the federal Interior Ministry, which usually followed up with petitions of its own.[73] In a similar bit of double-dipping, Guardians director Michael Calmes occupied the Panel's seat for "youth welfare" until his death in 1957, leaving the seat for "religious communities" open for another Christian activist (not from the Guardians, but sympathetic).[74] In 1956, the Guardians claimed responsibility for over half the items indexed—in private correspondence, since such information would hurt the cause if it were publicly known.[75] Other confessional institutions also submitted materials to petitioning agencies, though at a much slower rate; Protestant youth-protection leagues considered "filth and trash" to be a much lower priority than did the Guardians.[76]

Yet some of the law's early opponents credited the Panel with proceeding in a manner that alleviated their worst fears.[77] One important reason was Robert Schilling, who as chair of the Panel from 1954 to 1966 absorbed the brunt of criticism of its censoring activities and its evident prioritization of sexual danger. The sharpest attacks came in 1964, when the news show *Panorama* not only ridiculed the "little group of peculiarly prudish custodians of morals with a puberty-like penchant for seeking out [sexual] passages and a notable need to inform others" but also discredited its leader as "a man whose Nazi past completely compromises his office."[78]

In fact, Schilling was a moderating influence. Many items that appalled moral purity advocates did not meet the Panel's threshold for indexing, either because of the nature of their content or because of the Panel's interpretation of constitutional safeguards.[79] Schilling represented an important strand of cultural conservatism: one that deeply feared the influence of "unclean" writings on young people but that did not believe all things sexual were dangerous, and that was committed to constitutional principles.

Born in 1904, Schilling studied law and joined the office of the Cologne district attorney in 1932; he subsequently worked in several Rhenish cities before his military service. A member of the right-wing German National People's Party briefly in 1923, he joined the Nazi Party and the Sturmabteilung (or brownshirts) in 1933 and held positions in several party organizations. Schilling acknowledged that he had been a committed National Socialist for many years, with doubts emerging only toward the regime's end. His Nazi-era superiors considered him thoroughly reliable. When the Nazi state was defeated, Schilling assumed his career as a lawyer was over and took an apprenticeship as a mason. The denazification courts, however, classified him as a "fellow traveler," and in 1948 he was appointed district attorney in Cologne. There he embarked on his mission to clean that city of smut, developing a cozy working relationship with the Guardians (although he was Protestant) along the way.

Schilling believed in eternal moral standards (at least regarding sex) and feared the relativism implicit in the legal convention that the community's "general sense of modesty and morals" should define what was acceptable. What if recent events had corrupted the "general sense of modesty and morals," as he believed to be the case? On these grounds, he applauded a 1954 Constitutional Court decision upholding the prohibition on "procurement" and rejecting the notion that the widespread acceptance of premarital sex called for a revision of this portion of the 1900 vice law. Schilling used this decision to argue that standards for obscenity in word and image were likewise unchanging.[80] But Schilling was not cut from Guardians cloth. The Guardians fundamentally rejected such markers of modernity as materialism and liberalism, and considered youth protection to be a first step toward their real goal: to eliminate objectionable materials entirely. Schilling, by contrast, was firmly situated in the twentieth century—including that century's requirement of adaptability to changing political realities—and believed that a fully developed culture included materials that were not suitable for children.[81] As a result, Schilling publicly denounced portions of the Law on Youth-Endangering Texts—some because they were unconstitutional, to his eye, and others because he considered them unworkable given the social and cultural realities of the mid-twentieth century.

If Schilling's modernity made him more tolerant of sexual representation than many of his allies, it also enabled him to better understand sexual consumer culture. As decency advocates replayed Weimar-era battles by waging war on newsstands (and quaintly took aim at book peddlers), Schilling urged attention to the less visible, but more dynamic, mail-order houses. One of the first to take such firms seriously, Schilling's early research into the mail-order sector was for years *the* source of information for decency advocates and state officials who belatedly turned their attention to it.

Decency advocates valued Schilling's ability to contextualize their concerns in the political and commercial realities of the postwar setting, and he was their choice to chair the Indexing Panel. He was not, however, the first choice of the Ministry of the Interior, which feared that Schilling's Nazi past might prove embarrassing. The ministry may also have considered Schilling's close relationship with the Guardians a political liability: the Guardians' involvement in the passage of the Law on Youth-Endangering Texts had attracted much criticism in the press.[82] In the end, the ministry appointed Schilling, but Schilling's situation was strained. Having pushed through the legislation to please the cultural conservatives that formed an important part of the CDU/CSU's base, the government subsequently appeared ambivalent about the enterprise. Even critics of the law acknowledged that the Panel was poorly funded.[83] In over ten years of work, the Panel was not once mentioned in the government's Bulletin (which, by contrast, enthusiastically publicized the nongovernmental Film Self-Control Board).[84]

At the very least, the government made clear that the Panel's powers were limited. Constituents evoked an array of political and historical associations in their complaints about the marketplace in youth-endangering materials. Communist East Germany at least kept this sort of stuff under control.[85] Democracy's tolerance of smut made people nostalgic for Nazism.[86] Trashy novels were the products of those socialized by Nazism.[87] But in 1959 CDU Interior Minister Gerhard Schröder repeated the position the government had taken since it had drafted the law—a position Schilling shared—in response to those who asked whether the government couldn't "do something once and for all" about smut. The answer was no. The Film Self-Control Board and the Indexing Panel were important elements of a societywide commitment to protect youth, said Schröder. However, state censorship according to "moral" criteria—which according to a recent poll 54 percent of the population desired and only 20 percent opposed—was incompatible with democracy. Nazi Germany and East Germany both practiced such censorship, and so they appeared "cleaner" than West Germany. In both cases, however, "puritanically strict outer façades" veiled horrifying crimes—hardly a model for West Germany.[88]

Vested by moral purity advocates with hopes of turning back the clock a hundred years or so, alternately excoriated and ridiculed by Social Democrats, and held at arm's length by the government, Schilling steered a middle path. He seems to have been moved less by a political instinct to compromise than by a sense of lawyerly correctness, a commitment to balancing constitutional guarantees with youth protection, and recognition of the limits of social engineering. It is impossible to say what transformed this avowed Nazi into a conventional cultural conservative with a demonstrably greater commitment to liberal principles than many of his allies in the moral purity movement. Volumes of documentation, however—some intended for public and some for purely private consumption—attest to Schilling's concern for constitutional guarantees in applying the Law on Youth-Endangering Texts.

Schilling openly criticized the law for limiting adults' as well as children's access to reading materials, for putting inappropriate powers into the hands of civil servants and the police, for ignoring due process with "obviously deeply youth-endangering" materials, and for inadequately protecting freedom of artistic expression.[89] He went beyond clear-cut constitutional principles to defend interpretations of the law that baffled decency advocates. He insisted, for example, that even a work which, in the hands of young people, would unquestionably endanger their moral development was only indexable if it circulated in places that youth actually had access to.[90] A work that fell short of true artistry might be exempted from indexing in order to protect the "free development of art": how were budding artists to perfect their craft if they could not practice?[91] The Panel rejected many petitions regarding materials with sexual content, and petitioning bodies sometimes declined to forward items they found objectionable because the Panel's past practice made an indexing of the current item unlikely. Such works included sex manuals, books of nude photography, novels with sex scenes, erotica catalogs, and magazines that constituents considered homosexual propaganda.[92] While indexings of criminal, militaristic, or racist works almost always resulted from Panel hearings (374 of 393 such works indexed between 1954 and 1959), three-fifths of indexings of sexual works (472 of 804) resulted from confiscations of "obviously deeply youth-endangering" materials, which bypassed the Panel.[93] In his valedictory report of 1968, Schilling lashed out at decency advocates: by ensuring that sexual materials constituted the large majority of indexed items, they gave the Panel an undeserved reputation of being obsessed with sex to the exclusion of violence, racism, and crime.[94]

Schilling was not solely responsible for the direction of the Indexing Panel. Although moral purity activists occupied some seats on the Panel, others were filled by persons whose aim was to guard against too-easy censorship.[95] The Panel saw its domain to be popular literature and resisted cases concerning high literature, including the genre of "problem literature," whose point was to explore sexuality or violence in an unvarnished manner.[96] Panelists agreed far more than they disagreed: nearly all decisions were unanimous or had only one dissenting vote.[97] This outcome reflected not only many conservatives' respect for constitutional limitations but also agreement among liberals that taking action against "trashy" literature was appropriate. Representatives of literary and publishing circles focused on the protection of art and scholarship, both on the Panel and in more public forums. The occasional indexings of high literature, not the routine indexings of dime novels or illustrated magazines, moved them to protest.[98]

The Indexing Panel did not proceed with complete abandon, but its job was to index works, and this it did. The Panel's report on Frederic Gaston's *Die Verlorenen* (The Lost Ones), a work set in occupation Germany and indexed in 1957, illustrates its concerns about the ways a book might harm young people.[99] The black marketeers, drug smugglers, criminals, and prostitutes in the work used crude language: "broads," "ass," "whorehouse," "shut your trap." The author used the turbulence of the postwar period as an excuse to pile violent crime upon violent crime in a manner that "brutalized" the young reader: a pimp beats his prostitute, American soldiers knock the teeth out of the hero, a prostitute tempts a smuggler to a field of rubble where her accomplices kick and rob him. Yet when caught, perpetrators are rewarded rather than punished. The work furthered racial hatred by making the leader of a criminal gang a Jew who exploited postwar conditions to get rich before obeying his need to wander—but not to Israel, because Israel offered more work than prosperity, and, according to the book, "work was not Grünberg's strength."

Still, the most serious problem was the book's numerous sexually explicit passages. Four of the six single-spaced pages of the decision were given over to sex scenes—not without wit, as panelists clearly enjoyed poking fun at their poor literary quality. The sheer number of sex scenes was important: the Panel sometimes rejected works with only a few sex scenes on the grounds that they did not define the work as a whole. Yet the Panel's need to paraphrase so many sex scenes in order to demonstrate that the work was suitable to "stimulate young readers' sexual fantasy in a manner that harms their development" and to "confuse young readers' capacity for sexual-ethical judgment" is striking: a single paragraph demonstrated the brutalizing nature of the book's numerous violent scenes. This is the sort of decision that led *Panorama* to comment on the group's "puberty-like penchant for seeking out [sexual] passages and notable need to inform others."

Despite Schilling's relative liberalism—in comparison to the Guardians, at least—he too wished the Panel could better halt the spread of materials he considered dangerous to youth. But the law, to his mind, granted people not committed to the project too much power. The most serious problem was the petition system. Before the law's passage, decency advocates, convinced that they spoke for the silent majority, assumed that once a law was in place, citizens would stream forward with literature for indexing. The petitioning bodies could take it from there. But citizens did not do their part.[100] Decency advocates blamed Germans' Nazi-era socialization to expect the state to do everything for them.[101]

The petitioning bodies, therefore, had to take the initiative. They did so unevenly, as the provinces' disparate commitment to the project persisted. About 25 percent of the 771 petitions submitted through 1959 came from North Rhine–Westphalia and 37 percent from the Ministry of the Interior, most of these prompted by the Guardians. Rhineland-Palatinate and Bavaria also produced large numbers of petitions. Schleswig-Holstein, by contrast, submitted 2, Bremen 5, Hessen 10, and Baden-Württemberg 15.[102] In 1960, North Rhine–Westphalia spent DM 250,000 to fight youth-endangering materials, including a DM 10,000 subsidy for the Guardians. Hamburg had no budget for this purpose.[103] Even committed provinces had no mechanism for systematic observation of the marketplace. They thus submitted petitions for items that had long since been widely available or with print runs so tiny as to pose no danger, while failing to catch new mass-circulation works in time to hinder their spread.

To address these problems, and to streamline the linked struggles against obscene and youth-endangering materials, federal guidelines instructed each province to develop a Central Office for Combating Obscene and Youth-Endangering Texts. By sorting out tasteless-but-harmless, "youth-endangering," "obviously deeply youth-endangering," and "obscene" items, the Central Offices would funnel objectionable materials to the appropriate channels.[104] They would also coordinate efforts across provinces.

Again, provinces showed different levels of enthusiasm. Some had opened Central Offices before the passage of the law and used them aggressively to seek out objectionable materials. Others skipped planning meetings, were tardy in establishing their offices, invested them with minimal powers, and took action only when a citizen brought an item to them.[105] The Schleswig-Holstein district attorney charged with pursuing all cases regarding Beate Uhse informed the annual conference of Central Offices that he had the honor not because of any commitment to the cause, but rather because he had inherited responsibility for firms whose names began with the letter "U" from his predecessor.[106] Since each Central Office was to monitor publications of firms in its province, firms in inactive provinces escaped this moment of scrutiny. A stricter province might pick up an item from one of these firms once it was on the market—but in order to avoid duplicate (and possibly contradictory) judgments, the item was to be passed to the Central Office in the province where the item had originated. That Central Office would determine whether action was warranted. Schleswig-Holstein's Central Office was unimpressed by southern Catholics' constant demands for action on one item or another of Beate Uhse's, and Bavaria could do nothing about it.[107]

In short, a federal system required mechanisms for inter-provincial coordination, and the system developed for obscene and youth-endangering writings put a great deal of power into the hands of the more liberal provinces. Once an item made it to the Indexing Panel, its chances of being indexed were good. But to begin and end the story at the Panel (or, for obscenity, with cases that made it to court) is to ignore the ways that skeptics blocked most objects from getting this far. As Michael Calmes, head of the Guardians, fumed in 1955: "Certain firms, for example the mail-order firms Beate Uhse (Flensburg), Gisela (Stuttgart), and Delphin (Göttingen), can only persist in their unholy business because the district attorneys at the place of publication are too 'soft' and mostly file charges late or not at all; in such cases the district attorneys at the point of distribution are powerless."[108] In a response to a similar outcry from the Hamm (North Rhine–Westphalia) judiciary, the director of Schleswig-Holstein's Central Office proved more phlegmatic about regional difference: "The view expressed here, that the Federal Republic is being increasingly flooded with obscene and youth-endangering texts, is in my opinion not borne out by the facts. . . . It is however certainly possible that the measures of 'obscenity' are stricter in Hamm than in Schleswig-Holstein."[109]

The Difficulty of Discussing Sex

Divergent regional cultures and the complicated place of sexuality in liberalism made it difficult to enforce a conservative sexual-moral order. There was another reason, however, that it was so hard for public officials to resolve these matters: their own vexed relationship to sexually explicit materials and

talk about sex. Moral purity activists and members of the regulatory apparatus became consumers of sexually explicit materials. But unlike "private"
consumers, whose relationship to their wares is the subject of the next chapter, these were "public" consumers. In their professional capacity they consumed on the public's behalf, and the function of their consumption was to
shape not their private lives but rather public policy. Yet their response to the
wares they examined was inevitably informed by attitudes about sex that had
been shaped in the "private" spheres of home, neighborhood, and church.

The large-scale deaths of World War II meant that government and moral
purity organizations were dominated by older men. Their sexual socialization
often predated the First World War. Members of the CDU/CSU and moral purity organizations came from a social elite and religious milieu that defined
its distance from the masses in part by its sexual propriety. For these men,
examining arousing materials was shameful. Becoming aroused by them was
really shameful. Imagining sex with material objects, like imagining homosexual sex, evoked disgust. And although they might trade sexual innuendos
in all-male social settings or with "disreputable" women, the taboo against
speaking of sex was so strong that it made it difficult to do so, even when the
purpose was to combat indecency.[110]

Liberals, too, were older and usually had a deficient sex education. There
was a considerable gap between opposition to state regulation of sexuality,
on the one hand, and acceptance of nonconformist sexuality on the other.
Even Free Democrats and Social Democrats usually inculcated their children
with sexual shame and a double standard regarding acceptable behavior for
boys and girls, never mind regarding homo- versus heterosexuality. Yet liberals were more likely to have grown up in a milieu sympathetic with earlier reform movements like the legalization of contraceptives in the Weimar period.
Social Democrats came mainly from a working-class environment in which
the frequency of unwed motherhood required a more flexible attitude toward sexual morality. Like the bourgeois liberals of the Free Democratic Party
(FDP), Social Democrats were mainly Protestant, and both groups tended to
be less pious than the conservative Protestants who, like conservative Catholics, gravitated to the CDU/CSU. Coming from privileged households, Free
Democrats were less accustomed to single motherhood in their circles, but
they shared a dislike of church involvement in public affairs. In short, proponents of liberalization, if not unburdened, were less burdened by internal
shame regarding sex than were conservatives. Their greater (if still limited)
comfort with sex gave them an advantage in debates about it, which helped
to balance conservatives' numerical superiority in government.

In the case of images, decency advocates developed a highly differentiated,
if subjective, language to distinguish decent from indecent. For example, they

described the ways that light and shadow transformed a photograph of a woman engaged in decent activity, like exercising on the beach, into an indecent representation by focusing attention on her sexual organs.[111] By contrast, sustained discussion of sex aids and their use was simply too much for most decency advocates and their allies in government.[112]

Decency advocates were uncomfortable with the notion of a woman receiving pleasure from an object rather than the unmediated penis. Dildos required no penile penetration and thus were to be used in sex that was, according to moral purity advocates, necessarily indecent. By contrast, textured rings, sleeves, and condoms involved penetrative heterosexual sex. In decency advocates' minds, such aids thus transformed a decent act (if performed within marriage) into an indecent one. Yet they found it difficult to make this argument, since it required a language so much more explicit than the language describing the transformation of a decent image to an indecent one. While entrepreneurs and medical professionals spoke of sexually transmitted disease, frigidity, and the value of satisfying sex to marriage, decency advocates could not utter the words necessary to demonstrate that the objects were intended for indecent use.[113] Health exemptions and language about marital compatibility were important for proponents of aids not just for substantive reasons, but also because detractors had such trouble countering with words to explain their purported indecency.

Few of those who in an official capacity discussed sex aids, whether to defend or to excoriate them, were likely aroused by examining the objects. (The unsexy appearance of the items led Beate Uhse's staff to nickname them "dead mice."[114]) Sexual texts and images were a different story: protagonists had to come to terms with their own illicit desire. The taboo nature of that arousal, like the difficulty in describing just what was so abhorrent about sex aids, could be useful for the industry and its defenders.

Protagonists on both sides of the battle avoided speaking about their own arousal. Officials' language regarding a work's anticipated effect on consumers, however, was sometimes so strong that it suggested their sense of being overwhelmed by the material. Such was the case even years later with a district attorney's application to have Jörg Freimann's *Sex-Orgien im Ferienhaus* (Sex Orgies in the Vacation Home) examined as obscene: "Broadly painted and salaciously arousing scenes comprise the book. The instant, constant, and excessive satisfaction of lust is not only portrayed, but propagated as exemplary and natural, with no distancing devices. The portrayals are suitable for triggering such strong sexual reactions that nothing else remains in the thoughts of the average reader."[115]

Although protagonists were mum on the subject of their own arousal, they frequently speculated about their opponents' arousal. Anticipating ac-

ademic theories describing sexual taboos as providing sexual incitement, reformers portrayed decency advocates as men driven simultaneously by sexual impulses and a sense of shame, grateful for an officially sanctioned excuse
to pore over explicit material.[116] The complement to such armchair psycho-
analyzing was satire: cartoons portraying officials salivating as they examined objectionable film clips over and over, or the characterization of the
Panel by *Panorama*.[117]

Decency advocates, in short, were hypocrites. But even without the im-
plication of hypocrisy, to portray a respectable bourgeois man as aroused by
texts or images was to portray him as pathetic, his rational facilities disabled
by the crudest of materials. (Participants in the debate sometimes imagined
the arousal of female consumers by text or image, but they imagined aroused
activists and officials as purely male.) Those materials might succeed with
the primitive lower classes, but they really should not move the bourgeoisie.
Decency advocates revealed this class bias by linking "smutty" literature with
working-class delinquency and criminality. Liberalizers accused decency advocates of elitism, for example ridiculing a 1962 court decision that the memoirs of Restif de la Bretonne were acceptable—but not the insert that translated into German the sexual terms that had been left in Latin in the original
translation.[118] But even liberalizers never spoke of a stimulation by text and
image whose freedom from hypocrisy or whose more refined presentation
made it dignified. Instead, they revealed their own class bias by distinguishing between "filth and trash" or "obscenity," on the one hand, and "art" on
the other.[119]

Entrepreneurs were cut from a different cloth. Few came from an elite
background, even if some eventually became wealthy; neither Walter Schäfer
nor his father, for example, attended university, and many smaller entrepreneurs had only a primary school background. Rotermund was exceptional
in having two university-educated parents (though she bypassed university
herself), but she was also exceptional in that those parents were feminists
and lifestyle reformers. And postwar entrepreneurs were typically young.
They had received their sexual socialization either in the more liberal Weimar
period or under the Nazis, with their celebration of healthy sexuality among
the racial elite and their opportunities for mobility among young people.
Thus entrepreneurs, unlike even liberal politicians, spoke about the virtues,
and not just the harmlessness, of arousal by text and image. In early catalogs,
for example, Beate Uhse cited a statement by the former director of Berlin's
Institute for Sexual Science that erotic literature could help save marriages
by stimulating couples who had lost their erotic spark.[120] By attaching such
testimony to classic erotic works, Rotermund attributed a positive arousal by
text and image not just to the working class but also to the bourgeoisie.

Entrepreneurs, too, found opportunities both to psychoanalyze and to ridicule the sexual response of their opponents. In early 1952, Rotermund suggested to the provincial attorney general that only a sexual neurosis could account for the district attorney's urge to pursue her firm so relentlessly. The attorney general found the remark "tasteless," and there is no evidence of Rotermund having made such a suggestion again, as she refined her interactions with public officials.[121] But there was something of the technique in her orchestration, two decades later, of a reading of several cheap explicit novels in court. Officially, the reading was to demonstrate that the sex scenes were connected to other realms of life, which would mean that the work was not indecent (according to standards set by the Constitutional Court in 1969, not the standards of the 1950s). However, the tactic also guaranteed a supremely unsexy reading and a vivid demonstration of the works' poor literary qualities, practically daring any of the members of the court to admit that they might find such a work stimulating. Worst of all, it required that the judge and attorneys take turns reading out loud. The excruciatingly embarrassing nature of this task for men who were well trained not to speak of sex in public—much less before a woman, and least of all in the crude terms of these books—was a powerful disincentive for district attorneys to file charges and for judges to bring future cases to trial.

Doing Business: The Sexual Consumer Goods Industry Engages the State

Entrepreneurs required more than personal comfort with sex in order to succeed. As moral purity advocates organized confiscations behind the "erotica curtain" and spearheaded the drive for national legislation in the early 1950s, erotica entrepreneurs had reason to fear for their survival. The industry's skill and aggression in confronting legal challenges enabled it not only to survive but to thrive. Its strategies also helped to determine the form in which it would thrive. Mail-order firms were not just the beneficiaries of the loophole in the Law on Youth-Endangering Texts; they were also adept organizers, expanding their room for maneuver even as other retailers, like newsstands, saw theirs shrinking.

The idea of industrywide organizing for mail-order erotica originated with the first postwar giant of the sector, Walter Schäfer. When Schäfer, son of a Stuttgart shoe salesman, returned from the war, he pursued an eclectic range of business activities.[122] By 1948—at the age of twenty-two—he employed 320 people and did DM 300,000 of business per month. Currency reform in June 1948 bankrupted him, but a cache of condoms he had acquired in a black-market transaction in the Soviet zone enabled him to start anew. He founded International Mail-Order House Gisela, which by the winter of 1949–50 sold erotica to 200,000 customers, 60,000 of whom ordered monthly or bi-weekly.[123] Gisela's success enabled Schäfer to build an empire that included pharmaceutical laboratories (which, among other things, made virility tonics), cosmetic manufacturing (breast creams), food processing (aphrodisiac-filled chocolates), publishing houses (books on sex), printing presses (catalogs for all these items), and—reflecting his father's legacy—shoe stores. His first best seller was a cure for corns; later, a dieting aid made him a fortune.[124] Schäfer's diverse business concerns reflected his catholic interests as an avid reader and traveler.[125]

Such a businessman naturally employed a lawyer. Recognizing erotica's unstable legal status, Schäfer's lawyer founded the Verband deutscher Versandunternehmen (Alliance of German Mail-Order Businesses) in 1951.[126] The Alliance tried to keep its members out of legal trouble, helped them out if trouble came anyway, worked to expand the legal space in which the industry could operate, and sought to improve the public's perception of the industry. The first goal meant avoiding practices that would tempt lawsuits. One firm's sloppy practice could bring a negative ruling that constrained the entire industry, and so the Alliance pressured member firms to operate cautiously, tried to coax nonmembers into the organization, and rejected applicants who had a history of prior convictions.[127] The second goal required arming entrepreneurs with knowledge of positive legal precedents while enabling them to claim ignorance of negative precedents. Selective reporting in the Alliance newsletter helped members to gain acquittal on grounds that they had acted in good faith.[128] The third goal—expanding the space in which the industry could operate—involved two types of activity. The first was to help firms obtain acquittal on substantive grounds, prompting a verdict that other firms could cite in their own defense. The second was to press for reform. Finally, toward the fourth goal—improving the industry's public image—the organization circulated positive news about the industry to the media.

Compared to other industry groups the Alliance was a small operation, with around fifty member firms from the 1950s through the mid-1960s. Most were tiny: only three member firms in 1965 had more than five employees.[129] But then, the state institutions fighting the industry were also small. Schilling, still in Cologne at the time, wrote to his Munich counterpart in 1953 that decency advocates "are like orphans in regard to tactics, intensity, and communication, compared to the Alliance." It would be lovely to have a counterpart to the Alliance's monthly newsletter ("the Rotaprint method the Alliance uses would be ideal") "if it weren't for the pathetic question of who would do it and who would pay for it." Schilling's dream newsletter would inform colleagues "in the backcountry" of convictions and court-ordered confiscations, strengthening their will to act and arming them with supportive precedents. As it was, those colleagues received only the newsletter of the Alliance, which found it useful to publicize dismissed charges, acquittals, and overturned convictions, giving the impression that leniency was the law of the land.[130]

Nor was the Alliance shy about approaching the highest authorities. When the Bavarian Central Office announced in 1952 that its confiscation orders applied nationally, the Alliance argued to the federal Ministry of Justice that if this was true, then court rejections of applications for confiscation orders (like those routinely issued in Schleswig-Holstein) must also apply nationally.[131] In 1952, the Alliance submitted a petition to the Bundestag arguing that the proposed Law on Youth-Endangering Texts was unconstitutional, and in 1960 it approached the same body to oppose the inclusion of mail order in a revised Law on Youth-Endangering Texts.[132]

All of these petitions failed. The Alliance's real impact in those years was in helping members to negotiate the law as it stood. Member firms joined an effort to make the industry more legitimate, both by complying with the law and by stretching the boundaries of what was acceptable. They did so by avoiding objects and practices that were clearly illegal, and by defending themselves when they felt they could win a case or appeal. This strategy distinguished member firms from those that operated in a gray market, selling whatever they could get away with and disappearing when trouble came (perhaps to reemerge under a new name a few months later).[133] Thus while some entrepreneurs knowingly sold images and texts that were obscene under the current terms of the law, Alliance member firms hired lawyers to vet their materials in order to ensure their legality and to enable the firms to plead "good faith" if charges were filed anyway.[134] While publishers and authors of books for the pay library market rarely defended their works before the Indexing Panel, Alliance member firms frequently organized a defense.[135]

When erotica firms were sued despite careful practice, the setting was ripe for a defense that might establish by precedent more generous terms on which erotica firms could operate. Such cases tended to come from Rotermund, who often sought acquittal on subjective grounds (like good faith) but did not hesitate to challenge charges or appeal convictions on substantive grounds. When Rotermund was accused in 1952 of facilitating indecent relations by selling condoms to unwed persons, Rotermund retained Eberhard Strohm, well-heeled erotica firms' favorite attorney. Strohm prepared a defense arguing that nonmarital sex could no longer be classified as indecent, since Germans' behavior and mores had changed markedly since the law had been crafted. Given Rotermund's and Strohm's near-perfect record in the courtroom (both apart and together), it is worth imagining the impact an acquittal on these grounds might have had on the legal underpinnings of West German sexual conservatism in the 1950s.[136] But the case never got that far. First, the defense tracked down each recipient of condoms for the shipment at issue in the trial—and found that all were married, making the case moot.[137] Rotermund (with different lawyers) was behind the 1955 Constitutional Court case establishing that, with careful distribution methods, erotica catalogs did not endanger youth. The same decision determined that unsolicited catalogs did not violate the recipient's honor by implying, as the plaintiffs claimed, that something was amiss in the recipient's marriage.[138]

Lawyers were not the only professionals who helped in court. The industry cultivated allies in many academic disciplines—psychology, education, criminology, literary criticism, art history, medicine—who produced sympathetic affidavits when the need arose. These experts occupied university seats nationwide, but Frankfurt, historical home of the University of Frankfurt's progressive social science tradition and the base of the German Society for Sexological Research (Deutsche Gesellschaft für Sexualforschung), founded in 1951, was a particularly important nexus.[139]

Physicians were especially important in the earliest years. While freedom of speech and the press were newly anchored in the constitution and could be restricted to protect youth, an exception to the ban on selling indecent objects in the case of items serving medical functions dated from 1927.[140] The purpose of the exemption had been to enable the distribution of condoms to fight infection, but now the Federal Health Bureau approved a variety of dildos, rings, textured condoms, and other aids on the grounds that they addressed frigidity, a medical condition.[141] Compounding the weight of medical authority was the constitutional commitment to marriage. Once it was established that sex aids might further a healthy sexual life, it was easy to argue in court that they could strengthen marriages.[142]

Thus erotica firms hired medical experts to back them up in court. In her appeal of a 1951 conviction, Rotermund commissioned an affidavit from Wilhelm Hallermann, since 1941 director of the Institute of Legal and Social Medicine at the University of Kiel. Hallermann testified that 30–40 percent of women did not experience orgasm during intercourse, that failure to reach orgasm caused not only emotional but also physical symptoms in women, and that physicians often recommended mechanical aids to remedy the situation. Likewise, physicians sometimes prescribed the active ingredient in the ointment Beate Uhse sold to prolong erection. The appeals court overturned the conviction.[143]

Over the next two decades, members of the German Society for Sexological Research submitted affidavits in dozens of cases, and lists of signatures sometimes read like a who's who of sexual science.[144] Decency advocates (and not a few academic physicians) considered such expert witnesses to be hired hands of a disreputable industry, and indeed experts were paid for their efforts. But sexual scientists were also paid for their academic work; this did not negate their belief that more relaxed obscenity statutes were crucial to a healthy sexuality, and thus to a happier human experience. (Conservative academics were likewise paid for affidavits for the prosecution.) Erotica firms were wealthy patrons in a cause sexologists wished to fight. Indeed, erotica firms' payments to the German Society for Sexological Research indirectly subsidized research in areas that had less financial backing, like research on homosexuality.[145]

In time, alliances formed to fight legal battles evolved into deeper professional relationships, with benefits for both sides. Having examined sexual consumer goods to pen affidavits, sexologists drew on this knowledge for scholarly publications.[146] Doctoral students of sexual scientists found opportunities to do research with corporate records.[147] Sexologists even got research subjects in the form of customer lists.[148] Such collaboration helped to legitimize the industry, even outside the courtroom. In the early 1960s, Beate Uhse advertised its cooperation with the Institute for Sexological Research at the University of Hamburg, and the director of the firm's Scientific Division signed his blurb in the catalog as a member of the German Society for Sexological Research.[149]

Affidavits from academics did not guarantee victory in court. Erotica firms lost at least as many cases as they won, and even acquittals did not challenge the legal framework criminalizing obscenity. Verdicts varied from jurisdiction to jurisdiction and from year to year, and criteria were inevitably subjective, especially for objects that claimed no medical function.

Nude photographs provide a good example. The Law on Youth-Endangering Texts was a blow to naturalist organizations, but publishers who had exploited the naturalist label rechristened periodicals such as *Söhne der Sonne* (Friends of the Sun) with titles like *Kunst und Fotografie* (Art and Photography) and claimed artistic license rather than the protection of a worldview.[150] They thus simultaneously claimed a label that ensured some prejudice in their favor and helped to define the types of representations that counted as "art." In Panel hearings and obscenity trials of the 1950s, as in the Weimar period, the visual conventions of the naturalist movement—an outdoor setting, natural lighting, the subject in motion with gaze directed away from the viewer—were interpreted as nonsexual and became the markers of acceptable nude photography. Photos of nudes situated indoors, with artificial lighting or dramatic shadows (that might draw attention to the breasts or genitals), and with the subject meeting the viewer's gaze were ruled obscene or youth-endangering.[151]

Still, even these rules left room for interpretation.[152] Before the 1954 Constitutional Court decision asserting the timelessness of moral standards regarding premarital sex, courts formally acknowledged that what "injured the sense of modesty and morals in a sexual manner" was relative. And indeed, just a few months before that case, the same court had declared that context mattered in evaluating texts and images: a book on sexual perversions might be scholarly in a medical library but obscene in a mail-order erotica catalog.[153] Subjective interpretation characterized court and Panel decisions both before and after 1954.[154] Did a photo of a particularly curvaceous woman emphasize womanliness (nothing wrong with that) or sex (plenty wrong with that)?[155] Was a woman's facial expression unselfconscious (good), or did she appear aware of her beauty and thus inviting others to enjoy it (bad)? Was another woman's facial expression "steamy" or just "dull and stupid"?[156] Did unobjectionable photos and text become problematic when published together, since linking them drew attention to the sexual aspects of each?[157] Did the nude man's downward gaze at the nude woman end at her pubis, so the implicit story concerned his thoughts of sex?[158] Was the point of that "lingerie photo series" the lingerie, or the women in it?[159] In case after case, courts were called on to decide such matters. They produced one stack of verdicts that decency advocates could applaud and another that the erotica industry could tap to justify future publications.

This inconsistency created legal uncertainty for erotica firms and publishers. Thus a full range of legal tools, and not just debates over obscenity or youth endangerment per se, was important. Did the defendant *knowingly* sell an obscene image? If the defendant had solicited expert advice before publication, then the firm had acted in good faith—even if critics found entrepreneurs' practice of employing (reliably sympathetic) professionals to vet their materials suspect.[160] Had the firm informed itself about standards of obscenity and youth endangerment? If it read the Alliance newsletter and had considered the cases published there in choosing images, it had acted in good faith—it was not the firm's fault the Alliance was selective in the decisions it published.[161]

Then there was the matter of "technicalities." If the preliminaries could be dragged out long enough, then a case might be dismissed because staging a trial in 1959 to confiscate a book that had gone out of print in 1956 was a poor use of state funds.[162] Perhaps a retailer with advance proofs of obscene magazines confessed that he planned to sell the finished products once they were available; this arrangement did not constitute possession of obscene items with intent to sell, because the retailer did not intend to sell the advance proofs.[163] If a court decision did not describe which photographs in which magazines were obscene, a conviction might be overturned: it was not enough to demonstrate that the defendant sold "assorted" magazines with pictures of stripping, intercourse, and flagellation.[164] Technicalities, to be sure—but exploiting such technicalities was part of a carefully calculated business strategy. Nipping charges in the bud was another. Wealthier firms learned to appear at indictments armed with a stack of affidavits. Public prosecutors could not afford to commission affidavits for routine indictments. Working with only the evidence presented at the grand jury, courts might doubt the prosecution's ability to make a case in the same terms that the defense clearly had at its fingertips, and decline to bring the case to trial.[165]

Despite the restrictiveness of the law, the erotica industry flourished and developed ever more solid institutions. But this was a circular process: solid institutions helped firms to survive the hostile legal environment in the first place. Small firms sent ads as unsealed bulk mailings. Since Beate Uhse sent ads in sealed envelopes, an expensive practice but one less likely to result in children's accidental discovery, Rotermund was less vulnerable to charges of youth endangerment.[166]

It took money for erotica firms to operate cleanly, to dot all the i's and cross all the t's before testing legal boundaries, to bring well-prepared defenses when charges were filed and appeal unfavorable decisions, to choose a long-term strategy of improving the climate for the industry over immediate profit. Only large firms could commission affidavits or employ experts to vet materials in advance of publication.[167] Convictions, even indictments, resulted in "going-out-of-business" sales for many small operations, with one of the larger firms buying the smaller firm's assets cheaply.[168] Wealthier firms' legal advantage was an important element in the concentration of the industry.

Legal challenges also threatened large firms. Two years after the Constitutional Court determined that mailing unsolicited catalogs did not constitute insult, it reversed course and effectively banned such mailings.[169] This action was potentially catastrophic, as it eliminated one of erotica firms' most effective ways of locating new customers. Around the same time, a series of harsh lower-court and Panel rulings regarding magazine advertisements led magazine publishers to reject even discrete ads from erotica firms, cutting off erotica firms' second major avenue to new customers.[170] It was Rotermund who found a solution: unsolicited letters describing the firm (but not its products) and inviting recipients to return a coupon to claim their catalog. So innovative was this method that it won a prize from the American Direct Marketing Association—and it cut costs, since a higher proportion of catalogs went to potential first-time buyers who had confirmed an interest.[171]

Schäfer met legal problems with competence, but he did not share Rotermund's relish for the challenge. In 1956, Baden-Württemberg staged a "monster trial" involving charges against nearly every erotica item Schäfer sold.[172]

Although he could easily afford the fine eventually imposed on him, Schäfer decided that erotica was more trouble than it was worth.[173] His subsequent decision to scale back his erotica business cleared the way for Beate Uhse to become industry leader.

Conclusion

In chapter 10 of Rotermund's memoir, subtitled "Early, Prudish Years," the Guardians, Robert Schilling, and the Indexing Panel all make an appearance. In the next chapter, however—"The Momentum of the Early Years!"— we learn of Beate Uhse's breakthrough catalog of 1952, the thousands of customer letters she had received even before this catalog appeared, and the firm's rapid early growth. Rotermund implies a link between her success and the prudish environment. So repressive were the 1950s that West Germans, desperate for a basic sex education, snatched up her books explaining the "facts of life." So repressive were these years that people ordered erotic literature and sex aids by mail because they could not get such items anywhere else. There is much truth in this explanation of the industry's growth against a backdrop of state repression, but there is also something a bit too inevitable about it. If there had been no significant marketplace in erotica, its absence might likewise be seen as evidence of the decade's repressiveness.

Although Rotermund's autobiography is filled with stories of battles with the Schleswig-Holstein judiciary, the files of that office tell another story. There are, to be sure, records of numerous cases against Beate Uhse. But there are also piles of requests from Bavaria for charges against the firm—and Schleswig-Holstein's rejections of those requests. Schleswig-Holstein was dominated by the CDU, but the province protected Beate Uhse. So did the federal Ministry of the Interior when it declined the Guardians' request to submit a petition to have one of Beate Uhse's catalogs indexed. So did the Constitutional Court when it ruled that the firm's catalogs were not indecent, nor did mailing them unsolicited constitute insult. As the CDU-dominated state permitted the industry's growth, the limits of moral purity advocates' drive for a state-upheld conservative sexual order became evident.

Moral purity advocates argued that a conservative sexual-moral order was necessary to recover from Nazism. But if moral purity advocates (and much of the population) saw sexual dissoluteness as one result of Nazi rule, they also recalled the Nazis' campaign to clean up the "degenerate" face of Weimar Germany. These contradictory narratives weakened moral purity advocates' ability to speak with a clear voice—and contributed to schisms with some of their natural allies, representatives of political Christianity.

In earlier years, moral purity advocates had argued against liberalism; now they had to make a case on liberalism's terms. And this was tricky, since one could equally make the case that freedom from censorship was a necessary antidote to totalitarianism. Although the battle often appeared to be between Christian Democrats insisting on a conservative sexual-moral order and Social Democrats on a free press, the matter was not so simple. Social Democrats highlighted the importance of a free press, not a more liberal sexual-moral order, in opposing the Law on Youth-Endangering Texts. But they also defended potentially sexual images in fighting the blanket restrictions on nudist magazines, in ignoring the provision in provinces they governed such as Hessen, and in voting for its removal in the 1961 revision of the law. And although the CDU/CSU urged a conservative sexual-moral order, it took for granted that its efforts to implement such an order would be limited by constitutional protections. Given the censoring capacities of the Law on Youth-Endangering Texts and its proponents' obsession with sexual danger, it is all too easy to lose sight of just how weak a variant of censorship this was, even in regard to sexual materials. By the end of the 1950s, illustrated magazines whose covers featured barely clothed women had replaced nudist magazines on newsstands. Erotica ads were mailed by the millions. West Germans distraught by this turn of events were right: such widespread sexual consumer culture—clearly visible to young people—would have been impossible in Nazi Germany and in the Communist East.[174]

But if Christian Democrats and Social Democrats agreed that heavy-handed censorship was incompatible with liberalism, so did all parties agree that liberalism required a sexual-moral order. Nazism had upended the sexual-moral order with its support for nonmarital childbearing among the racial elite, the revision of marriage and divorce law according to racial criteria, and its unleashing of total war; Communism did the same by upsetting the distinct roles of husband and wife and by its scorn for the convention of "legitimacy." The criminal code's provisions against obscene writings and images went essentially unchallenged during this period, and if protagonists disagreed about how to protect youth from corruptive materials in a liberal state (in some cases, disputing that it was possible at all), almost all agreed that raising good citizens required attention to young people's sexual-moral development. Weimar Germany's failure in this regard had left Germans vulnerable to Nazism's appeal, and so the lesson must be learned: a liberal state could not afford to ignore sexual morality.

In other words, not only was there no consensus on sexual morality and liberalism in these years, but the lines were not neatly drawn between clearly defined positions. Rather, all positions involved some concern for a sexual-moral order, some concern for constitutional principles, and some sense that the Weimar past, the Nazi past, and the Communist counterexample had lessons to teach West Germans: it just wasn't clear what those lessons were. Was the bottom line for the SPD its opposition to the Law on Youth-Endangering Texts or its tacit acceptance of the criminalization of obscene texts and images? Christian conservatives were conspicuously split: all agreed on the seriousness of youth endangerment and obscenity, but their divisions on the priority of civil liberties ran deep. As a result, moral purity advocates were unable to dominate a single forum that might control youth-endangering or obscene materials—not the Central Offices, the courts, or the Indexing Panel. The consequences could be seen in the growth of the mail-order erotica industry.

After the Law on Youth-Endangering Texts dominated the agenda in the 1950s, the sexual-criminal code, including provisions restricting "obscene" texts and images, attracted vigorous debate in the 1960s. The resolution of that debate—which spanned the sex wave and the sexual revolution—was quite different than the compromise on youth-endangering materials of the 1950s. With two reforms of the sexual-criminal code in 1969 and 1973, the state formally relinquished its role of guarantor of a sexual-moral order in order to fully guarantee civil liberties. But the earlier effort to balance civil liberties with a state role in maintaining a sexual-moral order left its mark: it made possible the vast expansion of sexual consumer culture that helped to set the stage for more radical change half a generation later.

3 The Economic Miracle in the Bedroom

A Pessary, a Tube of Ointment, Thirty Photographs

In 1950, Gisela printed on its letterhead the boast "The leading mail order house." A decade later, Beate Uhse advertised with the slogan "Every 15 seconds, someone turns to Beate Uhse."[1] West German firms, however, were not just big. They also created a more holistic marketplace in sexual consumer goods than did their international counterparts. In the United States, Hugh Heffner built an empire in the 1950s around a single product—*Playboy* magazine—marketed to a single sex. The big West German firms of the 1950s, by contrast, offered everything sexual from A to Z as long as it was legal, and they reached out to a potential customer base of all adults.

The state enabled the erotica industry to survive in the 1950s, but the state did not cause the industry's spectacular growth. Nor did the state determine West German firms' unique standing internationally. To understand the scale and nature of the erotica marketplace, we must look to entrepreneurs and their customers.

In the first two postwar decades, informational texts and contraceptives were the mainstays of an industry serving a population struggling with the aftermath of war, Nazism, and a history of poor sex education. By increasing women's access to goods and providing a new forum for couples to discuss sex, big firms played a major role in the renegotiation of gender and sexuality within the couple. They did so in part through their product line and their language about sexuality and sexual consumption. Equally important, however, were features that had nothing to do with sex: the size and solidity of the firms, the department store–like breadth of their offerings, the mail-order format for purchasing.

Erotica firms found an enthusiastic marketplace. Following wartime separations and postwar shortages, West Germans made sexual consumption one strategy to recover from material want and emotional strain. With activist and official attention focused on more visible aspects of sexual (mis)behavior, mail-order erotica flew almost under the radar, growing rapidly as restrictive legislation limited the activities of other outlets. By the time the media discovered a "sex wave" in the mid-1960s, mail-order erotica firms had served half of West German households, which were progressing from recovery to plenty as the economic miracle finally reached the working class.[2] When it entered the public eye, sexual consumption was thus associated with affluence. Its role in recovery had been experienced as "private" and went unremarked on the public stage.

To illustrate sexual consumption in the early years of recovery, let us consider Hermann Grünewald (a pseudonym), who placed an order with Gisela in April 1952: one pessary, one tube of ointment to combat premature ejaculation, and a set of thirty photographs representing lesbian sex scenes.[3] Grünewald's shopping list illuminates not only his sex life but also his relationship with his intimate partner, probably his wife. The couple had surely conferred about the pessary, since Grünewald would not have ordered such an expensive item without confidence that his wife would use it. The couple had probably discussed frustrating experiences: although he had the satisfaction of orgasm, Grünewald knew enough about his wife's discontent to seek a remedy. Neither the pessary nor the ointment had much use outside the context of intercourse, most likely with a committed partner. The pictures, by contrast, were open to multiple uses. Probably Grünewald used them for his own pleasure; he might have passed them on to friends. The couple may have looked at the pictures together. Perhaps Frau Grünewald was the true fan of lesbian erotica, though asking her husband to obtain the pictures would have been an unusual strategy for pursuing such fantasies. The fact that the request for the photos appeared on a separate order form (slipped into the same envelope) suggests that the couple might have filled out the form for the pessary and ointment together, while the request for the photos came from Herr Grünewald alone.

Grünewald's history would also have informed his consumption. At thirty-seven, he was not a newcomer to sex.[4] His access to goods, the meanings he ascribed to them, and his ability to coordinate purchases with his partners, varied over time, and although Grünewald gives no details of his sexual history, we can reconstruct plausible contexts of prior consumption. Before the war, Grünewald might have obtained his ointment or condoms in a pharmacy—if he did not mind having others in his small town know about his sex life. But then, enjoying a youthful romance in the heady mid-1930s, he might not have worried about contraception or premature ejaculation. He and his future wife (or another partner) might instead have purchased a marriage manual, composed in accordance with Nazi racial ideology, or they might have read their parents' Weimar-era manual. If the couple practiced contraception during the war, they would have used condoms Grünewald obtained in the military to enable him to visit prostitutes safely. Erotic photos might have circulated at the front and in prison camp. Without contraceptives and in poor health after the war, Frau Grünewald might have had a miscarriage that made future pregnancies dangerous. Memories of all these events, and the products associated with them, would have informed the couple as they perused Gisela's offerings in 1952.

What did Grünewald's purchases mean to him and his wife? For consumers, goods obtained much of their meaning from their use in everyday life. And the first step in using an object was obtaining it. Mail order radically changed that experience.

This chapter begins with the growth of mail-order firms after the Second World War. It then turns to marketing and consumption. Advertising aimed to attract business, but it also expressed entrepreneurs' self-perception and communicated with employees.[5] The mechanics of marketing also shaped the gendered and social parameters of this marketplace. Purchasing behavior revealed consumers' priorities: controlling their fertility, remedying a deficient sex education, and experiencing greater pleasure in heterosexual partnership.

Big mail order provided, and consumers exploited, a vocabulary of options for understanding the gendered and social contexts of sexual consumption. This breadth constituted a real opening in comparison to earlier decades. Women's access improved, couples could shop in tandem more easily, the experiential gap between obtaining "legitimate" and "dubious" articles narrowed, and anonymity provided protection for customers who needed to keep their sexual practices secret from neighbors. Sexual consumption helped to reshape gender relations, sexuality, and domesticity in the aftermath of World War II.

"Mail-Order Houses for Marital Hygiene" Become Big Business

Germany ended the Second World War as a land of rubble. Over five million military personnel were dead and additional millions languished in prison camps. Nearly a million and a half civilians had died, and millions more had fled or been expelled from eastern territories. Refugees arrived in a truncated Germany whose economy had collapsed, whose cities had been destroyed by bombs, and which already housed millions of displaced persons. This was also a land of sexual suffering. The first postwar census of October 1946 showed seven million more women than men. Mass rapes had accompanied the Soviet conquest in the East; hunger, prostitution, and sexually transmitted disease followed across occupied Germany. Malnutrition and illness brought high rates of miscarriage, abortion, and maternal and infant mortality. Starvation, injury, and psychic trauma in war and prison camp took a toll on men's sexual response. Memories of wartime liaisons or suspicions about those of one's partner complicated reunions.[6]

In her 1989 "as-told-to" autobiography, Rotermund described shortages of sexual consumer goods in this environment. As a black marketeer dealing in toys, she saw women's joy upon their husbands' return crumble when they became pregnant. They wanted abortions, and they wanted to know how to protect themselves since "there weren't any condoms (any more)." Daughter of a physician, Rotermund had learned about the rhythm method as an adolescent. A trip to the library helped her to recall the details, and she published a pamphlet describing the method. Paper was scarce, however, and the printer demanded five pounds of butter. It took Rotermund three weeks to collect enough butter to print two thousand copies of "Schrift X" (Text X) and ten thousand flyers to advertise it.[7]

Rotermund's story contains reminders of sexual consumption in Nazi Germany. Women had used condoms until recently; Rotermund's local library still held a book on the rhythm method.[8] Postwar shortages and long-standing ignorance, not twelve years of Nazi rule, were the problem. The scarcity of paper slowed production of Rotermund's pamphlet, condoms had evidently vanished, and bereft of them, women did not know how to "protect themselves." In fact, condoms were available—for a price, and for those in the right place at the right time. While Rotermund was peddling "Schrift X," Walter Schäfer was acquiring condoms through black market transactions in the Soviet zone. Shortly after currency reform, Schäfer would use those condoms to found Gisela.[9]

Basic goods dominated the black market, and Germans sought sexual wares that could help them to protect themselves from further decline: condoms and writings on "natural" methods of contraception. Yet in one way, the marketplace in sexual consumer goods was atypical. For the most part, consumption had been women's work, and women had learned to negotiate black markets during the war. The military, however, had distributed sexual wares to men even as those goods disappeared from civilian sites. The first major changes to this marketplace were thus a relative equalization of consumer opportunity and sharing of consumer space—not because women's opportunities expanded, but because men's contracted. New distribution networks would have to accommodate a civilian world in which women played an unusual role.

With currency reform in June 1948, pinups suddenly hung from every newsstand. Alarmed, moral purity activists pursued legislation, eventually winning passage of the Law on Youth-Endangering Texts. Lobbying against a single but very visible object, decency advocates were late to recognize the real revolution in sexual consumer culture: the spread of mail order. Already in 1952, the Guardians counted 111 mail-order firms (using 145 names) that disseminated sexual wares.[10]

Since the nineteenth century, mail-order firms had offered "rubber goods," virility tonics, and books and pictures about sex. These firms were frequently small operations run from the home. After the war there was a revival of such businesses, as veterans discovered that their old jobs had disappeared (or, if younger, sought a niche despite a lack of civilian work experience), as widows had to make do with inadequate pensions, and as refugees struggled to build new existences. Small-scale mail order required only minimal capital investment and a corner of the kitchen table. Manufacturers and distributors provided cheap ads and catalogs, which retailers stamped with their own return addresses and sent to names on their mailing lists. Only when customers ordered did the resellers obtain the products from wholesalers, so the retailers required no warehousing space.

Others came to the sector with experience in business, craft, or bookselling but found themselves in erotica by chance or desperation. When Alfred Weber, artisanal manufacturer of sex aids, decided to make dildos, he approached the woodcutter across the street in his small town—a man who otherwise specialized in crucifixes—to carve models from which Weber could then make molds to manufacture the items.[11] When Walter Schäfer's varied enterprises went bankrupt with currency reform in June 1948, the wares he had on hand to start up again happened to be condoms. Booksellers found destitute customers reluctant to buy—until they added sexual literature and nude photo series to their offerings.[12] Underpaid women moonlighted as nude models. Female entrepreneurs were common in this industry, though not all firms with women's names were run by women: men sometimes registered their businesses under their wives' names, or simply gave their firms women's names to make them alluring to the largely male customer base.[13]

Running one's own business was risky, doubly so when the products attracted legal complaints. Many businesses went belly-up after court-ordered confiscations.[14] In other cases, entrepreneurs gladly sold their businesses when a safer job came along.[15] But some firms grew. By the time of the passage of the Law on Youth-Endangering Texts, Beate Uhse had fourteen employees and 100,000 customers.[16] Christiane Schumacher (a pseudonym), a waitress who took evening courses in business when her husband was imprisoned for disseminating obscenity, opened her own mail-order firm in Tübingen (Baden) and by 1956 employed twenty-six people.[17] The real giant, however, was Gisela. Already in the winter of 1949–50, Gisela served 200,000 customers, 60,000 of them monthly or biweekly. By the late 1950s Schäfer's firms collectively constituted the largest mail-order business of any type in

Europe, with mailing lists of four million names.[18] The big firms also supplied smaller retailers and exported wares—up to 50 percent of revenues, in Gisela's case.[19] But their greatest impact was in their contact with West German customers.

Consumers found mail-order opportunities in magazine ads, and direct marketing reached more potential buyers. In 1947, Rotermund mailed 10,000 flyers for "Schrift X" to addresses copied from city directories. Professional directories, registries of marriages and births, and address lists from commercial agencies all provided new contacts. West Germans who approached a firm, even if they made no purchase, were added to mailing lists. As legal constraints prohibited the mailing of unsolicited catalogs in the late 1950s, firms sent unsolicited letters inviting recipients to request a catalog.[20] In other words, erotica firms, which had no storefront to attract customers, had to keep their magazine advertisements modest, and could not hang placards in public places, pioneered the flood of junk mail that has become such a familiar part of consumer society.

Mail order grew rapidly after the war, accounting for 5 percent of all retail sales in 1955, over twice the prewar figure.[21] Still, household names like Neckermann, whose offerings resembled those of Sears, never dominated their sectors the way mail-order dominated erotica. The Law on Youth-Endangering Texts gave mail-order firms a near monopoly in "youth-endangering" works, and they were essentially the only outlets for sex aids. They found a hungry market. Millions lacked basic sex education. Poverty made contraception crucial. People who would not have sought a mechanical or chemical aid before the war reconsidered in light of stress or injury. More leisure meant time to read erotic literature. And mail order reached millions who could not patronize alternative outlets: customers in rural areas or in towns with strict local controls, customers afraid to purchase in public. "Until now," a new mail-order customer wrote, "my local source knew every intimate detail of my married life."[22] At least he had persisted: many had found neighbors' scrutiny too much to bear and had simply gone without.

By roughly 1957, 8 million West Germans—out of a population of 54 million—were on erotica firms' mailing lists.[23] Many purchased for themselves and their partners, making the true circle of consumers larger. Five years later, industry insiders felt that by conservative estimate, half of West German households had patronized a mail-order erotica firm.[24] These were large numbers in their own right, and they represented dominance of the sector. In 1960 Schäfer's firms accounted for 30–40 percent of all condom sales in West Germany[25]—and mail order surely commanded a larger portion of sales of items that were not also available in vending machines and pharmacies. In a decade and a half, mail order had grown from marginal business to West Germans' primary source of sexual consumer goods.

Telling Stories about Sexual Consumption: Gender, History, and Marketing

Catalogs were mail-order firms' main means of presenting themselves and their products. Gisela's and Beate Uhse's catalogs shared common features but also established distinct corporate profiles. Collectively, the big firms offered consumers a vocabulary of options regarding how to interpret sexual consumption and their wares: neither a single norm, nor complete openness.

Gisela and Beate Uhse offered similar goods, both based product descriptions on suppliers' blurbs, and portions of text in their catalogs were identical. Weimar-era sexology informed both firms' advertising. Rotermund, product of a reformist household, educated herself by reading Weimar-era classics, and even in the early 1960s she gave new employees her revised edition of Emilie and Paul Fried's 1929 *Love Life and Marital Life*.[26] Bibliophile Schäfer made his collection of old sexological works available to staff working on advertising, product development, and legal defense. Yet the two firms communicated different messages about sexual consumption. Identifying her person with her firm, Rotermund emphasized women's burdens after the war, urged customers to end women's sexual misery, and made the companionate couple the imaginative context for sexually oriented products. Hers was one model for "integrating" the sexual marketplace: not only did the firm bring all products under one roof, but it also created a narrative framework that placed all products within a holistic sexual world. By contrast, although there was a real Gisela (Walter's wife), the company Gisela was not associated with any identifiable individual, nor did it explicitly locate customers' needs in time and place. Gisela addressed not only the couple but also men measuring themselves against their peers. Gisela offered a different model of integration: a single firm offering multiple products and interpretive frameworks to consumers with varied sexual wants.

Distinct corporate cultures explain the firms' divergent messages. Having started with one woman's black market activity and informed by her husband's business expertise, Beate Uhse had the feel of a family enterprise.[27] The firm was the founder's sole project, and she publicly identified herself with it. Even as she hired specialized staff, Rotermund strictly controlled the firm's external image, devoting painstaking attention to advertising materials. She also worked to compensate staff for the firm's dubious reputation in its small home city of Flensburg, in the poor, rural province of Schleswig-Holstein.

Superior pay and benefits were part of the answer; assuring employees that they were embarked on an important social mission, not a dirty business, was another.[28] Respectable catalogs bound both customers and staff to the firm, and they fulfilled Rotermund's perfectionist drive for advertising materials she could consider not only defensible in court but also aesthetically and philosophically unassailable .

With flyers and short catalogs, Beate Uhse built a solid customer base between 1948 and 1951. These largely unillustrated catalogs, authored in part by Rotermund's husband, emphasized conjugal harmony but addressed men with comments such as "The foundation for success in life is a peaceful home and a satisfied wife."[29] In 1952 Rotermund authored a thirty-two-page catalog that eliminated such sex-specific wording and, even more significantly, introduced the trope that would become the firm's trademark: the identification of the firm with the person.[30] In prominent spots in general catalogs for the next fifteen years, the founder introduced herself and her firm. As catalogs grew, so did the frames: from three paragraphs in the 32-page catalog of 1952 to twelve pages in a 162-page catalog of 1958. Well into the 1960s, catalogs employed Rotermund's biography to link the firm to a feminized history of the recent past and a philosophy of sexuality identifying women as the anchor of conjugal life.[31] The firm thus drew on the language of Weimar reformers, popular memories of the "hour of the women," and a broad consensus that the family was the best hope for a West Germany that could resist both Nazism and Communism.[32] Yet the firm persistently omitted sexist subtexts to these popular discourses: Weimar reformers' instructions regarding male leadership in sexual matters, the notion that women required rescue from their "forced emancipation" during and after the war, and metaphors of the man as "head" and the woman as "heart" of the family.

The 1952 catalog, the first to use photography, featured on its cover the head of a woman, dramatically lit in the style of Weimar-era expressionism (which had enjoyed a renaissance in early postwar film), who stared intently into the camera and implicitly posed the question of the catalog's title: "Is everything all right in our marriage?" The catalog located the firm's origin in the immediate postwar period. Couples had grown apart, and pregnancy was a disaster. As Rotermund explained, "it's the woman who suffers the most from [sexual] dissonances." Although she was a happily married mother of four, a doctor had told Rotermund of his patients' problems. Inspired to "help married couples in need," Rotermund found that "for me as a woman I could only imagine promoting women's happiness and the preservation of marriage in this way with the greatest idealism."[33]

In fact, Rotermund knew the world of male comradeship as well as the world of domesticity. The only woman among sixty students in her pilot-training

3.1. "Is Everything All Right in Our Marriage?" Beate Uhse's breakthrough 1952 catalog portrayed the customer as a woman worried about her marriage in the hard postwar years.

course in 1937 (she was seventeen at the time), Rotermund passed the war in the overwhelmingly male environment of the Luftwaffe, experiencing her first sexual contact, marriage, and motherhood as "one of the boys." In the 1950s, though, Rotermund did not publicize this history, drawing instead on memories of the postwar "hour of the women." She was equally selective in describing women's strategies for ensuring family harmony. Rotermund knew from customer letters that although some women needed contraceptives upon their husbands' return, others used them in hopes that a pregnancy would not betray their infidelities during their husbands' absence.[34] But there was no need to broadcast the firm's aid to adulterers.

Product presentation underlined the goal of saving marriages by improving women's sexual experience. Descriptions of goods continually returned to one point: women should have orgasm during sex, but men's practice meant that this was too rarely the case. Using exquisitely delicate language, Beate Uhse's catalogs made the following points: Men who rush lovemaking because their minds are cluttered by work disappoint their wives. (An erotic novel would get them into the mood.) Without contraception, women sought

... sie sind glücklich!

3.2. "They're Happy!" Beate Uhse's 1958 catalog portrayed customers as couples whose path to conjugal harmony during the economic miracle was paved with consumption and education.

unsafe abortions. Furthermore, fear of pregnancy made women emotionally incapable of orgasm, while withdrawal made it physiologically impossible. (Couples might consider a wide array of contraceptives.) If a woman appeared "frigid," it was probably because her husband didn't know how to make love to her; he might not know that she, too, was capable of climax. (He should read a sex manual, and perhaps try a device that increased the stimulation of his wife during intercourse.) Impotence or genital injury might diminish a man's confidence, but his wife also suffers if intercourse is impossible. (A hormone pill, a pneumatic device, or a genital prosthetic might compensate.) If he climaxed too quickly, he would frustrate his wife, whom nature equipped to take more time to reach orgasm. (An ointment to prevent premature ejaculation would help.) The 1952 catalog did not offer photos of nude women, and its single sketch of a lingerie-clad woman was modest. Catalogs avoided mention of condom use to prevent STDs, which implied illicit sex.

As the decade progressed, customers and the firm progressed from recovery to greater plenty. The firm walked a careful line in representing customers, in its public relations, as desperately needing help, yet in its catalogs as healthy and upbeat.[35] Catalogs made greater use of photography and

3.3. The entrepreneur in domestic guise. This photo of Rotermund washing the car appeared in catalogs of the late 1950s and early 1960s, and was reprinted in one of the first lengthy articles on Rotermund in the local Flensburg press in 1961. *Lustvoll in den Markt* dates it to 1952. Courtesy of FZH.

grew to 162 pages in 1958.[36] Covers no longer posed customers' anxious question of whether everything was all right in their marriages. Instead, portraying couples embracing or talking, catalog titles declared, "They're happy!" "The best years of our lives," or "Healthy marriage, happy marriage." Images portrayed presumed customers as sometimes content, sometimes worried, but always dressed in style. Such customers not only expected prompt service and quality goods; they also had the kind of hectic lives that called for some help in the romance department. Sometimes the very comforts of the economic miracle—heavy food or too much drink—interfered with their sex lives.[37] But Beate Uhse, likewise at home in this fast-paced world, could help. Illustrated "tours" of the firm showed a busy mailroom, a nicely decorated reception area, and a sea of filing cabinets, while graphs of fertility cycles and stages of arousal underlined the firm's scientific approach.

Yet even as catalogs portrayed a successful firm, they domesticated the entrepreneur behind it. Rather than dwell on Rotermund's long hours and professional drive, catalogs featured photos of Rotermund and her sons at the beach or washing the car, mentioned her homey touch of sending foreign stamps (from international orders) to children of customers who ordered her "birds

1,7 Millionen Kunden unter einem Dach. Umsorgt, betreut, behütet als Vertretung unserer Kunden: die Kartei.

Gesprächspartner bei Sorgen und in persönlichen Fragen — die geschulten Fachkräfte der Korrespondenzabteilung.

Aus über 300 Büchern und mehr als 1 400 Erzeugnissen treffen täglich Tausende ihre Wahl. Prompte Belieferung und sorgfältige Verpackung schaffen hier zufriedene Kunden.

3.4. Women in the erotica industry. A "tour" of the firm in Beate Uhse's 1963 catalog shows a feminized workplace in which women answer phones, pack customer orders, and respond to queries about personal problems. *Source: Gesunde Ehe—Glückliche Ehe* (1963).

and bees" book for children, and—despite her tendency to hire men in top positions—showed a feminized workplace with women answering phones, opening mail, and perusing the firm's library.[38] Linking women's agency with the firm's approach to sexuality, catalogs declared that "courtesy and honest engagement with the cares and concerns of others" had given the firm a good reputation.[39]

Still, Rotermund knew that men dominated her customer base. Beate Uhse fulfilled men's requests for photos of nude women, even if they shared those photos with their friends, not their wives. It would have been senseless to ignore impotent men whose main concern was their own virility, not their wives' pleasure. If men could cause their wives distress, the catalogs granted, the reverse was also true: a woman's neglect of her appearance or criticism of her husband might explain his apparent impotence. But Beate Uhse wove male-centered wishes into its narrative of companionate harmony, in which women's experience was always equally important. Arousing photographs were a physician-recommended remedy for a marriage dulled by routine.[40] On men whose war wounds left them incapable of coitus, the catalog declared, "These people—and certainly their wives as well—have a particular right to help."[41]

By emphasizing women's satisfaction, Beate Uhse did not ignore men's desires. Rather, the firm created a less guilty language for such desires.[42]

Men seeking goods for solitary sex, exploitative relationships, or circulation among male friends could find what they wanted with Beate Uhse. Established customers received specialized catalogs with images of nude and near-nude women, which were absent from the general catalogs that went to new contacts.[43] Yet however pleasurable passing around risqué photos among friends and using condoms with prostitutes may have been, such activities did not create the happy marriages that men also wanted. Some men rejected illicit sex and "obscenity" outright but cared deeply about relations with their wives. Or they were conflicted: they liked arousing images and texts, they accepted nonmarital sex, they sought pleasure for themselves (not just for their partners), but they felt guilty because it was so hard to interpret such pleasures as legitimate. Beate Uhse's emphasis on "marital hygiene" and good sex for women offered an alternative not only to the condemnatory language of decency advocates but also to the "dirty" talk of the Wehrmacht and the pub.

Beate Uhse's "clean," companionate sexuality helped the firm attract more women than its competitors, while also providing a less guilty language for men. Most of all, it made sexual consumption compatible with customers' hopes for a "normal" family life that blended security and deep feeling: a couple who bore healthy children but not too many, and a sex life that fulfilled the erotic passions of both partners. Using this strategy, the business grew to serve a million and a half customers and employ two hundred people by 1962.[44]

With a different tone stemming from a different corporate culture, Gisela grew even bigger. While Beate Uhse's male managers had to contend with a dynamic female boss, the men at the top of Schäfer's firms were independent of authoritative female voices. Schäfer's admen drafted texts to sell erotica, pharmaceuticals, and shoes; they did not share their competitor's focus on shaping a positive image for sexual goods. The village near Stuttgart in which the firm was located was even more provincial than Flensburg, but the conglomerate's breadth meant that the staff's self-perception and social reputation did not depend on Gisela.[45] The catalog needed to sell products and avoid legal trouble. It did not need to tell stories about sexual consumption that pleased the boss or reassured his staff.

In its earliest years, Gisela's flyers for a pessary argued that, in these hard times, women must be empowered to control their fertility. Gisela also advertised the type of photo series that circulated among men and claimed no role in women's emancipation: "Rita and the Whip," "Rita and the Donkey," "Rita with Jo and the Negro."[46] Contemporary references and voyeurism intersected in gag items like "Miss Trizonia," "Holla Fräulein," and "Miss Demontage," photos whose movable parts permitted the viewer to undress the

*Ich könnte
genauso gut
mit einem
Kühlschrank
verheiratet sein -*

sagte einmal ein Mann zu seinem
Freunde, als das Gespräch — wie
könnte es auch anders sein — wieder mal beim Thema „Frauen" an-
gelangt war. Er wollte damit sagen,
daß seine Frau eine äußerst kühle Natur sei, daß sie anscheinend kein Tempe-
rament besitze, daß sie sozusagen ein „Ehe-Fräulein" wäre. Spaß beiseite: Das
Problem der Gefühlskälte (Frigidität) bei der Frau ist in Wirklichkeit alles

3.5. "I could just as well be married to a refrigerator." Walter Schäfer's catalogs parlayed men's complaints about their wives' supposed frigidity, even as some product listings suggested that men's own performance might be to blame. *Source: Preislist Nr. 7 (1957).*

woman pictured.[47] As business grew, Gisela developed comprehensive price lists and, by 1956, illustrated catalogs. The catalogs did not, however, craft a consistent narrative to establish a "face" for the firm, as Beate Uhse's did.[48]

Both firms started with manufacturers' descriptions, but Beate Uhse edited them to ensure delicacy and consistency. Schäfer's catalogs more often copied descriptions verbatim, untroubled by raw language or inconsistencies.[49] The same difference characterized ads for products of the firms' own make. Thus Schäfer's catalogs advertised a numbing ointment by explaining that men's too-rapid climax was behind most supposed female frigidity. Pages later, readers learned that many women, "due to some nervous physical or psychological cause or other," did not experience orgasm, leaving their husbands to feel that they "may as well be married to a refrigerator."[50] Following the refrigerator analogy with a command to leave "all jokes aside," the catalog employed a humor banned from Beate Uhse's catalogs. Most illustrations, like Beate Uhse's, portrayed products or presumed customers, but Schäfer's general catalogs also included nearly nude women whose flirtatious winks indicated their availability.

Although Gisela, like Beate Uhse, sold heterosexual companionship, Schäfer offered a second setting for sexual consumption: the male group. Gisela's 1957 catalog opens with a fictional talk between two friends over a beer, which leads one of the men to seek the advice of a Gisela salesman.[51] In the ensuing man-to-man session, "Rainer" and the reader learn of various sexual problems and wares to alleviate them; all gain their meaning in the context of male comradeship. Rainer, it turns out, is not alone with his potency problems: 80 percent of men suffer from impotence at some point. Rainer's friends laugh at his inexperience and inability to follow their sexual banter; the salesman advises him to read scholarly works to correct his ignorance and erotic fiction so he can brag about sexual adventures he's never had. The catalog suggests that the customer buy gag items in bulk and sell extras to his friends. Even on birth control, the text highlights neither Rainer's wife nor the couple as (potential) parents; rather, it concludes that Rainer's approval of contraception places him in the company of forward thinkers. Photographs identified Rainer's community as men of the war generation. Rainer, his buddy, and the salesman are middle aged; Rainer is haggard and drawn. The talk in a pub evoked men recounting war stories (and affairs) in that environment, and readers would have recognized the trope of sexual problems among veterans. The catalogs' headlining of condoms as "Strong Weapons in the Battle against Sexually Transmitted Disease," with its martial imagery and relegation of contraception to a secondary function, evoked condoms' military legacy. Customer testimony printed in catalogs came entirely from men.[52]

Yet this emphasis on men's satisfaction, friendship, and experience of war was not diametrically opposed to Beate Uhse's accent on female satisfaction, marital harmony, and women's postwar trials. Pages offering contraceptives noted women's distress at unplanned pregnancies, and descriptions of aids urged attention to women's sexual satisfaction. The firm mailed thirty million leaflets for an aid ("invented by a woman") with the slogan, "Marital strife will be no more / if you have O-GARANT in store!"[53] Schäfer offered a subscription for monthly delivery of tampons and sanitary napkins,[54] and his catalogs promoted the literature proffered by Pro Familia (Planned Parenthood), which one of his presses published. The covers of two 1957 catalogs resembled Beate Uhse's "Is Everything All Right in Our Marriage?" (which remained in circulation throughout the decade), with a woman posing an intimate question as she stared piercingly into the camera.[55] A catalog otherwise identical to the "Rainer" catalog replaced the dialogues with an interview with an American marriage counselor, which originally had been published in the *Ladies' Home Journal*.[56]

Beate Uhse anchored its products in a single context and employed a consistent, delicate tone. Schäfer's firms described two sites where its products found meaning and alternated between seriousness and slightly ribald humor. Still, Schäfer's approach was hardly a free-for-all. Gisela and its sister firms, like Beate Uhse, avoided mention of settings that might attract legal trouble or alienate too many potential customers. Neither firm acknowledged homoerotic uses for its products, although both sold books and photographs suited to homoerotic fantasy.[57] Nor did they acknowledge customers' likely assumption

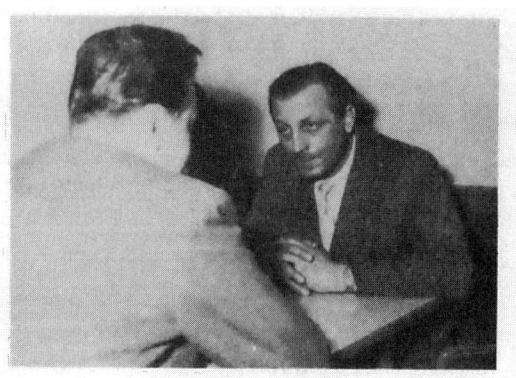

*Am Stamm-
tisch werden
nicht nur
Witze erzählt*
sondern auch manch-
mal recht ernsthafte
Gespräche geführt !

3.6. "More than jokes are exchanged at the pub." In a man-to-man talk, "Rainer" commiserates with his friend about problems in his marriage. The friend suggests a visit to Gisela. *Source: Preislist Nr. 7 (1957).*

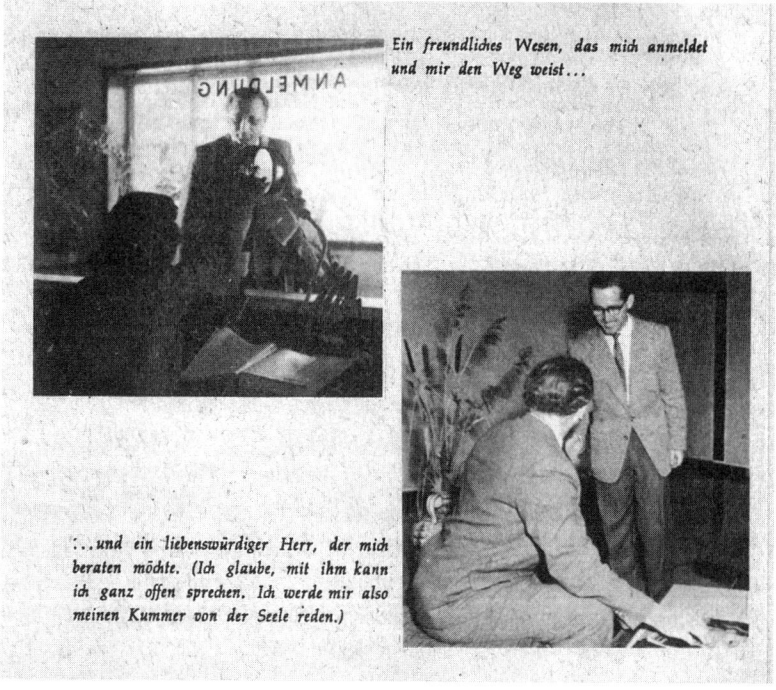

*Ein freundliches Wesen, das mich anmeldet
und mir den Weg weist . . .*

*. . . und ein liebenswürdiger Herr, der mich
beraten möchte. (Ich glaube, mit ihm kann
ich ganz offen sprechen. Ich werde mir also
meinen Kummer von der Seele reden.)*

3.7. "An amiable fellow who'd like to advise me." "Rainer" discovers a trustworthy male advisor at Gisela. "I think I can speak openly with him. I'll get my problems off my chest." *Source: Preislist Nr. 7 (1957).*

that their "women's teas" (to "regulate menstruation") were abortifacients.[58] Neither firm mentioned solitary sex, despite the common use of erotic materials for this purpose. Beate Uhse's suggestion of woman-to-woman discussion, rather than wives learning from their husbands, was notable,[59] but there was no female equivalent to Gisela's image of men bragging and joking about sex.

A defined vocabulary of options—neither a single, prescriptive rhetoric nor complete openness—characterized large firms' marketing of sexual consumer goods. According to erotica firms, partnership was as important as motherhood in women's domestic experience, erotic pleasure as important as security, and sexual partnership must be egalitarian. By emphasizing women's sexual pleasure, the industry underlined a goal that had been marginal in previous consumer regimes. Furthermore, it claimed that a good husband was sensitive to his wife's sexual needs, echoing a larger postwar shift from militarized to domestic masculinity.[60] But sexual consumption could still enhance men's standing with their friends.

For all their differences, both firms domesticated sexual consumption, even as they hinted that procreative marital sex was not the only legitimate sex. Yet language about sexual consumption was only one element of the catalogs' appeal. After years of shortage, consumer demand in general was high. It sufficed to publicize a product's availability and to deliver quality goods promptly to turn first-time customers into repeat customers.[61] Customers who had many catalogs might favor the one that best suited their tastes. Customers with only one catalog could overlook displeasing or irrelevant language to obtain the goods they wanted.

Nevertheless, catalogs shaped the experience of sexual consumption. If the military and men's restrooms were the outlets for condoms, then obtaining condoms was men's job. Catalogs that arrived in the home enabled women to buy. If bookstores sold works by sexologists but only fly-by-night businesses sold sex aids, then a vast gulf separated "legitimate" from "illegitimate" goods. If catalogs offered both products on the same pages, then the distance between them was not so great. Ruinous rumors could follow a single woman who sought condoms in a pharmacy, or a man who bought a book about homosexuality in a bookstore. The same purchases by mail order were safe. Mail order integrated a variety of goods, opened the door to women, and placed consumption in the home while easing the way for customers whose sex life was not conjugal. The medium of the catalog was as important as its tone.

Consumers in the Domesticated Marketplace

For Germans whose sources had been sex-segregated (the military, men's restrooms), meager (the black market), public (pharmacies, newsstands), and fragmented (with different sources for different products), mail order brought profound change. The catalogs of the 1950s offered a cornucopia of goods and inhabited a space that was both private and sexually integrated. Millions ordered from them, but catalogs were also texts on sexuality and consumption in their own right, perused by readers who placed orders seldom or not at all.

Mail-order firms served West Germans of all social classes. Condoms came three for a mark (the same price as a kilo of bread), and customers could find aids, cosmetics, and nude photo series for under five marks. Short paperbacks could be had for four marks and best-selling hardbacks for under ten. Both firms, however, also carried expensive, limited-edition books, and handmade genital prosthetics were pricey. When, in the late 1950s, Beate Uhse began selling short films showing striptease or nude gymnastics, the firm also offered film projectors (up to DM 225) and screens (up to DM 70)—extravagances when millions still lived in substandard housing.[62] Early on, Beate Uhse targeted professionals, but by the early 1960s customers reflected the population in class composition, with professionals only slightly overrepresented.[63]

How sexually integrated were these customers? Customer lists were overwhelmingly male. A 1954 analysis of 691 customer records of two firms carrying a wide variety of items but no contraceptives found that over 96 percent of customers were male.[64] A 1957 seizure of mailings for Gisela customers yielded 185 stuffed envelopes, 84 percent addressed to men.[65] Veterans of Beate Uhse recall that about 70 percent of customer cards in the 1950s listed male names, although data collected in 1968 give a figure of 80 percent.[66]

Yet such data mask as much as they reveal.[67] In previous decades, couples needing condoms dispatched the man to the pharmacy. Now, when couples sought erotica by mail, the woman might fill out the form but pen in her husband's name. When Beate Uhse informally polled employees in 1962, asking why they believed customers liked the firm, one gave a doubly revealing answer: "Confessor! You know, people come to us because they can trust us with their intimate cares as they would a Confessor. A woman, for example, can buy everything for her husband with us by mail and there's no further fuss, and you wouldn't believe how often that happens."[68]

The 1954 study—the only surviving data that included marital status, unfortunately with only a tiny number of women—illustrates the veiling of wives' purchases. Among customers, 21 percent of men but 53 percent of women had never married. Either single status increased women's chances of buying far more than it did for men, or married women ordered under their husbands' names, leaving wives underrepresented.[69] Beate Uhse's mailings to new mothers in the late 1950s showed mail order's appeal to women; the mailings prompted a response rate 50 percent higher than did those to newlyweds, and three to five times greater than did untargeted mailings.[70]

The "new mothers" campaign, however, was exceptional. The simplest explanation for men's overrepresentation is that nearly all mailings to potential customers went to men. When she culled city directories, Rotermund found men: couples appeared under the husband's name, and few single women lived on their own. Professional directories were another heavily male source.[71] Firms rented addresses of proven customers from commercial services and bought address lists from failing erotica firms—practices that recycled largely male lists.[72] By the early 1970s, most men had received a catalog at some point, even if they had never approached a mail-order firm. Women had received catalogs only if they had requested them or had purchased under their own names.[73] When a couple responded to an unsolicited mailing, the man's name or a number keyed to it was already on the order form.

How did catalogs circulate inside the home? Most landed straight in the trash: response rates for nontargeted mailings were in the single digits.[74] Men could easily discard catalogs without their partners' knowledge, or hide them and order goods to be sent to a post office box.[75] Yet after the Second World War, wives' voice in family decision-making grew.[76] Erotica firms urged couples to discuss the catalogs; Metropol, a short-lived Stuttgart firm, recommended that they read it in bed.[77] Customers described joint shopping in letters to Beate Uhse: "My wife and I read your little booklet with great interest. Both of us agreed that it contained very good tips that could be decisive for a marriage."[78]

Privacy was one advantage of mail order. Time was another: couples could extend delicate discussions with no pressure to buy or get out of the store. Sometimes erotica firms joined conversations under way. A veteran wrote to Gisela in 1953 that a wartime injury had left him incapable of penetration. At fifty-three, he could adapt, but his younger wife suffered from unrelieved sexual tension. Perhaps Gisela could suggest something to give him a firmer erection.[79] Catalogs could also prod couples who shied from discussing sex. "Even between spouses, sexual questions are wrongly suppressed," wrote a customer. "Your catalogs forced us to have a 'heart-to-heart' talk."[80]

By the mid-1950s, many catalogs included lengthy expositions on sexuality. Beate Uhse's catalogs evolved into detailed primers, covering sexual development, response, and dysfunction; conception and contraception; and social problems of sexuality such as nonmarital births, divorce, the "population bomb," and the sexual politics of contraception.[81] Gisela's catalogs, although less thorough, included informative introductions and digressions. Millions of households owned no other literature on sexuality, or they had a work they found difficult. In such cases, catalogs, mailed by the millions, with their accessible language and concise format, could become reference works, reopened as new questions came up, and passed on to friends.[82]

Customers bewailed their sexual ignorance in letters to erotica firms, but West Germans had some reference points for thinking about sexual pleasure, education, and reproduction. Erotica catalogs were compatible with existing frameworks but offered a novel blend of information, accessibility, and promise of easy solutions. Readers found enough that was familiar to make the catalogs convincing, and enough that was new to make them exciting.

Older customers would have recognized Weimar reformers' language of "marital hygiene" in erotica catalogs. Younger readers, too, absorbed this idiom as Weimar-era texts came back into print and new works echoed their language.[83] But developments since 1933 also made West Germans receptive to the language of erotica catalogs. The emigration of much of the psychoanalytic community meant that psychoanalytic explanations for sexual problems were not as broadly popularized in Central Europe as in the United States.[84] Psychoanalytic models rendered sex education, better communication between partners, and improved sexual technique irrelevant in addressing unhappy sexual lives—yet these were the solutions erotica firms recommended. West German sexual science instead focused on physiology (with particular attention to hormones), criminality, and deviance.[85] The latter two subjects lent themselves to sensationalistic books; the former was compatible with efforts to inculcate faith in performance-enhancing potions. In the United States, Freud's theory that a mature female orgasm was a vaginal orgasm evolved into a pathologization of the clitoris, leaving Americans to wait for Masters and Johnson to "discover" the complementarity of vaginal and clitoral stimulation in the late 1960s. Spared this privileging of vaginal orgasm, West Germans could accept erotica catalogs' agnosticism about clitoral versus vaginal stimulation, as they offered aids and informative texts to enhance both.

Erotica catalogs also spoke to healthy reproduction, a long-standing concern. Weimar Germany had tried to improve maternal and infant health, at least partly along eugenic lines, and race-conscious breeding had been central to the Nazi project. While rejecting Nazi racism, West Germany pursued pronatalist policies. It also maintained the eugenic indication for abortion and warned of the demographic danger posed by Germany's low birthrate and "asocials" like promiscuous women. When West Germans turned to erotica firms, they saw a sunnier vision, one that celebrated healthy reproduction but was less fraught with danger. No Germans endangered reproductive health in erotica catalogs, nor did threatening races. "Exotics" in faraway lands might titillate the reader but were irrelevant to reproductive concerns. Customers were thus spared worries about racial-eugenic danger, as discussions of reproduction focused inward and thus assumed whiteness. Customers also saw their faith in their sound genetic stock confirmed: economic or emotional factors, not eugenic indications, made some limit the size of their families.[86]

The racial context of reproduction was strictly "Aryan," but the racial context of eroticism was not. In keeping with European traditions of eroticizing people of color, firms marketed titles like *Love Lives of Natural Peoples*; *Love Lives of Cultural Peoples*; *Distant Lands, Strange Morals*; and the *Kama Sutra*.[87] Photo series included titles like "Japanese Models" and "American Negresses."[88] Yet nonwhites were the subject of only a handful of photo series, and although a few books promised displays of African and Asian sexuality, the market in such works evidently did not warrant the composition of new books or new translations. Instead, the same titles were marketed over and over.

For postwar West Germans, the "exotic erotic" was France. Translations of French novels dominated literary offerings in the first years, and their numbers increased even as more German-authored works and translations from other languages joined the lists. Exposés of French prostitution and French striptease clubs were heavily promoted, as were French advice books on how to increase your sex appeal. Schäfer advertised French specialty condoms (textured condoms), Parisian Love Drops (an aphrodisiac), and French perfumes.[89] Beate Uhse permitted customers either to domesticate the exotic erotic or to leave it exotic, as they pleased. The French had long used the *godemiché* (dildo) for pleasure, the firm explained, but in Germany the item was known as an "artificial member" and had therapeutic applications for wounded veterans.[90]

In favoring French eroticism, Germans drew on a long tradition of imagining France as a land of sexual refinement. Unlike the delights of more distant lands, those of France were within reach. Indeed, they were within recent memory. During the war, France had been a coveted assignment not only because there was little fighting there but also because of real and imagined erotic opportunities. Men's wartime experiences there and the tales they told upon their return further fed the myth.[91]

This wartime history may explain the striking absence of other Mediterranean reference points. Tourism to Italy had always included a component of erotic fantasy, and this aspect increased as West Germans began vacationing there in the late 1950s.[92] Yet there were few references to Italy in the marketing of erotica. Germans' recent memories of Italy (and Iberia) simply did not provide the same fodder for sexual fantasy as their recent memories of France did. Furthermore, whereas France had long produced sexual consumer goods, some of which could be exported as is and some translated, the rest of the Mediterranean had less to offer. Since the object of marketable exotic-erotic fantasy was typically female, even the growing presence of male guest workers from southern Europe in West Germany did nothing to change the equation. Only in luxury editions about sexuality in the classical and medieval worlds did Italy make an appearance.

The Anglo-American presence was mainly scientific and pedagogical. In light of West Germans' sense that the Nazi years had left them behind the rest of the Western world, translations of British and American works such as Eustace Chesser's were popular.[93] But the most influential Anglo-American imports were the Kinsey Reports. Years before the text was available in German, a cover story in Der Spiegel disseminated Kinsey's findings.[94] Critics bemoaned Kinsey's lack of romance, but his preference for dispassionate descriptions of sexual experience over a deep interrogation of his subjects' emotional lives complemented the language of erotica firms. Kinsey's teachings also included a reassuring subtext: if sexual behavior was so varied, then buying erotica was probably not deviant, and curiosity about sexual practices beyond the missionary position was reasonable.

Even the churches, which excoriated sexual consumption and sex outside marriage, taught that sexual harmony within marriage was important, even sacred. Christians might feel justified in buying a marriage manual—perhaps one whose author was identified as a Christian marriage counselor, or one that had been approved by the Guardians—to strengthen their matrimonial bonds.[95] A former Catholic youth leader described having ordered Chesser's book from Beate Uhse before his 1954 wedding: "In this way at least I wasn't entirely ignorant, since my wife, too, was completely inexperienced."[96] Catholics might feel reassured by clerical defenses of birth control reprinted in erotica catalogs, bypassing the condoms to buy a book explaining the rhythm method.[97]

By using recognizable languages of sexuality but offering confident solutions, erotica catalogs gained the trust of millions of West Germans. So assured did customers feel of the firms' expertise and open-mindedness that the firms became favored addressees for questions about sex. Rotermund initially hired a physician to answer such letters; the task, however, soon required assembly-line procedures employing prefabricated paragraphs and dozens of letter writers.[98] The responses offered accurate information and referred to products in an enclosed catalog. Schäfer turned the job over to "Frau Renate," whose qualifications lay in her experience as wife and mother, her reliability as a longtime employee, and her forthright yet tactful approach to sexuality.[99]

For erotica firms, education had an instrumental function: knowledgeable people would feel more comfortable as consumers, would understand the benefits of particular products, and would be loyal to the firm that had answered their questions. In terms of social impact, however, the provision of information—through catalogs, books, and correspondence—was anything but secondary. In the 1950s, when there was no sex education in the schools, the popular media had yet to take up sex, and the Law on Youth-Endangering Texts effectively banned books about sex from bookstores, these firms were West Germany's sex educators. In 1963, both the Humanistic Union, a prominent voice of liberalism, and the leading women's magazine *Constanze* credited erotica firms with doing the work performed in other countries by publicly supported facilities for contraception and sex education.[100]

What do purchasing decisions tell us about customers' hopes? Skeptics mocked customers' faith in performance-enhancing potions, but they exaggerated such products' importance.[101] Most sales were of items whose chances of producing success were good. Books and photos instructed or aroused the reader; contraceptives prevented pregnancy. Customers' choices reveal not only their needs but also what they thought bought goods could achieve.

Customers prioritized contraception, knowledge, and heterosexual compatibility over improved experiences for one individual. Rotermund's stepson, then an apprentice in the firm, recalls condoms as having constituted up to 80 percent of sales in the late 1950s. This impressionistic figure is probably too high, but it reflects the firm's understanding that condoms were the core of the business.[102] The earliest available written records of sales date from the early 1960s, when slightly over 30 percent of sales were in contraceptives, overwhelmingly condoms.[103] Books accounted for 25–30 percent of sales, with basic manuals dominating this category. Also selling well were items that described good technique and thus promised to enhance both partners' experience; ointments to prolong erection, which extended both partners' pleasure; and aphrodisiac chocolates, which helped to create a setting of erotic foreplay and which functioned only if both partners wanted them to function.[104] Objects to enhance one partner's experience or masturbation fared less well. Mechanical aids promised to help women whose husbands' injury or impotence prevented penetration or for whom penetration provided inadequate stimulation. Yet textured condoms, dildos, rings and sleeves, and pneumatic devices reduced the man's sensitivity or marked his inadequacy; they accounted for only one-tenth of sales. Photos of nudes, which nearly half of men but only 10 percent of women considered arousing, claimed under 8 percent of sales.[105] Erotic fiction, described by Beate Uhse's medical advisor as "an introverted form of pleasure-seeking . . . 'experienced' in the realm of one's own fantasy," was the least popular type of book.[106]

These figures do not perfectly reflect the larger marketplace. If we take into account other outlets, the proportion of mechanical and chemical aids sold would probably drop, whereas that of books, contraceptives, and photographs would rise. Still, these figures reveal the priorities of customers who used the dominant form of commerce in erotica: contraception and information first, better sex for both partners second, and greater pleasure for one partner or a solitary pleasure-seeker last.

Was eroticism in the 1950s safely domesticated; was the 1950s domicile refreshingly erotic? Perhaps, but purchasing behavior does not transparently expose customers' use of their wares, and illicit uses could range from loving to exploitative. Erotica firms recommended contraceptives to improve family life, but customers also used condoms outside marriage. "Artificial members" sold as aids for wounded men turned up in photo shoots of lesbian sex.[107] Still, the domestic setting for purchasing; evidence of joint decision-making; the high priority of contraception, information, and mutual pleasure; and customers' reliance on erotica firms for advice—all suggest that many customers hoped mail-order erotica would enhance stability and pleasure within the committed couple.

Customer letters, too, reveal such hopes for erotica. In 1955, a man wrote to Beate Uhse (upon receiving an unsolicited catalog) that "my wife and I have little experience due to our upbringing, and I would like to obtain books that give thorough information about all questions relating to marriage." He asked that van de Velde's Weimar-era classic *Ideal Marriage* and Richard Wunderer's postwar *Hygiene of Sexual Life* be sent to his wife's address, since sexual ignorance was not the couple's only problem: lack of housing meant that he roomed near his workplace and visited his wife sporadically. Five years later, he had solved his housing problem and was ordering lingerie.[108] Other customers described sexual consumption itself as saving a marriage: "So much is clearer now. My marriage is saved, and I have my wife back. . . . If I'd had your books before, this crisis would never have occurred."[109]

Conclusion

For postwar West Germans, sex was a cheap pleasure at a time when memories of pain were near and extravagant pleasures out of reach. Of course, sex was not cheap if the result was unwanted pregnancy, and it ceased to be pleasurable if it led to domestic tensions. But if these hazards could be avoided, then a good sex life could help make the family not only a refuge from a dangerous world, but also a site of passion. In the early years of reconstruction, the sexual consumer goods industry addressed West Germans' simultaneous quest for security and intense feeling.

Three factors converged to make this possible. One was the form of consumption. The domestic site of mail order and the inclusion of all wares in a single catalog made it easier for women to shop and for couples to consult. The second was erotica firms' role as sex educators. In linking conjugal harmony and women's sexual empowerment to consumption, erotica firms ensured a broader dissemination of the message than sexual reformers of the 1920s could achieve. The third was the appeal of the family as a location for emotional and physical passion after the Second World War. Indeed, the very breadth of the erotica industry enhanced its appeal to couples seeking stability on the one hand, heightened experience on the other. At the same time, the features that made mail order conducive to conjugal decision-making—privacy, breadth of offerings, a language of open-mindedness—also created opportunities for those whose sexual activity fell outside marital bounds.

The 1950s, when young firms battled hostile courts and church organizations to bring contraceptives and information to a needy public, can easily appear as the "heroic age" of the West German erotica industry. When pornography became the industry's mainstay in the 1970s, it became harder to attribute to firms like Beate Uhse a compelling social function, even for those who favored the dismantling of the obscenity statutes. Yet even antipornography feminists of the 1980s, who reviled Rotermund, praised her contribution in the 1950s to sexual emancipation.[110] Indeed, the emergence of big mail-order erotica a generation before the legalization of pornography gave West Germans a form of sexual consumption whose relative (if incomplete) egalitarianism was unique. When big comprehensive firms emerged elsewhere in the 1970s, they did not replicate the product line, the language, or the functions of the West German firms of the 1950s.

By the early 1960s, most West German adults used sexual consumer goods. Just as consumers could enjoy meat after having sated their hunger with potatoes, so could they think about sexual "luxuries" once access to condoms and informational works became routine. In the mid-1960s, West Germans described a "sex wave" that followed the other "waves" of consumption that had marked the economic miracle: the food wave, the housing wave, the car wave. This transition from a consumer regime of subsistence to one of plenty helps to explain the next generation's difficulty understanding their parents' sexual worlds.[111] Interpreting sexual conservatism as common to fascism and postwar bourgeois society, sexual revolutionaries found the term "marital hygiene" an easy target, saw their parents' manuals as hopelessly moralistic, and interpreted sex aids as evidence of sexual repression. Yet the marketplace transformed West Germans' experience of sex while sexual revolutionaries were still children. Mail-order firms sold "marital hygiene" but enabled single people to buy condoms without alerting the local pharmacist to their activity. Even when addressing men, they made it easier for women to shop. Mail-order firms routinized access to good information about sex, helped to normalize the goal of women's sexual satisfaction, and eased the way for couples to talk about sex. By the time commentators described the "sex wave" and then the sexual revolution, erotica firms had reshaped sexual knowledge and experience for millions of West Germans.

4 Interlude   *The Beate Uhse Myth*

From Wife and Mother to Flier for Hitler's Luftwaffe

If sexual consumption was part of Germans' "private" journey from Nazi-era optimism through defeat and poverty to recovery and finally plenty, then the Beate Uhse myth created a "public" narrative linking sexuality, history, and consumption. Reflecting Rotermund's instincts as much as calculated marketing decisions, Rotermund's changing narratives reflected the delicate interplay of sex, gender, social class, and history in establishing respectability in the early Federal Republic.

In her catalogs, Rotermund placed her story squarely in the context of German history. The project of creating a cohesive narrative for the larger public began in the late 1950s, when public relations were introduced at Beate Uhse; it intensified in the early and mid-1960s, as Rotermund became a celebrity. Over the ensuing decades, Rotermund elaborated a public biography that continued to grow with German history. This "public biography" became part of West Germans' common vocabulary, with Rotermund enjoying a name recognition of 87 percent in 1974 and 94 percent in 1982.

If Rotermund's biography appeared to parallel Germany's, then we should not be surprised if her ways of telling it changed over the years: Germans' understanding of their national history shifted through the postwar decades. And Rotermund had many opportunities to revise, since her media were advertising and public relations, not (until 1989) a memoir between hard covers.

Although she didn't know it at the time, Rotermund began to create the Beate Uhse myth when she started using her life story as a marketing device in 1952. In her early catalogs, as we saw in chapter 3, Rotermund presented what would become central elements of the myth: feminine suffering and Rotermund's nascent entrepreneurship during the "rubble years," and the subsequent building of a modern business that aided conjugal harmony. Rotermund made erotica respectable by integrating her firm's origins in the "hour of the women" with a language of domestic, companionate eroticism during the economic miracle.

Against this backdrop, Rotermund's self-presentation in her 1963 catalog may appear as a bolt from the blue. From her mother, a doctor, she had learned of "the joys and pains of her fellow humans." Always strong-willed, she learned to fly despite her parents' worries, and "'stuck by her guns' as a test pilot during the war." Her last flight was a daring escape from a besieged Berlin in April 1945. The postwar story became a ménage of unordered (and ungendered) images of homelessness, poverty, endangered marriages, and "the idea of helping people [not "women"] in need of advice."[1] Her infant son was with her on that plane out of Berlin, but the husband and other children nearly vanished. This narrative represented a profound change in Rotermund's presentation of herself and German history: from a wife and mother to a highly unconventional woman, from postwar suffering to Nazi-era military prowess. Occurring just as Rotermund began to attract media attention, this shift also coincided with the transition from the "private" sexual consumption of the 1950s to the public consumption that defined the "sex wave."

If grounding the business in Rotermund's biography as a wife and mother had been so successful, why exchange that biography for one that was doubly risky in calling forth images of women far outside traditional roles and directing attention toward Nazi Germany? Perhaps changing times and the firm's success made its leaders confident enough to take risks: to branch out from customers who needed reassurance of sexual consumption's respectability to customers who wanted something a little more daring. But veterans of the firm, asked in the early 2000s about the new marketing strategy of 1963, did not recall an environment that encouraged risk taking.[2] Rather, they described a sense of siege. They desperately needed to demonstrate their respectability. And so they introduced the Luftwaffe story.

The notion that a firm could enhance its respectability by transforming its founder from a struggling wife and mother to a flier for Hitler's Luftwaffe may seem counterintuitive. The story this chapter thus tells—the early development of the Beate Uhse myth—concerns the tricky terms of "respectability" during the first decade and a half of the Federal Republic. Rotermund spoke to multiple audiences, and those audiences changed over time. Even in the beginning, Beate Uhse's advertising was not aimed only at customers. Product catalogs also addressed employees and expressed the founder's self-perception. And the "outside world" with which advertising communicated did not consist only of customers. It also included the courts, and by the early 1960s, the media. Yet in no location was the function of Rotermund's biography transparent. Marketing was an expression of corporate culture and the entrepreneur's sense of self, not just an effort to sell products.[3] The courtroom was a social space, not just a setting where legal issues were resolved.[4] Journalists did not simply cover the news in a transparent manner; rather,

their concerns helped to determine what was newsworthy, and their prejudices shaped the manner of coverage.[5]

Not only did audiences vary, but the times truly were changing—for the
firm, its customers, and Rotermund herself. When Rotermund introduced
the Luftwaffe story, West Germans were increasingly turning to sexual consumption for pleasure even apart from recovery. Rotermund was becoming a
celebrity, and her firm a household name. Where isolated elements of her autobiography had served specific marketing or legal concerns, a neatly packaged
biography now became the Beate Uhse myth. In this context, the Luftwaffe
story blended a history of respectability with a story of excitement, thrill,
and risk. At the same time, the story of postwar crisis and companionate harmony retained its valence as a tale of survival and recovery.

Sexuality and the recent past constituted a complicated subject for postwar West Germans. But through her personalized marketing and, later, celebrity, Rotermund transformed what might have been an inchoate set of associations into distinct images: the female Luftwaffe veteran, the woman of the
rubble, the unashamed entrepreneur. A narrative initially patched together
from fragmentary signals of an evolving postwar culture became a seamless
story that encouraged West Germans to understand the Nazi past, the rubble
years, the economic miracle, and sexual liberation as a natural progression.

From a Good Family: Respectability in the Courthouse

By 1962, Beate Uhse had a million and a half customers and employed two
hundred people.[6] Yet in her 1989 autobiography, Rotermund introduces 1963
with two stories that describe a sense of embattlement. The first describes
the Flensburg Tennis Club's rejection of her application for membership—
although her firm was one of Flensburg's largest taxpayers and employers,
and although she came recommended by two prominent members of the local business community. The second story explains the reasons for "my reputation, my hermaphroditic existence [*Zwitterdasein*] between social disre-
pute and undeniable success." The explanation consists of a lengthy excerpt
from an indictment filed with the Flensburg court.[7]

By the early 1960s, Rotermund's feminized narratives of entrepreneurship,
history, and sexual consumption had established her respectability with staff
and customers. She had not, however, convinced the judiciary or the Flensburg Tennis Club. By juxtaposing them in her autobiography, Rotermund revealed how closely the two were linked: both consisted of the local elite. The
courts could impose crippling fines, shut down her business, or send her to
jail. The worst the tennis club could do was make it necessary for her to learn
to play tennis during her vacations in France. As Rotermund suggests, how-

ever, this elite was of a piece—and its withholding of social recognition was troubling, just as negative legal rulings were. In such circles, "respectability" referred not only to sexuality and gender—so important in relations with customers, and thus emphasized in catalogs—but also to social class. And the elite did not just distinguish according to wealth. It also distinguished between the established bourgeoisie and new money.

The tennis club episode was isolated, but Rotermund made frequent visits to the Flensburg courthouse. Legal proceedings were time-consuming, expensive, and risky: the firm could not know then that it would emerge triumphant from its long string of suits. Furthermore, the association of the firm with its founder meant that attacks on the firm were attacks on the person. Although distant complainants usually filed the charges, Rotermund defended herself in face-to-face confrontations with district attorneys and judges. Establishing respectability in this environment was not the same as writing good catalog copy for couples in small towns who needed condoms. In other words: customers and employees were not the only audiences the firm needed to impress. Long before Rotermund became a celebrity, she had a smaller public whose goodwill was essential, whether or not they bought her products. Rotermund learned important lessons about public relations in court.

Courts determined whether particular practices violated statutes on subjects as varied as obscenity, youth endangerment, fraud, and insult. If a court ruled a practice illegal, then the whole industry had to pay heed. Furthermore, such cases tested broad constitutional matters like freedom of expression and freedom of commerce.

Courts also, however, evaluated the defendant's character to address intent, extenuating circumstances, and likelihood of repeat offense. A sympathetic ruling on character did not establish that an activity was acceptable, and therefore a safe practice for the industry, but it could bring acquittal or a reduced sentence. Legal proceedings were by nature adversarial, but a court in which judges and attorneys respected the defendant differed from a court in which they did not. In other words: the courtroom was a social space. Courts did not just evaluate abstracted actions in light of the law: they also established and acted on personal relationships. When a defendant appeared repeatedly before the same small group of district attorneys and judges, those relationships became especially important. Rotermund quickly learned to make a good impression, and she understood the significance of lines like the following, from a 1953 judgment: "The court evaluates the defendant's offense mildly. As already stated, the defendant made a good impression on the court. She presents herself openly and freely, and does not attempt to cover anything up. It could not be established that she acted out of dishonorable motives; rather the contrary."[8]

Who populated the courts? Jurists had been raised in privileged house-holds and had enjoyed a university education. They lived in what Germans called "ordered circumstances," with tidy family relations and finances. And they were well enough established to have risen to the upper ranks of the civil service. In the 1950s, this professional status meant that they had served the Nazi state.

Even in the context of the reintegration of former Nazis in West Germany, the "renazification" of the Schleswig-Holstein civil service was notable. In 1959, a national scandal resulted from the discovery that a key figure in the Nazi "euthanasia" program, who had been implicated in tens of thousands of deaths, had reestablished himself in Flensburg and had thrived in provincial administration with the knowledge of colleagues and superiors.[9] The personnel files of the attorneys and judges whom Rotermund encountered show how old Nazis so easily reentered the courts: thick white tape covers crucial lines, even whole paragraphs, of the curricula vitae, professional reports, and superiors' evaluations from the Nazi period.[10] With files that no longer revealed any smoking guns, denazification and reentry into the profession were relatively easy, and men who had executed Nazi justice quickly returned to the Schleswig-Holstein judiciary.

In West Germany, civil servants enjoyed a nearly unbroken sense of status, privilege, and political reliability.[11] The same was true of the business elite to which Rotermund belonged economically, but not socially, by the late 1950s.[12] This self-perception was more important than specifically Nazi sentiments in establishing the culture of respectability that would judge Rotermund. This social world did, however, link a history of service to the Nazi state with a sense of culture and cultivation learned not only at school but also in the privileged home of one's origin.[13]

Socialized by upper-middle-class standards that were reinforced by Nazi campaigns against "degeneracy," jurists were well versed in stereotypes of "asocials"—the sort of people who presumably peddled condoms from their kitchen table, as Rotermund did early on. Such a person might be expected to combine low socioeconomic status with moral dissoluteness. Instead, court records described Rotermund's surprising biography: She had been born to a "good family" on an East Prussian estate. She had enjoyed a good education. She had joined the aristocratic ranks of flyers and had served in the wartime Luftwaffe. Her first husband, likewise a pilot, had fallen at war. After the war, women had sought her advice on sexual matters because they knew her mother had been a physician. In 1949 she had married the son of an established Flensburg shipping family, himself a wounded veteran. They now lived—in "ordered circumstances"—with their children.[14] Rotermund, in short, had far more in common with judges and lawyers than with the "degenerates" and "asocials" with whom they associated obscenity. The police likewise recognized Rotermund as a woman cut from their cloth: between raids of her offices, they invited her to apply for a position.[15]

The legal implications of Rotermund's sociohistorical respectability were not immediately clear. In early trials, her standing sometimes constituted an argument that she should have known better. Noting that she targeted physicians and academics for her mailings, a court in 1951 concluded that Rotermund, due to her "good upbringing and education," must have known that such recipients would find the catalogs offensive.[16] Yet even such language acknowledged Rotermund's place in respectable circles. Rotermund made the most of this point. Complaining to the attorney general in 1952 about a particularly insulting district attorney, she harrumphed (in writing): "I was born a Köstlin and come from family of well-known Württemberg jurists. I was raised to have a deep faith in the law." She apparently expected the attorney general to recognize her family name.[17]

Significantly, suggestions that Rotermund acted inappropriately *as a woman* disappeared from proceedings early on. In 1951, the court suggested that her sex made her actions particularly reprehensible; around the same time, the particularly insulting district attorney suggested that she give up her "dirty business" and knit sweaters if she needed to support her family.[18] Subsequent judgments, however, did not concern themselves with Rotermund's sex. "Dirty talk" was so strongly linked with male voices that Rotermund's identification of her careful language with female authorship helped her not just with customers but also in the courts.[19]

By contrast, Rotermund's social background and that of her customers never ceased to interest the court. Rotermund responded by reiterating both. Aware that elite men condemned sexual consumption among working-class men and women generally, but tolerated it for men of high social status, Rotermund repeatedly noted that her customers were professional men.[20] Indeed, Rotermund *performed* her status by entering court surrounded by lawyers with long pedigrees and carrying affidavits by expert witnesses with advanced degrees.[21] Such associates aided Rotermund's defense, but in the spatial environment of the courtroom they also demonstrated that she kept good company.

The goal, however, was not to establish that success had enabled Rotermund to hire good lawyers. This conclusion would suggest that Rotermund had aimed to make money. In a capitalist economy, such an accusation was perhaps strange, but the accusation of "profit motive" haunted entrepreneurs who sold products of dubious social value.[22] The Rosemarie Nitribitt scandal, regarding the unsolved 1957 murder of a high-priced prostitute who had served Frankfurt's business elite, revealed broad anxieties about a capitalism whose amorality was evident by its involvement with illicit sex.[23] If a "low-class" peddler of erotica was "asocial," then her successful counterpart was an amoral profiteer. A virtuous entrepreneur, by contrast, was an idealist whose economic activity served the common good.

Rotermund, of course, argued that her business served the common good, and descriptions of her products' positive social impact—such as saving marriages—peppered both her catalogs and her courtroom testimony. But her biography also helped to establish her as an idealist. Her paternal line consisted of well-known jurists. Her mother had been a physician. She had grown up on an East Prussian estate. She had served in the Luftwaffe.

In a highly stratified social environment, the Luftwaffe story served many functions. It marked Rotermund as someone born into a well-off family: flight training was a preserve of the wealthy. It demonstrated that "profit motive" was not at her core, since her choice as a young adult had not been for a career in business. It established that she had been a reliable servant to state and *Volk* during the Nazi era, just like jurists. The Luftwaffe story emphasized the respectability of social class and political conformity, rather than the sexual and gendered respectability highlighted in catalogs. Rotermund's insistence on her social respectability did not get her into the tennis club, but the court's acknowledgment of her status was an important partial victory.

By the late 1950s, Beate Uhse's management knew the Luftwaffe story not just as an anecdote about the founder's youth, but also as an important part of the firm's history—just not a part that was known to customers, because its usefulness was in court. But advertising had always been understood holistically at Beate Uhse. Catalog copy that lent confidence to the firm's staff did the same for customers. Advertising materials presented in court showed judges that Beate Uhse's language was not obscene.[24] In the firm's experience, language that established respectability in one environment never hurt in another. If the Luftwaffe story impressed judges, then perhaps it would impress customers as well.

Yet the courts that alerted Rotermund to the value of the Luftwaffe story and the public that would hear the story were two different audiences. Among other things, they were separated in time. The Luftwaffe story impressed jurists in the 1950s. Customers read the new catalog in the mid-1960s.

In addition, by the time the 1963 catalog was released, a new actor was joining the mix: the mass media. Through the 1950s, only local papers had mentioned Beate Uhse, and then only with curt coverage of the firm's legal troubles in the back pages.[25] By the mid-1960s, Rotermund was a fixture in the national media. Her biography now did more than introduce an understanding confidant to customers and an honorable entrepreneur to the court. It also presented a celebrity to West Germans with no direct contact to the business.

The Free Development of the Personality: Respectability and the Liberal Press

By the late 1950s, Beate Uhse was confronting an ironic cost of its success. In the early years, Beate Uhse had been one of dozens of small, unknown firms. A few years later, the firm was a known quantity not only to its customers but also to antiobscenity activists (if not yet to the general public). The firm's financial and legal successes, combined with Rotermund's open association of herself with her firm, prompted ever more complaints: opponents could now attach a name and a face to an industry that previously had been frustratingly elusive. The firm's inner circle determined that it needed to take a more active hand in shaping the firm's reputation among noncustomers. In other words, it was time for public relations.

But PR was not a purely defensive measure. After attending a direct marketing seminar in the United States in 1961, Rotermund decided to make Beate Uhse a recognized name brand, a synonym for erotica, as Kleenex is for tissue.[26] This endeavor would require educating the general public, not just customers and courts, to associate Beate Uhse with desirable functions. The field of organized public relations, complete with institutions and specialized professionals, arrived in West Germany (from the United States) only in the 1950s.[27] It was a natural fit for this firm, which already considered multiple audiences in its advertising: not only customers but also families of potential employees, doctors who might recommend products to their patients or write legal affidavits, and judges who would determine whether the materials were obscene.

Beate Uhse published its first PR brochure no later than 1958.[28] In early 1961, the firm hired Hannes Baiko, who founded a press office.[29] Baiko was the central figure in creating a version of Rotermund's biography for public consumption, although the entire management team cooperated in crafting all advertising and PR materials. In what appears to have been a partly intuitive, partly calculated process, Rotermund and Baiko plucked from Rotermund's biography such valuable tidbits as her mother's history as a doctor, while omitting elements of her background that had less marketing value. Most fatefully, the firm hammered out a telling of Rotermund's Luftwaffe history which, intentionally or not, presented flying as rather like enlightened sex. Like better sex, flying was a fantasy of untold millions: in the early 1960s few Germans had ever boarded a plane. Despite the aura of danger surrounding flying, in the end it saved the day: the oldest surviving PR brochure explained that Rotermund's ability to fly had enabled her to escape a besieged Berlin with her infant son.[30] In other words, taking risks would simultaneously make life more exciting and bring greater security.

Public relations paid off. When the Constitutional Court heard a case of Beate Uhse's in late 1961, the press departed from its habit of running terse summaries based on court reports. Instead, local newspapers ran longer stories that were informed by the firm's own materials, and national coverage included biographical background.[31] So inviting was the PR that one reporter approached Rotermund for an interview and was clearly charmed; the resulting article described an unpretentious, down-to-earth entrepreneur and included a fetching photo (fig. 3.3).[32]

An even bigger breakthrough came when the firm announced a year later that it was opening the world's first "shop for marital hygiene."[33] The opening attracted nationwide notice and introduced journalists to an articulate, photogenic speaker on sexuality. Rotermund appreciated the value of media attention for her business, and she thrived personally under the spotlight. Press packets provided journalists with a brief biography of Rotermund, a brochure describing the business, the latest catalog, and product samples (of inexpensive, relatively mainstream items like condoms). Press coverage ensured that by 1964, a quarter of the West German population knew of the firm.[34]

Some early coverage did not concern itself with her previous career but simply tapped Rotermund's sexual expertise: for example, a 1963 series on "sex education for adults" in West Germany's leading women's magazine and a 1966 television broadcast on abortion.[35] Most reports, however, delightedly linked Rotermund's first and second careers, describing a peppy entrepreneur aiding a sadly repressed population. With a wink and a nod (and a wartime photograph of Rotermund in uniform), *Der Spiegel* wrote of the "jet- and marriage-pilot" in 1965: "In the Second World War she ferried the *Jagdmaschinen* Me 109 and Fw 190, the *Sturzkampfbomber* Ju 87, and the *Strahljäger* Me 262 to the front. After the war she helped to steer the German people to seventh heaven."[36]

In part, the press's dissemination of Rotermund's dual career simply reflected the fact that this was a good story: it sold papers. But Rotermund's story did not just serve the media's commercial interests. It also helped journalists to articulate a relationship between liberalism and sexuality, a relationship that had vexed them through the 1950s and which was becoming yet more complicated in the early 1960s.

The intersection of Germany's midcentury traumas, sexuality, and liberalism had been a frequent, if complicated, theme in the 1950s. The media had sometimes described a satisfactory sex life as a weapon against totalitarianism or as a strategy for recovering from it. Editorial pages had opposed punitive attitudes toward war widows who cohabited rather than marry in order to preserve their widows' pensions.[37] News outlets had described returning POWs as rediscovering their individuality in the private (eroticized) sphere of the family after years of forced conformity and anonymity in Soviet prison

4.1. "Seventh heaven." The photo of Rotermund in uniform that appeared in *Der Spiegel* in 1965, with the caption "To seventh heaven: Me—109 Pilot Beate Uhse, 1944." Courtesy of FZH.

camps.[38] Sensitive to their own interests, the press had protested the Law on Youth-Endangering Texts.[39]

Sexuality did not always fit neatly into the battle between liberalism and totalitarianism, however. The Nazi-era tenet that sexuality's true meaning was in its function for the collective found echoes in the Basic Law's declaration that the family was the cell of the state and in subsequent pronatalist policies. Even liberals who denounced state regulation of sexuality often legitimized the search for sexual contentment with references to the common good. Thus returning POWs might find private happiness with their wives and children—but in being good husbands and fathers, they also made themselves and their dependents into democratic citizens. When it came to the search for individual pleasure per se, journalists mainly described it as a social problem ("endangered girls" around military bases) or as a scandal (the Nitribitt case).[40]

Beate Uhse's catalogs, however, made clear that customers were not responsible for serving state, society, or *Volk* through their sexual pleasures. Nor would they find those pleasures in state, society, or *Volk*. Beate Uhse's domestic, rational sexuality contrasted with the uncontrolled and public eroticism that some observers had linked to Nazism, and which others now saw in postwar popular culture.[41] Beate Uhse's customers would not faint from the excitement of a Bill Haley concert or a political rally. Instead, they would experience pleasure by learning where their clitorises were, by curling up with an erotic book, or by being aroused by their partner clad in a negligee or wearing a musk perfume.

The bodily comforts of the economic miracle—including a cozy domestic erotic life—provided relief after the war and hunger years. Yet reportage on sexuality that acknowledged only this therapeutic function, or that justified a liberal position on sexuality as a test of other, presumably larger matters (like opposition to censorship), remained incomplete: it neglected sexual pleasure and denied pleasurable associations with the Nazi years.

With the introduction of the birth control pill in 1961, journalists were confronted with the inadequacy of their vocabulary for sexuality. Here was a story that concerned sex for pleasure, not procreation—and not among marginal populations but among the "mainstream," and supported by modern science.[42] For ill-equipped journalists, Rotermund appeared at just the right moment, providing a vocabulary about pleasure in an age that acknowledged the sovereignty of the individual and that saw the link between consumer opportunity and personal happiness as a source of pride, not anxiety.

Rotermund enabled journalists to tell a sexual story that blended recovery with a search for pleasure, a story that made liberalism compatible not just with the sober task of fending off totalitarianism but also with the search for happiness. Rotermund offered a language on sexuality that rejected fascism's collective vision in favor of a liberal, individualistic valuation of pleasure, but that always remained polite and anything but hedonistic. The Luftwaffe story, for its part, evoked pleasurable associations for which the Nazi years, but not the early years of recovery, offered a vocabulary, while excluding aspects of Nazism that evoked danger.

The fantasy of flying linked technological modernity to sensual corporeality: high speeds, physical risk, freedom from the bonds of the earth.[43] As a result of her experience, the Luftwaffe story implied, Rotermund understood not only suffering and its remedy, comfort, but also thrills, excitement. She had found excitement in service to the state, not while disrupting the social order—but hers were not the threatening thrills of the mass rally. Rather, they were the individualistic thrills of a flier: in an era of mass institutions and conscription, flying had remained a solo experience and the Luftwaffe an elite club. Rotermund's membership in this elite constituted assurance that her brand of excitement had met the exacting standards of very strict masters indeed: the Nazi regime. As the courts had learned, it was hard to reconcile this marker of wealth and political conformity with images of "asocial" sexuality. But the press's more breathless language about Rotermund's flying blurred socioeconomic and political criteria of elite status—which might have suggested a certain stuffiness—with memories of a racial elite exciting in its capacity for physical exertion, mastery of technology, and sexual virility. The firm could not help but notice just how many functions Rotermund's story served: "The [firm] noticed that the mixture of sex and independent woman and Luftwaffe was apparently a good one," Rotermund's stepson recalled. "It made one unassailable, and it was great for the press."[44]

Beate Uhse's catalogs, which accompanied PR brochures in press packets, offered a domestic counterpart to the Luftwaffe story: a vision of pleasure that was likewise socially responsible yet individualistic, but which unlike piloting was accessible to all. Catalogs portrayed customers who sought pleasure for themselves and their partners by reading an erotic book, sharing "aphrodisiac" chocolates, or having a baby at just the right time. In their emphasis on various products' ability to preserve marriages, the catalogs could have legitimized erotica by emphasizing the Basic Law's commitment to marriage. But when the 1963 catalog cited the Basic Law, it was to quote the guarantee of the unfettered development of the individual's personality.[45] Beate Uhse enabled journalists, whose defense of sexual liberties had required collective goals, to describe the search for sexual pleasure as equally legitimized by individualistic liberal principles.

The gender upheaval suggested by the Luftwaffe story was also useful to journalists. Media reference to the war years typically portrayed a sex-segregated world—men at the front, women at home—and discussion of the postwar "sexual crisis" took wartime alienation of the sexes as a given. How, then, to describe a world in which the pill had seemingly eliminated the most significant difference between women's and men's sexual experience—the ability of one sex but not the other to enjoy sex without fear of unwanted pregnancy? Beate Uhse had always rejected the notion of a profound alienation between the sexes. Instead, men and women wanted the same thing—conjugal harmony—and were hindered only by ignorance and lack of access to contraceptives and sex aids. Rotermund in uniform personified a path from war through recovery to pleasure made more plausible by emerging from a holistically gendered Nazi-era experience. Rotermund personified the "Aryan superwoman" who enjoyed romance, bore strong babies, *and* enjoyed sport and adventure. But she also knew the military experience that had shaped a generation of men. Rotermund thus transformed the common narrative of sexual alienation into a story that more easily progressed from war to healing and then to "seventh heaven."

In its individuality, even within a totalitarian context, the Luftwaffe story underscored Beate Uhse's claims for a sexuality of a liberal age: individualistic, consumer-oriented, but socially responsible. At the same time, in its hermaphrodism, it overcame war's damaging sex-segregation. Finally, it captured an excitement that the language of social stabilization and economic recovery had been unable to convey. The integration of legal, public relations, and commercial concerns and the merging of various aspects of respectability are clear in the comments of a veteran of the firm regarding the new advertising strategy:

> She was trying to get erotica out of the gutter. And [as she presented herself] she was predestined for this: she was the daughter of a doctor, she came from an estate, she was with the Luftwaffe, she flew, she had three children. . . . And she was married, and directed a firm, and so she couldn't be what people imagined about her. Somehow the whole packet, doctor's daughter, daughter of the countryside, test pilot, wife and mother . . . that was all in all a positive image. And naturally it also made it easier to stand before the court, when one [had] this whole aura.[46]

Conclusion

Within the context of the Beate Uhse myth, the Luftwaffe story was never just a story about an unusual woman's activities in Nazi Germany. Only flight clubs were interested in Rotermund's Luftwaffe career in its own right.[47] The Luftwaffe episode found true meaning only in conjunction with the postwar chapters, which themselves reflected a thick layering of concerns of gender, sexuality, class, entrepreneurship, and liberalism in the early Federal Republic. By implying an elevated social status and service to the state in the Nazi era, the Luftwaffe story helped to establish an elevated social status and service to the common good in the postwar years. By portraying an individualistic experience of corporeal pleasure in a totalitarian context, the Luftwaffe story suggested the compatibility of sexual pleasure and liberal individualism. And in connection with Rotermund's initiative in addressing women's need for contraception, her conviction in expanding her business, and her resoluteness against those who would shut her down, the Luftwaffe story signaled self-assuredness, willingness to buck convention, and strength against adversity.

As the Beate Uhse myth became part of the West German vocabulary, it was naturalized. Those who drew on it presented it as self-contained, logical, and complete, even as they emphasized different episodes or drew different lessons from it. When the Beate Uhse myth is now evoked in reference to the 1950s, it is to illustrate the prudish nature of that decade. The myth tells us that Rotermund battled obscenity suits, even as she provided much-needed sex education and as consumer demand demonstrated the need for her goods. But Rotermund's story was never only about sex. If it had been, the myth would not have become so useful as a shorthand for German history. As diverse aspects of the battle for respectability informed the making of the myth, they helped to create a vocabulary for understanding Germany's transformations in the mid-twentieth century.

Rotermund's sex and domestic situation helped to establish her respectability among her customers and staff in the early years, and so feminized stories of her personal life found their way into the myth: her marriages, her experience as a widow with a young child, her concern for women during the rubble years. Once ensconced in the myth, such stories helped to anchor women's strength and vulnerability in tellings of postwar history. But in the courtroom, social standing and membership in a productive entrepreneurial class were equally critical in establishing respectability. As these elements of respectability were woven into the myth, they lay the groundwork for Rotermund to personify the opportunities offered by the economic miracle. Finally, journalists valued Rotermund's ability to explain the quest for pleasure in liberal terms. In the myth, Rotermund became not only a sex educator and productive entrepreneur, but also a defender of liberty in a fragile democracy.

This remarkable tangle of associations knit together past and present concerns. Equally remarkable was the way this story positioned Rotermund for the future. Sexual mores and sexual commerce were about to undergo rapid change. By the late 1960s, the world of the early 1960s would seem almost unrecognizable. Yet Beate Rotermund, who had so perfectly captured the mood of the 1950s and now did the same for the early 1960s, did not become obsolete. Instead, she was only on the cusp of her true celebrity: the era in which, for millions of West Germans, Beate Uhse became synonymous with sex.

5 The Sex Wave

Sexual Consumption Goes Public

On December 23, 1962, Beate Uhse opened what she claimed was the world's first aboveground erotica boutique, modestly labeled a "specialty shop for marital hygiene." The shop's opening attracted national media attention. Journalists not only reported on the novelty of a store carrying books on sex, contraceptives, and sex aids. They also revealed a fascination with the shop's founder: a woman who spoke easily and articulately about sex, who had already been educating West Germans about sex for ten years, and who to boot had flown with the Luftwaffe. Rotermund became famous, and her firm the world's largest erotica concern.

The opening of Beate Uhse's storefront and Rotermund's transformation into a celebrity were only two markers of the increasingly public sexual commerce in the early 1960s. During the economic miracle, contemporaries described West Germans as embarking on consecutive "waves" of consumption: the food wave, the clothing wave, the housing wave, the car wave. In the mid-1960s, the media discovered a sex wave, a burst of consumption of things sexual.[1] In fact, erotica was already big business in West Germany. But in the 1950s sexual consumption had been discrete, with catalogs mailed in plain brown wrappers. Now it became visible. Ten years after the opening of Beate Uhse's first shop, there were some 350 sex shops across West Germany, and 87 percent of West Germans knew Beate Uhse's name.

This chapter focuses on the years of the sex wave, roughly 1959 to 1968. The first stages of the sex wave occurred outside the erotica industry proper. Illustrated magazines showed ever more female flesh on their covers and told ever more salacious stories of adultery within; advertisers relied on sexual images to sell all manner of goods. With the introduction of the birth control pill in 1961, the media heralded the arrival of a new sexual world—in stories that contributed further to the seeming saturation of the environment with sex. Finally, the erotica industry, starting with Beate Uhse, emerged from its self-protective anonymity.

West Germany's increasing wealth gave rise to much discussion about the relationship between consumption and national strength. Finance Minister Ludwig Erhard, regarded as the architect of the economic miracle, had long claimed that consumption was a school of democracy, as consumers learned to make choices and to consider the consequences of those choices for themselves and others. By the early 1960s, the notion that affluent consumer society had created a more demanding but also more discerning citizenry was commonplace among Cold War liberals, a counterweight to conservatives' fears that consumer society was decadent and thus a weak defense against Communism.[2]

By eradicating the poverty of the early postwar years, the economic miracle lessened the number of West Germans who clung to a conservative cultural code as their sole anchor in desperate times.[3] The economic miracle shaped more liberal attitudes toward sexuality generally and toward sexual consumption in particular. Christian conservatives had vilified materialism since the late nineteenth century. Yet even as the sex wave triggered unease at the commercialization of sex, a condemnation of materialism per se had ever less valence. When West Germans objected to the legalization of pornography more strenuously than to other reforms in the early 1970s, they were not singling out consumption. Rather, they were distinguishing between personal liberties exercised in private (like gay sex in the bedroom) and in public (like the sale of pornography on the street).

The sex wave represented a new type of behavior in the marketplace; it was not triggered by state action. In the world of regulation, not much changed. Loopholes and ambivalent institutions had permitted mail-order erotica to expand during the 1950s despite official sexual conservatism. From the late 1950s to the mid-1960s, courts and parliament confirmed the stalemate: neither liberalization nor effective enforcement of a conservative sexual-moral order. A federal prosecutor's description of a standoff regarding vending machines selling condoms could easily have applied to the scene more broadly: "It appears that the leaders of both groups have long since become accustomed to holding monologues past each other."[4] The stalemate was broken only by the Constitutional Court's *Fanny Hill* decision in 1969, which invalidated the sexual-criminal code's provisions on "obscenity in text and image" and transformed the sex wave into a porn wave—the subject of the next chapter.

The deadlock reflected familiar divides: should the state uphold a sexual-moral order, or should it limit itself to protecting citizens from injury? With the sex wave, however, another question became important. Was consumption a central problem of illicit sexuality, or was it marginal to the larger matter of sexual morality? In the 1950s, indecency in text and image had been prosecuted far less frequently than violations like male homosexual acts or indecent exposure. The increasingly public sexual commerce, however, complicated matters. Liberal arguments about *Rechtsgut* had not differentiated between sexual acts and sexual consumption. As long as individuals hurt no one—whether by engaging in consensual same-sex acts or by reading erotic literature—the state had no business limiting their activity. But what if the vehicle for delivering erotic literature to the consumer *did* harm others, for example in exposing children to sexual imagery and thus undermining parents' constitutional right to raise their children as they saw fit? As sexual consumption moved from shipments in plain brown wrappers to sex shops and movie theaters, this question became more pertinent. The sex wave redefined sexual consumption as central to sexual morality generally.

In the meantime, the erotica industry continued to sell its wares. Neither the goods themselves, however, nor the manner of marketing them became notably racier in the first half of the 1960s. For established firms, this was the moment to realize the potential of a market that had remained stunted, despite its growth in the 1950s. In a narrow sense, the increasingly explicit magazine covers and articles about celebrities' affairs made it easier to demonstrate before the Indexing Panel that a work in Beate Uhse's or Walter Schäfer's list was no worse than what was available on the newsstands.[5] In a broader sense, it enabled established firms to present themselves almost as prophets. They had long argued against the conservative grip on sexual norms. But unlike those who cynically employed bikini-clad girls to sell liquor, erotica firms addressed sex and relationships with educational literature, contraceptives, and items to help couples develop intimacy through positive erotic experience.

At the same time, if backlash ensued, erotica firms would surely suffer. This was no time to pour fat onto the fire with especially risqué materials. Instead, this was the time to combine bold marketing strategies with restrained content and presentation. It was in this environment that Beate Uhse moved her business from the private home to the public square. And it was in this environment that Rotermund took the supremely polite language developed for customers of the 1950s to the media.

Mail order may have increased women's access to contraceptives and information about sex, and it may have eased joint decision-making in the conjugal home, but it hardly eliminated women's sexual vulnerability. If it had, there would not have been an estimated one million illegal abortions annually in West Germany in the early 1960s. In many ways, the sex wave looked like an era not just of sexual liberation in general but of sexual liberation specifically for women. The first sex shops emphasized conjugal harmony, just as Weimar-era reformers, postwar Christian churches, and 1950s catalogs had done—and now, the birth control pill put contraception in women's hands. Rotermund gave a female face to enlightened sexuality, and she spread to an ever-wider audience her gospel of egalitarian relationships and sexual self-determination for both halves of the heterosexual couple.

In the last third of the decade, political and sexual culture underwent rapid change in tandem. Already in the late 1950s and early 1960s, trials of Nazi-era crimes and the discovery of the Adenauer administration's efforts to censor critical media shook West Germany's conservative consensus and lent credence to more liberal voices. The year 1963 marked the end of the Adenauer era, and with it the dominance of political Catholicism on the national scene. The CDU/CSU remained in power in Bonn until 1966, but under the reins of Ludwig Erhard, who was associated with economic growth, not cultural conservatism. During 1966–69 the CDU/CSU shared power with the SPD in a Grand Coalition, before the SPD took over (in coalition with the FDP) in 1969. In the meantime, increasing numbers of West Germans had become involved with grass-roots political organizing. The ascendant SPD embraced this more participatory model of politics with the slogan "Dare more democracy!" and talk of the *mündiger Bürger*, or the "citizen who has come of age."[6]

To be "of age" implied both political and sexual maturity. Enlightenment thinkers had disparaged *unmündige Bürger*, who were intellectually captive to suspicion and ignorance. In the political sphere, before the spread of the term *mündiger Bürger* to describe a more participatory citizenship in the late 1960s, *mündig* had referred to a legal adult (and the word retained this meaning). Someone who was *mündig* could sign a contract, could vote—and could consent to sex or marriage. A wedding between underage partners was invalid; sex with an underage partner was statutory rape. Persons who were of age, by contrast, could make decisions for themselves; for example, they could marry despite their families' disapproval.

In fact, though, even West Germans "of age" could not make their own sexual decisions. They could simply engage in a narrow range of approved activities. Now politicians spoke of the "citizen who has come of age": the citizen who did not need to be treated as a child. Intentionally or not, this choice of words evoked the language of adulthood in intimate affairs. If citizens were "of age," should they not also be able to chart their own sexual paths?

Nowhere were discussions of *Mündigkeit* more striking than in the Catholic Church—and nowhere was the connection between challenges to authority and the relaxation of sexual norms more evident. After the Second Vatican Council, hopes ran high that the Church would reform its sexual dictates, especially by ending its ban on contraceptives. Yet in 1968, a Papal Encyclical reiterated the ban. In response, West German Catholics openly questioned not only the ruling on contraception but, more broadly, Catholics' duty to obey papal dictates unquestioningly. Both lay and ordained Catholics demanded that the Church recognize Catholics as *mündig*: responsible for considering Church teachings, their personal situations, and social questions such as overpopulation; endowed with the capacity to discuss these subjects seriously with coreligionists; and equipped then to follow their own consciences.[7]

By the end of the 1960s, sexuality in the public sphere looked very different. Sexual texts and images became simultaneously more explicit and more visible. Young radicals employed unorthodox sexual behavior and bodily deportment as theater. Looking back from the close of the decade, the early 1960s looked decorous, proper, conservatively dressed. But this was the period when sexual consumption went public.

The Not-Quite-So-Clean Streets

During the 1950s, mail-order firms were the major source for sexual consumer goods. The Law on Youth-Endangering Texts restricted more visible outlets, and customers valued the privacy and discretion of mail order. Commerce in sexual wares never vanished from the streets, however. Gay-themed magazines disappeared from the newsstands, but magazines that had once displayed female nudes on their covers and run articles about nonmarital sex simply slapped bathing suits onto their models and concluding paragraphs about the triumph of marriage onto their articles about sex. As the decade wore on, the bathing suits became smaller and smaller, while celebrity reporting gave the boulevard press an excuse to write about affairs whose proper ending—marriage—lay somewhere in the future, if anywhere at all. In addition, condoms could be found not only in pharmacies and mail-order catalogs, but also in vending machines, which migrated from men's restrooms to city streets. By the late 1950s, young people in towns without strict local controls routinely encountered sex in the newsstands and vending machines.

The "illustrateds," a category encompassing a wide array of weekly and biweekly publications, had some twenty-five million regular readers in West Germany by 1962.[8] Millions more leafed through the magazines in coffee shops, waiting rooms, and other public spaces, and anyone who walked by a newsstand saw the covers. With themes like fashion, gossip, sports, and television and radio, the illustrateds carried stories that decency advocates felt promoted poor moral values, even if they stopped short of sexual explicitness. They featured photos of female celebrities and models in alluring poses. They ran sex surveys. Their advertisements used suggestive pictures to sell everything from cosmetics to cars. Their back pages included classified ads for mail-order erotica firms.[9] The Working Group for Advice on Journals rated only two nonconfessional publications as "unobjectionable" in spring 1962.[10]

This Catholic organization had admittedly strict standards, but publishers of erotica agreed that the illustrateds were sexual indeed. Those publishers found it useful to bring a stack of illustrateds to Panel hearings. By doing so, they demonstrated that their works were no more risqué than what consumers saw every day on the newsstands.[11] Decency advocates, frustrated at the government's inaction, urged publishers of illustrateds to form a body to impose self-censorship, just as the film industry had done (under threat of government intervention).[12] But film making was concentrated in the hands of a few major studios. The publishing industry was far too diffuse for this model to be effective, and all efforts at "voluntary self-control" failed.

Illustrateds were not all that consumers could buy on the streets. They could also buy condoms. The Reichswehr had introduced vending machines dispensing condoms into military barracks toward the end of the First World War, and shortly thereafter the Prussian government established them in police barracks. The 1927 Law on the Prevention of Sexually Transmitted Disease legalized the advertisement and display of prophylactics, as long as the manner was not injurious to public morals. By 1932, at least 1,600 vending machines sold condoms around Germany. Some were contracted by the Reichswehr or municipalities for barracks or public men's restrooms; others were set up in locations of private commerce centered on male sociability, such as barbershops and pubs.[13] We lack data for the Nazi years, but the number of machines almost certainly rose. The improving economy enabled more businesses to lease machines in the absence of new restrictions limiting them. At the same time, mass organizations and the militarization of German society meant the removal of millions of men to barrack settings by a regime deeply concerned with reproductive health and worker and military morale. Tolerating illicit sex served the latter; encouraging men to use condoms abetted the former.[14] Vending machines went up in foreign laborers' barracks during the war: sexually transmitted disease could affect their working capacity, too, and could harm the reproductive potential of the German women with whom so many established sexual relationships.[15]

It was after the war, however, that vending machines became the single most important source of condoms, accounting for between one-third and one-half of all sales by the late the 1950s.[16] Already in 1951, a single firm, Westav-Automaten, had 8,225 machines around West Germany.[17] Furthermore, businesses like drug stores and barbershops now placed vending machines outside as well as inside their shops. Proponents of public health welcomed this development: most people, after all, needed condoms after hours, when stores were closed.[18] Some proponents of machines noted their special importance in light of the foreign—especially the African American—troop presence.[19] Decency advocates opposed them for exactly the same reasons: sex in which

couples discovered at the last minute that they needed a condom was probably illicit, and easy access to prophylactics presumably made restraint less
likely.[20] It was also distressing to see women patronizing vending machines.[21]
As long as sales had been concentrated in barbershops and men's restrooms,
planning for nonprocreative sex had been a male prerogative. In any case, the
1927 law (updated in 1953) legalized the advertisement and display of condoms
for prophylaxis, not for birth control. To decency advocates, the fact that condoms were used for contraceptive purposes was argument enough against
vending machines.

Most serious, however, was the incontrovertible fact that outdoor vending machines were in children's line of vision, and that there was no immediate instrument of social control, such as the person behind the counter, to
shoo them away.[22] Some vending machines sold candy from some slots, condoms from others, and vending machines appeared not only in big northern
cities but also in tiny Catholic villages.[23] Level heads cited studies indicating that few children noticed the machines and doubted that those who did
would spend precious pocket money on a condom rather than on candy once
their curiosity had been satisfied.[24] Nevertheless, children did occasionally
make mischief with the condoms, and some who grew up in those days recall
the condom vending machine as an introduction to things sexual.[25]

The Regulatory Stalemate

The increasingly public commerce in sexual wares prompted a flurry of regulatory and courtroom activity in the late 1950s and early 1960s—which resolved nothing at all. State efforts to regulate sexual morals were utterly mired
in stalemate. It proved impossible to chip away at restrictive legislation, and
equally impossible to deploy it to enforce a conservative sexual-moral order.
Consumption maintained an uneasy place in state regulation of sexuality.

Yet the terms of the debate shifted in important ways during these years,
which helped set the agenda by which the sexual-criminal code would finally
be reformed in 1969 and 1973. If liberalism protected citizens from intrusions
by the state, then how were those citizens imagined? In opposing censorship,
liberals had typically focused on the producer and disseminator of protected
speech. Developments between 1958 and 1961, however, suggested that the
rights of the consumer-citizen were at issue as well.[26]

Even more important was the evolution of disputes about the purpose of
the law in the liberal state. For conservatives, the law was to protect the moral
order. Liberal legal theorists had long argued that the proper object of the
law, or *Rechtsgut*, was limited to the protection of individuals from personal
or material injury. Through the 1950s, however, positions were not neatly

drawn; most conservatives were committed to certain liberal principles, and most liberals presumed that the liberal state should foster—if not enforce—a sexual-moral order. When two high courts delivered contradictory decisions on vending machine sales of condoms in 1959 and 1960, however, they demonstrated the irreconcilability of these two philosophies—and suggested that consumption might be a source of special friction. Two years later, the government's reactionary draft of a reformed sexual-criminal code prompted a howl of protest that brought to the front pages the most starkly drawn iteration of liberals' position: that preserving a sexual-moral order was simply not the purview of the law.

Both conservatives and liberals remained unhappy with the Law on Youth-Endangering Texts through the 1950s. In 1958, the Constitutional Court determined that the blanket indexing of naturalist publications violated parents' constitutional right to raise their children as they saw fit.[27] Although the clause it invalidated was narrow, this decision was important: while the court had traditionally focused on the rights of producers and distributors of restricted materials, it now turned its attention to the consumer. The Bundestag was again faced with questions about the constitutionality of the Law on Youth-Endangering Texts, and it opened hearings on revising the code.

Although some liberals continued to argue that the law was inevitably unconstitutional, most had reconciled themselves to it—not least because they were reassured by the Panel's generally cautious indexing practice.[28] They continued, however, to protest the automatic restriction of naturalist publications, since it was not clear whether the court's decision invalidated the entire provision or just required modifications to ensure parental rights. Liberals' further demands emphasized the rights of producers and distributors, and liberalizers joined industry interests in urging a repeal of the provisions regarding "obviously deeply youth-endangering" materials. These provisions, liberals argued, were problematic in many ways. They violated due process in that retailers were criminally liable for carrying publications that were nowhere listed. They failed to guarantee equal treatment before the law because they left newsstand owners in conservative towns more vulnerable than those in liberal regions. They contravened proportionality by permitting the state to initiate action against a newsstand owner for carrying the wrong magazine, although it could prosecute statutory rape only if the guardian of the injured party sued. Finally, liberals wished to eliminate the Panel's ability to decide what qualified for exemption on artistic grounds.

Decency advocates had their own wish list, beginning with the demand that mail-order firms and pay libraries be prohibited from carrying indexed materials. Decency advocates also wanted the Panel empowered to initiate proceedings on objectionable items. They certainly did not want the artistic exemption relaxed; the Guardians wanted it eliminated entirely.[29]

Schilling refused to fall neatly into either camp. The present system, in his mind, was deeply flawed. Effective youth protection would require clamping down on pulp publications about the war, since "You can't impart an understanding of the Third Reich when these sorts of mendacious utterances remain uncontested."[30] The Panel, however, could act only on petitions submitted to it, and no one filed petitions for this genre. Nevertheless, Schilling did not want the Panel empowered to initiate proceedings. *This*, in his mind, would make the Panel into a central censoring agency that functioned simultaneously as prosecutor, judge, and jury. He sought the removal of special provisions for "obviously deeply youth-endangering" materials and naturalist publications, because he considered those provisions unconstitutional and the cause of well-justified hostility toward the whole enterprise.[31] And he agreed that the Panel should not determine what was art. The Panel should exempt all items that made a serious claim for artistic intent, whatever the qualities of the finished product.[32] Schilling seconded decency advocates' demands in only one regard: he wished to see mail-order firms and pay libraries added to the list of outlets prohibited from selling youth-endangering publications.

The 1961 revision satisfied decency advocates on most points.[33] Mail-order firms and pay libraries were forbidden from carrying youth-endangering works. The prohibition against display and advertisement of naturalist magazines and "obviously deeply youth-endangering" works stood, with a new clause allowing parents to authorize their children's exposure to naturalist publications. The Panel was to continue to distinguish between works that claimed to be art and works that really were art. Only the proposal to give the Panel authority to initiate proceedings and the Guardians' dream of eliminating the artistic exemption were defeated.

These modifications, however, did not resolve debates about the law. Barely six months later, the Flensburg court questioned the constitutionality of the new restrictions concerning mail order.[34] Beate Uhse had brought the case and, not surprisingly, much of it focused on the rights of distributors. The court found that the provision unconstitutionally disadvantaged a professional group by prohibiting mail-order businesses from activities permitted to storefront retailers. A portion of the decision, however, focused on consumers' rights. The court determined that freedom of opinion and information included not just the right to express oneself but also the right to inform oneself. This principle included the right to educate oneself about sex by obtaining reading materials from mail-order sources. In perhaps the most striking portion of the ruling, the court cited the Basic Law's guarantee of the right to the free and unfettered development of the personality. This right, the court said, must include the development of one's sexuality, if so desired, by purchasing sex literature.

The Constitutional Court rejected the arguments of the Flensburg court. The Flensburg case, however, did not just signal that the constitutionality of the Law on Youth-Endangering Texts was still in play. It also highlighted a critical new argument regarding sexual consumption. Previous protests against restrictions on commerce in erotica had focused on freedom of the press, freedom of artistic expression, freedom of commerce, and health-related exemptions. Now the Flensburg court cited the constitutional guarantee of the free development of the personality, and it named sexuality as constitutive of that personality.

In the meantime, however, mail-order firms could no longer sell youth-endangering materials. Or at least, they could not sell materials that were indexed—firms that had wanted to operate aboveground had long avoided anything that might be "obviously deeply youth-endangering." So mail-order firms did quick advertising blitzes for potentially indexable works and sold their lot before anyone had a chance to petition for a Panel hearing. In any case, the era when mail order was practically the only source for sexual works was nearly over.

Decency advocates also targeted vending machines that sold condoms. By the late 1950s, courts all over West Germany were hearing cases concerning whether one machine or another injured morals and decency. Technically, such cases hinged on details of presentation. Was the word "condom" or one of its colloquial synonyms visible? Was the machine on a popular route for schoolchildren? In reality, those who opposed vending machines opposed them anywhere, in any form. Vending machines on busy streets offended decency by suggesting that condoms were everyday items, but such machines tucked in alleyways enabled people who shouldn't be having sex at all to draw their wares unobserved. The word "condom" was a no-no, but simply permitting the brand name to show was no better, since everyone knew what a Blausiegels was.[35] In other words, such machines' very existence was injurious to morals and decency. Yet the 1953 revision to the 1927 Law on Sexually Transmitted Disease confirmed the legality of discrete display and advertisement of condoms, adding no new language to suggest that outdoor machines might require special attention. The Bundesrat nixed legislation that would have banned outdoor machines in 1956, and the German Conference of Cities joined in opposition to such a ban.[36]

In 1959, the Constitutional Court determined that outdoor vending machines were necessarily injurious to morals and decency, since condoms "by their very nature concerned sex." Less than a year later, the High Administrative Court determined the opposite, specifically, that police could take no action against a machine unless it had particular offensive characteristics, since such machines were not in and of themselves injurious.[37] Some states aggressively used the 1959 decision to crack down. Other states did not, and the industry exploited the confusion. Manufacturers provided retailers with instructions on how to cite the 1960 decision if hassled by the authorities, and they offered legal aid to those facing prosecution.[38] Decisions turned on questions only a lawyer could love, such as whether a machine's placement and display constituted "having items available for sale" (*feilhalten*, which was acceptable) or "offering items for sale" (*feilbieten*, which was not).[39] In 1960 parliament rejected a proposal to ban vending machine sales entirely, but approved a ban on vending machines on "public streets and squares."[40] The revision, however, left plenty of room for wrangling on such questions as whether a vending machine 2.15 meters into the entryway of a barbershop— but still out of doors—was in a public place, whether a machine on the street selling cigarettes could bear a sign informing passersby that a machine in the entryway sold condoms, and what the fine distinctions were between placing a vending machine *an der Strasse* versus *auf der Strasse*.[41]

For sellers and buyers, the situation was familiar. Enforcement was inconsistent and depended heavily on location, so outdoor vending machines were rare in some areas, routine in others. But the contradictory decisions of the two High Courts attracted much attention. In theory, if lower courts arrived at inconsistent rulings, then one was in error, and a High Court decision revealed the correct answer. The contradictory decisions of the two High Courts suggested that there *was* no correct answer. The rational state was not equipped to divine and adjudicate standards of decency.

This inference, of course, was exactly what liberals had long argued. Their claims became more public and consequential in debates over the government's 1962 draft revision of the sexual-criminal code. Lawmakers had begun and abandoned efforts to update the code many times since the Wilhelmine era, and it was on the agenda again in the early years of the Federal Republic. After a government-appointed grand commission of jurists and legislators recommended significant areas of liberalization, the Ministry of Justice disregarded those recommendations in a reactionary proposal of 1962. The draft law was roundly criticized and never taken up by parliament. A monument to the official sexual conservatism of the 1950s, it turned into a memorial as it backfired. Rather than solidifying conservative mores, it instead rallied opponents of state-imposed sexual conservatism, and this led eventually to two dramatic revisions of the sexual-criminal code in 1969 and 1973. But whereas the legalization of pornography provoked greater public passion than any other portion of those reforms, the debates around the 1962 draft barely touched on consumption.

In 1954, the grand commission opened discussions on the code. In 1957, a subcommittee considered obscene writings and images, as well as objects intended for obscene use. The subcommittee recommended that the exemption to the ban on advertising and displaying "items intended for indecent use" include not only prophylactics but also contraceptives. A minority recommended permitting advertising and display of any object whose distribution was legal.[42] The grand commission declined the minority position but adopted the subcommittee's recommendation that (decent) advertisement and display of contraceptives, not just prophylactics, be permitted. The Ministry of Justice, however, proposed a resolution that would have made the revised code even stricter than the 1900 original. Arguing that if an item was intended for indecent use it should not be tolerated at all, the ministry's draft did not stop at banning advertisement and display of such objects but rather prohibited their distribution entirely.[43]

The subcommittee and grand commission were clearly more liberal than the ministry (whose draft also maintained the criminalization of male homosexual acts, adultery, and abortion, and other measures that liberalizers opposed). Even these more reformist bodies, however, did not question the state's ability to prohibit the dissemination of obscenity. The recommendation regarding advertisement and display of contraceptives was the sole challenge to the state's control over commerce in sexual wares. There was no substantive discussion of stipulations regarding indecent writings and images (as opposed to objects intended for indecent use). Liberals had long raised objections to such stipulations: the subjective criteria for determining "indecency," the possibility that the dissemination of such materials might not rise to the level of criminal offense, and the claim that the prohibition contradicted such basic rights as freedom of the press. Not one of these objections was raised in the meetings of the subcommittee or the grand commission. In light of the lengthy discussions about birth control, abortion, and male homosexual acts, the utterly uncontroversial nature of the prohibition on "indecent" wares—the heart of state regulation of commerce in sexual goods—was striking.

Equally notable was the continued quiet as the ministry's draft sparked public controversy. Critics accused the ministry of ignoring the recent research on sexuality that the grand commission had consulted. Instead, as the editors of an influential anthology put it, "The draft shows the clear tendency to substitute prejudice and religious confession for experience-based knowledge."[44] Furthermore, the draft violated the fundamental principle of *Rechtsgut*. Instead, the government justified its draft by citing its duty to uphold the moral order.

According to liberals, claims of a "moral order" had not just enforced church teachings in an increasingly pluralistic society. Stripped of its divine connotations, the "moral order" had been cited by the Nazis in their claims to defend the "moral sensibility of the people" with ruthlessly punitive measures toward outsiders, including sexual minorities. In the debates surrounding the 1953 Law on Youth-Endangering Texts, liberals had contrasted Nazi censorship, on the one hand, with liberalism's protection of a free press on the other. With the release of the 1962 draft, liberals contrasted the Nazis' denial of reproductive autonomy and its persecution of homosexual men with the liberal state's responsibility to protect individual autonomy unless the exercise of that autonomy injured others.

Few critics, however, challenged the state's claim to protect the moral order by banning distribution of indecent writings, images, and objects. They objected to the ban on the narrow grounds that it endangered freedom of artistic expression, or that restrictions on contraceptives contributed to high rates of illegal abortion.[45] But critics did not pose the fundamental question: which *Rechtsgüter* were harmed by "indecent" images, writings, and objects that did not serve art, scholarship, or health?

The outraged response to the 1962 draft helped to make the conservative position untenable. Parliament never took up the bill. By the time the Bundestag revisited the sexual-criminal code in the mid-1960s under a "Grand Coalition" of Christian and Social Democrats, the liberal position regarding the primacy of *Rechtsgut* was dominant. But the place of consumption remained uncertain, reflecting the transitional moment in the visibility of sexual consumption. The Constitutional Court had protected the rights of consumer-parents in 1958 when it invalidated the Law on Youth-Endangering Texts's blanket restrictions on naturalist publications. The 1961 Flensburg ruling described consumers whose sexual personalities enjoyed constitutional protection. But sexual consumption was off the radar screen of the liberal intellectuals who protested the government's 1962 draft reform of the sexual-criminal code. Since those objections formed the heart of arguments for reform later in the decade, the blind spot regarding consumption would have serious consequences.

Sex Shops

One reason for the protests against the government's draft was the rapid change in public cultures of sex. The grand commission began its deliberations the year after the passage of the Law on Youth-Endangering Texts, a highpoint of public sexual conservatism. By the time the government presented its draft, the birth control pill was on the market, sexual images had become routine in advertising, and the press was avidly discussing the apparent overthrow of centuries-old sexual mores.

Although the pill promised a new stage in sexual liberation, it threatened condom sales, long the erotica industry's bread and butter. The Alliance of German Mail-Order Businesses briefly considered lobbying to make the pill available without a prescription. It dropped the idea, however, fearful that the result might be prescription-free sales permitted in pharmacies only, which would draw customers to pharmacies for other products such as chemical remedies for impotence.[46]

Contrary to the industry's worries, however, condom sales continued to climb. Fear of side effects made West German women slower than their U.S. counterparts to adopt the pill. In its advertising the industry exploited this concern, comparing the disadvantages of the pill to the advantages of condoms.[47] Journalists too contrasted the pros and cons of various methods of contraception. As a result, information about condoms, once passed along by whispers, now appeared in respectable media—and condoms, finally, were openly linked to contraception and not just prophylaxis. Even in the early 1980s, when pornography had been legal for years and lowered dosages had eased fears of the pill's side effects (and before the rise in condom sales associated with AIDS), condoms still constituted one-third of sales in Beate Uhse shops.[48]

Media coverage of the pill and its anticipated effects on sexual mores gave erotica firms an opening. In this new environment, people needed to banish their sexual ignorance once and for all—and erotica firms had the instructional manuals to help. If the medical community had invested in nonprocreational sex by developing the pill, then it must be all right for sex to be fun—so why not buy a piece of lingerie? West Germans might want to read books about this new sexual world, such as accounts of the supposed sexual avant-garde. But more important than the firms' strategies for selling particular products was the increasingly public face of an industry that in the 1950s had maintained a low profile.

The most striking emblem of this transitional moment was Beate Uhse's first sex shop. Already in the early 1950s, Beate Uhse's catalogs invited customers to visit the firm's Flensburg home. At first few did so. A hundred kilometers north of Hamburg, Flensburg was, to say the least, an out-of-the-way location. By the late 1950s, however, ever more West Germans could afford a vacation, and Danish beaches were a favorite destination. Mail-order customers began to make visits to Beate Uhse part of their itinerary.

There they were met by Hans-Dieter Thomsen.[49] In 1958 Thomsen, then twenty years old, had answered a help-wanted ad for Beate Uhse, a company he'd never heard of. Within a couple of months he took over "marriage counseling" for the firm. His training consisted of reading a few books: Theodor van de Velde's Weimar-era classic *Die vollkommene Ehe* (The Ideal Marriage), the pseudonymously authored *Unter vier Augen: Die hohe Schule der Gattenliebe* (Between Us: The Academy of Marital Love, 1949), and the more accessible *Liebes- und Eheleben* (Love Life and Marital Life), written by physician Emilie Fried and her Ph.D. husband, Paul Fried, in 1929, reissued in 1950, and acquired and heavily revised by Beate Uhse's press in 1957. This minimal preparation equipped Thomsen to aid customers suffering from severe sexual ignorance. More important than formal training in human sexuality were Thomsen's personal qualities—his easy manner of speaking and his empathy with tongue-tied customers—and confidence-boosting visual cues, such as sitting behind a kidney-shaped table and wearing a white lab coat.

By offering counseling, Beate Uhse mimicked a model developed during the Weimar years, expanded upon under the Nazis, and revived in some cities after the war. But whereas public marriage counseling centers had to bow to political mandates around issues such as contraception, homosexuality, and premarital sex, Thomsen was not thus constrained. Furthermore, public marriage counseling centers offered information only—no books to take home to a partner, no contraceptives with which to practice newly learned lessons about controlling fertility. A visitor to Beate Uhse could identify helpful products during counseling and take them home that same day.

Although such an encounter may seem a recipe for counseling oriented toward the longest possible shopping list, it was not. Thomsen dissuaded unhappy couples from purchasing exotic aids and potions. Without a basic level of comfort with sex, couples would remain frustrated, and their disappointment—perhaps even disgust—with their purchases would make them unlikely to return. Instead, Thomsen steered clients toward a book that would clear up their ignorance, and whose reading would provide couples with an opportunity for discussing sex. Grateful for having had their real problems—ignorance and poor communication—addressed, such customers returned for more, perhaps in the form of another book or a pack of condoms. A series of modest purchases by loyal customers was better than a single large purchase by a customer who would never return.

In 1961, Rotermund learned in a marketing seminar in the United States that successful mail-order businesses also had bricks-and-mortar shops. Thus she opened a shop on December 23, 1962—a date astutely chosen so holiday cheer would lessen the likelihood of protests. By all accounts, Rotermund and her staff were surprised when the Flensburg store did not simply absorb the tourist and counseling traffic to the mail-order firm but attracted local customers interested in shopping in person.[50] In February 1965, the firm opened a shop in Hamburg, which, during the first half of 1966, attracted 40,000 customers.[51] By the end of that year, Beate Uhse shops graced downtown Frankfurt and Berlin as well; in 1971 there were twenty-five Beate Uhse shops nationwide.[52] Other firms, encouraged by the increasingly permissive environment (and Beate Uhse's success), opened shops of their own. By 1973 West Germany had 350 sex shops in addition to Beate Uhse's, with 25 in Munich alone.

Through the 1960s many shops maintained the language of "marital hygiene" and the offer of counseling. Responding to press coverage of illegal abortion in 1963, Schäfer considered shops that would draw on the name Pro Familia (Planned Parenthood), which published its literature with one of Schäfer's presses.[53] As late as 1971, FCV (First-Class-Versand), with its fifteen shops second only to those of Beate Uhse, dressed its sales personnel in white lab coats, set up its shops to resemble pharmacies, and, like Beate Uhse, made half its sales with "hygienic" items such as condoms and chemical and mechanical aids.[54] In most other shops, stimulating books and magazines claimed some 60 percent of sales by the early 1970s.[55]

Even in the early 1960s, storefront sales of erotica were not new. Pharmacies had long carried condoms and tonics; bookshops had sold sex literature, albeit under the counter. What was new—just as in the expansion of mail order a decade earlier—was the opportunity for one-stop shopping. Catalog designers knew that packaging, cover design, framing texts, product blurbs, illustration, and organization of wares into subgroups all offered frameworks for interpreting sexual consumption. With shops, the street address, décor, interior layout, and service personnel did the same.

Beate Uhse's first shops blended aspects of a marriage counseling center, a library, and a pharmacy. Customers entered a "Reading and Information Room," where they could browse through books on sex education, contraception, partnership problems, and sexual science, with no direct pressure to buy and no need to enter the rest of the shop. Customers who wanted advice or other goods could discuss their needs with a counselor in a private room. The counselor retrieved items the customer desired, wrapped them, and made available a mail-order catalog. Customers could examine lingerie in a separate room, where it too would be wrapped. The customer approached the cash register with packages marked with product numbers only; customers could not identify each others' purchases. When self-service was introduced, customers retrieved neutral packages from bins under display models, which preserved discretion at the cash register. Carrying the objects in an unmarked, opaque bag, the customer exited past a staff member stationed at the shop's entrance to ensure that underage passersby did not linger.[56] Beate Uhse placed its shops on prime shopping streets and prepared sober and informative window

5.1. Early days at Beate Uhse's Berlin shop. In the reading room, customers could peruse books without encountering other objects or pressure to buy. An attendant was available for consultation, away from the cash register. Courtesy of FZH.

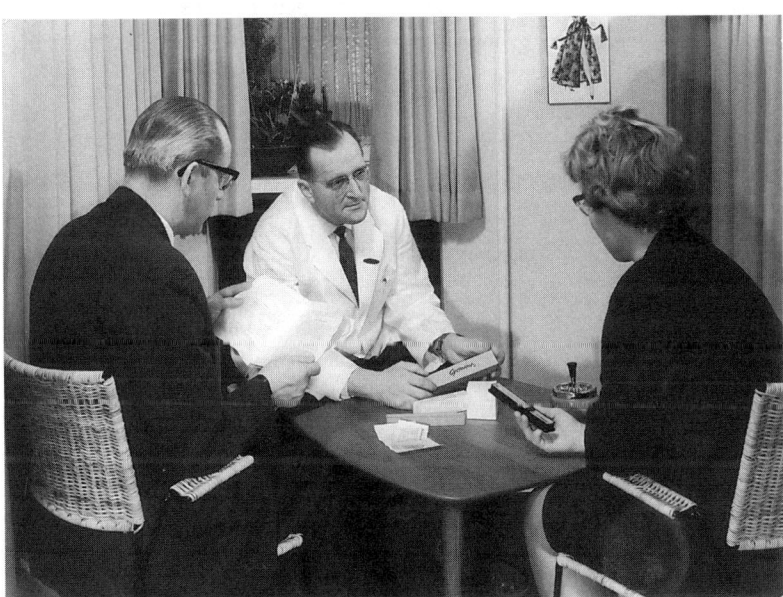

5.2. Counseling in Hamburg. Shop customers discuss their needs with a counselor (in white lab coat) in a private room; he shows them products and wraps the items before the couple proceeds to the cash register. Courtesy of FZH.

displays. This arrangement seemed comfortable to women, who constituted nearly a third of customers in the Flensburg shop—similar to their proportion on customer lists.[57]

Rotermund and her staff wavered between the hope that shops would bring more customers to mail order and the fear that shops would take customers from the firm's mail-order base. Neither scenario ensued. Instead, it turned out that mail-order and shop customers were two distinct breeds. Mail-order customers, who shied from face-to-face contact, weren't much tempted by the shops: mail-order sales barely declined in areas where a shop opened. Shop customers, who did not want their names on a mailing list, or who liked to see and hold objects before purchasing them, could not be coaxed into mail order: few orders came from catalogs distributed at the shops. In 1973, the firm estimated that over 70 percent of sales in storefronts were to customers who would not otherwise shop by mail. In other words, shops attracted a new group of customers. At the same time, the shops' visibility enhanced the firm's name recognition, helping mail-order sales to double between 1962 and 1972, despite the loss of some business to the storefronts. Furthermore, shops enabled the firm to test-market new items without the high advertising costs that mail order entailed.[58] Revenues for shops matched revenues for mail-order sales in 1972, and this figure represented twice as many shop customers as mail-order customers, since mail-order customers spent twice as much on average as shop customers. Both groups bought mainly contraceptives and informational books.[59]

Like catalogs, which in some cases were read by people who ordered rarely or not at all, the shops' influence was not limited to customers. Shops were visible to all passersby. With the firm's insistence on busy central locations, Beate Uhse shops were not only more numerous but also more visible than other sex shops. They established sex shops as part of the urban landscape—and not just in seedy areas—and their windows provided a few quick lessons even to those who walked quickly by. Large banners informed passersby of opportunities for self-service, no-strings-attached consultation, and mail order. Even larger banners described available goods: NUDE PHOTO BOOKS—CONTRACEPTION—SEXUAL SCIENCE. Display books illustrated the genres of sexual science, self-help, and fiction. Contraceptives and chemical remedies, in their packages, educated passersby further about what sexual consumption had to offer. Photos of attractive adults linked sexual consumption to desirability and happiness.

The catalog format of the 1950s had communicated important messages about sexual consumption, regardless of a catalog's precise content. So, too, did storefronts communicate messages about sexual consumption simply by appearing on city streets. If catalogs had established that sexual consump-

5.3. Attracting passersby. The exterior window display sympathizes with customers' desires to understand their intimate partners, describes the services and goods offered in the shop, highlights contraceptives and marriage manuals, and offers "the newest from the USA." Courtesy of FZH.

tion belonged not just in the back alley but also in the home, then shops established that sexual consumption belonged not just in the home but also on the public square. If catalogs had declared that sex aids and nude photo series should share catalog space with sexual-scientific works and contraceptives, then shops declared that erotica should share street space with clothing outlets and electronics shops. Or, in the case of FCV, which favored suburban locations, with single-family homes and corner bakeries.[60]

The expansion of storefronts forced some old-timers out of business. In the 1950s, 95 percent of the books published by Walter Schäfer's presses went to some three hundred mail-order firms specializing in sexual wares. By 1971, Schäfer's presses had increased production tenfold but could count only eleven mail-order retailers among their customers, and they purchased a mere 1.9 percent of Schäfer's books. The rest went to erotica shops, kiosks in train stations, and department stores.[61]

As an industry giant, Schäfer had the resources to open storefronts but opted not to, opening the way for Beate Uhse to dominate the sector. Exasperated by the "monster trial" of 1956–63, Schäfer considered giving up erotica and focusing on goods that caused less trouble.[62] But Gisela remained profitable in the early 1960s, and so Schäfer kept the business running. The expansion of sex shops, together with the blockbuster success of two of his pharmaceutical products (a dieting aid and a remedy for varicose veins), however, put matters into a new perspective. The firm briefly considered establishing "marital counseling centers" with attached shops, "à la Uhse."[63] But Schäfer had no interest in opening shops just for erotica; aside from his shoe stores, he retailed by mail order and made even more of his fortune as a wholesaler. Furthermore, while Beate Uhse's mail-order business boomed even as storefronts expanded, Schäfer's catalogs were so out-of-date that they failed to cover costs, which made even the mail-order enterprise questionable.[64] Eventually Schäfer permitted Gisela and its sister firms to shrink; he continued serving established customers but ceased active marketing. By the summer of 1969, only 22,000 private customers remained.[65] Schäfer continued to wholesale chemical aids, and he exploited the increased openness in publishing late in the decade, producing pornographic novels, sensationalistic reportages, and how-to books. Gisela and Schäfer's other direct-marketing erotica firms, however, disappeared from company records after 1969.[66] Beate Uhse had acquired them.

Trade was by nature a public activity, but moral purity activists had fought at least to limit the visibility of commerce in erotica. Perhaps it was impossible to deny adults access to materials that were short of indecent—but if those items were endangering to youth, then they should be available only under the counter. Perhaps it was impossible to ban condoms from the marketplace, but they should not be sold in outdoor vending machines. Yet by the early 1960s, newsstands were full of magazines with titillating covers, vending machines still sold condoms, and the media enthusiastically covered the birth control pill. Still, magazines offered a limited range of sexual goods: pictures, stories about celebrity adulterers, advice columns discussing sex. Women could obtain the pill only by visiting their doctor. Sex shops were different. By displaying all possible goods in their windows and creating new physical spaces for shopping, sex shops made sexual consumption public in a new way.

Sex Celebrities

Sex shops did not become a common part of the streetscape until the early 1970s. Beate Uhse's storefronts, however, did more than create a new site of consumption. They also helped to spread Rotermund's renown beyond her customers and moral purity activists, and to the general public. Rotermund became West Germany's first sex celebrity: West Germans henceforth consumed not only Beate Uhse's products but Rotermund herself. They bought magazines to read about her business and marriage; they turned on their televisions to watch journalists plumb her expertise on sex.

The media's flattering portrayals of Rotermund, starting in the mid-1960s, made her someone to take seriously. Physicians attended continuing-education courses at the firm's headquarters. Members of Hamburg's Task Force on Sexual Education and Frankfurt high school students met with representatives of the firm to discuss the sexual problems of youth. Nor was Rotermund's role as educator limited to sex: the firm took on interns completing their business degrees.[67] And Rotermund attracted international attention. Newspapers in countries as diverse as Italy, Denmark, Iran, and South Africa ran stories on her in 1966 alone.[68]

Around the same time that Rotermund became well known, a second celebrity sex educator emerged: journalist Oswalt Kolle. Born in 1928, Kolle credited his psychiatrist father with exposing him to problems of "crippled sexuality."[69] In 1964, his series on child-rearing, originally published in West Germany's largest illustrated periodical, became a best seller in book form. *Dein Kind, das unbekannte Wesen* (Your Child, the Unknown Being) argued for an enlightened approach to childhood sexuality and sex education. The flood of letters that ensued indicated that parents needed to educate themselves and overcome their own shame before they could educate their children. When Kolle embarked on a series of articles on adult sexuality, the letters continued to pour in. Those letters, and Kolle's analyses of the problems they described, formed the basis of his next two books: *Deine Frau, das unbekannte Wesen* and *Dein Mann, das unbekannte Wesen* (both 1967). *Das Wunder der Liebe* (The Wonder of Love) appeared in 1968.[70] Beginning in 1968, "enlightenment films" based on Kolle's books broadened Kolle's reach yet further.[71]

With Rotermund and Kolle, West Germans witnessed a sort of "he said—she said" dialogue regarding a more liberated sexuality, in which "he" and "she" were generally on the same page. The careful listener, however, could detect differences. Although both promoted equality in matters sexual, Rotermund linked this equality to greater independence for women in other realms (like economic life), whereas Kolle assumed a housewife role for women. Yet as an entrepreneur, Rotermund was more careful than Kolle not to come down too hard on men.

Rotermund lay much of the responsibility for women's sexual unhappiness at men's doorstep, but she didn't blame men: poor sex education had left men ignorant of women's anatomy and sexual response. If information were made available, well-meaning men would do all they could for their partners' happiness. In *Deine Frau*, Kolle was considerably harsher. By keeping girls ignorant about sex, parents, schools, and churches practically ensured that they would grow up to have sexual difficulties as adults. Romantic partners, however, did more than their share by groping under the skirts of girls who

5.4. "Your Husband, the Unknown Being." Like Rotermund, Oswalt Kolle emphasized the need for basic education and good communication in order to solidify committed relationships. The films' titillating come-ons (as in this poster), combined with their determinedly sober execution, earned them the scorn of sexual revolutionaries.

wanted to be caressed through their blouses, making a woman's first intercourse a race to the man's own orgasm, and raping their wives when the latter did not want sex. Men who studied their cars' technical specifications to the last detail thought it unnecessary to learn about women's physiology. Men who paid painstaking attention to their bosses' tastes and moods couldn't be troubled to do the same for their wives.[72] If men were ignorant, it was because they did not want knowledge that might disrupt their single-minded quest for their own pleasure. Selfishness, not ignorance, was men's problem.

Both Rotermund and Kolle were true celebrities: their personal lives were as interesting as their teachings to West German audiences. As journalists knew from the press packets provided to them by Beate Uhse, not only was Rotermund an expert on sex, but she also had a media-worthy personal history: Luftwaffe pilot turned sex guru. And who wouldn't want to know about the private life of the country's most famous erotica entrepreneur? The young women's magazine *Jasmin* satisfied readers' curiosity with a 1968 article titled "What Does Mr. Uhse Think of Mrs. Uhse?"[73] The tabloid press covered the double wedding of two of Rotermund's sons in the summer of 1972. By far the greatest "press event" in Rotermund's personal life, however, was her acrimonious divorce shortly before the sons' nuptials. The press got an added bonus in the form of Rotermund's relationship with an African American man a generation her junior. (Her husband had been openly carrying on with the nanny for two decades.) Disgusted with the press's racism and sexual double standard in treating both partners' affairs, Rotermund gave no interviews for several years.[74] Upon her return, Rotermund became a media fixture and remained one for the rest of her life.

The effect was overwhelmingly positive. In 1972, even as West Germany was wracked with debates about legalizing pornography, which the overwhelming majority opposed, most West Germans attributed positive qualities to the person most associated with commerce in sexual goods.[75] That year, 87 percent of West Germans recognized the name Beate Uhse. By 1984 the figure had risen to an astounding 94 percent, making Rotermund by far West Germany's best-known personality.[76]

Rotermund also stood out internationally. Hugh Heffner, whose renown as the publisher of *Playboy* predated Rotermund's, was her closest parallel. Yet Heffner was associated with a single product, a magazine whose gospel of male pleasure with interchangeable women was reinforced by its publisher's self-presentation: the bachelor in his bathrobe, surrounded by Playboy Bunnies in the Playboy Mansion. Rotermund had built her reputation with education, talk of marital harmony, and expertise in sexual health. Furthermore, her public image was that of a wholesome woman who loved sport and the outdoors, was happily married (until 1972, after which she emphasized the seriousness of her new relationship), and took great pride in her children.

Like Heffner's, Rotermund's gospel was one of pleasure, but pleasure of a different kind. Heffner's pleasure, designed for men (although some women might incidentally enjoy being Bunnies), required throwing off the constraints of marriage, family, and bourgeois respectability. Rotermund's pleasure, intended for men and women equally, required throwing off the constraints of ignorance and shame so that marriage, family, and bourgeois respectability could be sites of pleasure.[77] Heffner's pleasure rejected a way of life that was not only socially valued but in which millions sought, and often found, happiness. Rotermund's was a purely affirmative pleasure, embracing parenthood, companionate and passionate marriage, and enlightened nonmarital relationships. Her own example showed that she did not consider marriage necessary to a good partnership, nor were conventional standards of age and race important. Beate Uhse's publication, at around the same time, of a book of male nudes featuring Rotermund's sons—which they surely knew would appeal to gay men—suggested the entrepreneur was equally open on sexual orientation.[78] Yet although she always insisted that any activities between consenting adults were fine as long as they hurt no one, she never ceased to preach the gospel of committed relationships.

Kolle provided a variation on the same tune: rejecting the constraints of bourgeois convention while embracing their rewards. Kolle's film *Dein Kind, das unbekannte Wesen* (Your Child: The Unknown Being) featured his own family, including his teenaged daughter and son, at a nude beach. Candid about his bisexuality, he explained to journalists that he and his wife had an open marriage. He thus personalized the message of his film *Zum Beispiel: Ehebruch* (For Example: Adultery) that adultery need not destroy a marriage: most important was that the couple openly discuss their needs. The aim of all this unconventional behavior was to strengthen relationships and to prepare children for healthy partnerships.

Starting in the late 1960s, young people alternately mocked and pilloried Rotermund and Kolle for their emphasis on the sexually fulfilled marriage. Although their critics did not articulate the issue in this way, Kolle and Rotermund took the sexual revolution only halfway in insisting on women's equality in sex but leaving intact the privileges of marital status and age. Adolescents should enjoy healthy sexual relationships, but the greatest value in those relationships was that they trained teenagers for the more mature bonds that would come later.

Another way of putting it was that Kolle and Rotermund engaged in a different sexual revolution than did sexual revolutionaries. Rotermund and Kolle argued—like their Weimar-era forebears—for women's equality in sex, but they privileged marriage, or at least the adult committed relationship, as the site of greatest passion. Later in the decade, young men demanded sexual liberties outside committed relationships—and displayed striking disregard for women's wishes. By the mid-1970s, young women were accusing their male peers of crassly sexist behavior.[79] According to feminists' disappointed tellings, the pill ended women's fear of unwanted pregnancy—and then made them available to men regardless of their own desires, since they could no longer claim fear of pregnancy when saying no. And it did all this while imposing potentially serious medical side effects on women.

But sexual commerce, and not just the pill, also defined the emancipatory moment of the early 1960s. In important ways, sexual consumption of those years resembled that of the previous decade. Condom sales rose even as the pill took off, and educational texts remained best sellers. With Beate Uhse now the industry giant, that firm's catalogs—with their egalitarian orientation—became the standard for West Germans. Beate Uhse shops' language of "marital hygiene" militated against an environment that made men the consumers, women the consumed. As sexual consumption went public, its prime spokesperson, aided by West Germany's best-known sex educator, delivered an unerringly feminist message about women's sexual self-determination to the West German public.

Alternative Sexual Cultures

The illicit sexuality of alternative youth cultures formed a final component of the sex wave. Although young adults formed only a small minority of customers of erotica firms,[80] conservative commentators had long expressed distress at young people's tastes for objects and leisure activities with sexual overtones: tight jeans, rock and roll, fan magazines. In the second half of the 1960s, youth-oriented music and fashion became yet more daring.

The most alarming change, however, was not young people's shopping habits but rather their behavior. Young people insisted on their right to a sexual expression that was not furtive but part of a healthy and happy maturation. Acquiring this right required that youth openly challenge the norms with which they had grown up.

And so high school students petitioned not only for sex education classes but also, on occasion, for school rooms to be set aside for sexual encounters. Members of the media-savvy Kommune 1 in Berlin staged displays of their sexual openness to fascinated reporters. Communes less hungry for publicity established rules discouraging exclusive relationships. And young people simply began to have sex at an earlier age.[81] Yet members of the diverse youth movements of that era were anything but unified about the meaning of such activity.

The environment of radical change that characterized most Western cultures in the late 1960s and early 1970s encompassed both political movements and lifestyle choices. In a sense, everything was political: if drug use, for example, was illegal, then simply using drugs challenged state authority. In a sense, everything was lifestyle: to purchase a political tract was to participate in consumer culture and to choose to spend one's leisure time reading and discussing the text. Contemporaries often described a "sexual revolution" characterized by both radical rhetoric and nonconformist behavior. Nevertheless, there was a distinction between politicized youth whose explicit aim was to challenge the political order, and countercultural hedonists who expressed the desire to escape the bourgeois expectations of deferred gratification and self-denial.[82]

New Left sexual revolutionaries fell into the first category. Emerging from the student movement and committed to theoretical exploration of political problems, sexual revolutionaries linked sexual repression to capitalism and to fascism. In doing so, they acknowledged their debt to "Old Left" scholars who had written on the subject during the Weimar and Nazi years (in the latter case, while in exile), and who now updated their theories in light of political stability and economic well-being.[83]

It was this climate of prosperity that underlay sexual revolutionaries' critique of countercultural hedonists. According to sexual revolutionaries, the churches' antagonism toward sexuality had complemented economic interests during early industrialization. The working class needed to be convinced to set aside hedonistic interests in order to create a disciplined work force. So far so good: rejecting the work ethic in favor of pleasure was central to countercultural hedonists' program. But for sexual revolutionaries, the conditions of late capitalism had changed the equation. By drawing the proletariat into consumer culture, late capitalism gave workers both a stake in the system and an escape valve through which pleasure during leisure hours compensated for an alienating and exploitative workplace. In other words, in the current conditions, consumption and pleasure simply reinforced capitalism.[84]

Sexual revolutionaries and conservatives thus shared a suspicion of consumption and pleasure. Whether it distracted from work discipline or from the discipline necessary to carry out revolution, pleasure was dangerous. Capitalism had managed to ensnare all options into its web, and so sexual liberation, like women's liberation, would have to wait until after the revolution. This view, at least, was one logical consequence of sexual revolutionaries' theories of sexuality and capitalism. And indeed, a portion of the radical New Left moved in an ascetic direction.[85]

Yet many members of the politicized New Left, not to mention adherents of alternative lifestyles, experienced consumption, pleasure, and politics as complementary. The enjoyment and expansion of leisure, which included travel and consumption of drugs and music as well as uninhibited sex, was a hedonist program, not a blueprint for political change. Yet it remained a rebuke to the ethic of self-denial and delayed gratification that underpinned the educational, economic, and political establishment.

The complementarity of pleasure, politics, and consumption was a given for producers of youth-oriented music and publications: reading alternative literature and listening to alternative music were part of both a culturally alternative and a politicized lifestyle.[86] Yet the complementarity could be pragmatic, even cynical, as well as principled. Thus the preeminent left journal *Konkret* began featuring women in various states of undress on its cover in late 1964, appealing to "prurient" interests to break into profitability even as it seriously covered the politics of sexuality and other New Left themes.[87]

Much of the West German public would have been surprised to learn that the sexual revolutionaries they read about and the hippies they saw in city parks had very different interpretations of sexuality and politics. Indeed, it was the very diversity and complexity of the movements subsumed under references to "1968" that made the environment feel like one of such confusing and rapid change.[88] Theories of sexuality and politics mattered less than the fact that young people's behavior and deportment had changed radically in just a few years. The sex wave was not just articles in newspapers, images in magazines and advertising, and goods at the sex shop. The sex wave was *sex*, practiced by young people, openly and outside marriage.

Conclusion

The 1953 Law on Youth-Endangering Texts offered only temporary relief from what conservatives considered an overly sexualized culture. Within a few years, illustrated magazines displayed nearly nude women on their covers, vending machines selling condoms were commonplace, and advertisers used sex to sell all manner of products. This environment posed both an opportunity and a challenge for erotica firms. There was clearly a public appetite for sexual wares, but the very fact that so much of it was now on display rendered old marketing techniques, calibrated to the cautious mood of the 1950s, obsolete. Yet experience told erotica entrepreneurs that they dare not race ahead of what the law and public opinion would tolerate.

At this juncture, the paths of Walter Schäfer and Beate Rotermund diverged. The imperative to adopt new strategies at a time when the law seemed a great hazard—the "monster trial" was just over—seemed more trouble than it was worth to Schäfer, who had other profitable businesses. Rotermund likewise could not count on the law to back her, but the Schleswig-Holstein courts were more sympathetic than those of Baden-Württemberg: it was the Flensburg court that challenged the constitutionality of the revised Law on Youth-Endangering Texts in 1961. And developing new marketing strategies was an exciting challenge to Rotermund, who in any case had little choice unless she wanted to lose her business.

Lacking the desire to innovate and to become a public figure, Schäfer retreated from retail. Newcomers were busy learning the ropes and lacked the credibility of over a decade in the business. The fact that Rotermund bridged the conservative 1950s and the liberalizing 1960s became central to her celebrity.

Rotermund was not yet a symbol of the triumph of pornography—that would come in the 1970s. At this juncture, she personified Nazi-era athleticism and adventure, the striving for conjugal happiness despite an antisex environment in the 1950s, and sexual liberation in the 1960s. With the pill as the catalyst for discussions of a liberated sexuality, and with Rotermund as sex educator, the liberation of sexuality and the liberation of women appeared to go hand in hand. Yet the proliferation of women striking sexual poses on magazine covers was equally a marker of the new sexual world—and these were unmediated objects of consumption, whereas the pill was available only with a doctor's prescription. The law constrained the erotica industry from participating fully in the circulation of sexual images and texts, but this stance would change with the *Fanny Hill* decision of 1969.

That decision, which voided the codes on obscenity in text and image, ended the regulatory stalemate that persisted through the late 1950s and most of the 1960s. For all the back and forth on vending machines selling condoms and on youth-endangering texts, the state's authority to ban dissemination of indecent texts and images, as well as objects intended for indecent use, remained essentially unquestioned. The free speech issues raised by the ban, liberals felt, could be addressed with exemptions for items of artistic, scholarly, or health value. Materials lacking such value hardly warranted a fight, unlike the human beings hurt by the criminalization of male homosexual acts or adultery. When liberals carried the day in 1969 with the *Fanny Hill* decision, they were unprepared for the fact that the main impact would be on popular, not high, literature.

For years, liberals had decried the gap between sexual-criminal law, on the one hand, and Germans' sexual behavior and mores on the other. In doing so, they had pointed to the widespread acceptance of such practices as premarital sex and contraception. But these practices occurred behind closed doors, which enabled conservatives to imagine that a world in which such things did not happen was still within grasp. The sex wave, which brought sex to public spaces well before student radicals' media-enhanced performance of their rebellious sexuality, made such fantasies impossible. As a result, sexual consumption aggravated conservatives in a way that even homosexuality did not. It also, however, caught liberals off guard. In the meantime, entrepreneurs and publishers focused on the commercial possibilities of an ever-less-restrained marketing environment.

6 The Porn Wave

Pleasure, Consumption, and Liberalism

The spread of sexual consumption in the 1950s and 1960s required no reform of the regulatory apparatus. Indeed, the government confirmed its restrictive approach with the 1961 revision of the Law on Youth-Endangering Texts and the 1962 draft reform of the sexual-criminal code. In 1969, however, a partial reform of the sexual-criminal code legalized such behaviors as adultery and "simple procurement" (which was commonly understood to make premarital sex illegal).[1] A month later, the Constitutional Court ruled that John Cleland's 1748–49 novel *Fanny Hill* was not obscene. The new law and the court decision seemed to confirm the affinity of liberalism and democracy in sexual matters: few West Germans believed that literary classics should be banned as indecent; few believed the state should restrict the sexual activity of straight adults.

Yet the 1969 reform also served as a reminder that liberalism and democracy—if this meant ruling according to popular sentiment—were not in complete harmony. Although lawmakers ended the criminalization of consensual, noncommercial sex between adult men, they reinscribed popular prejudices by setting the age of consent at twenty-one, although it was fourteen for heterosexual sex. A second reform in 1973 lowered the age of consent for homosexual male sex, but only to eighteen. This unique limit on the liberties of gay male adolescents prompted no public outrage.

It was the aftermath of the *Fanny Hill* decision that made the tension between liberalism and democracy in sexual matters alarming. The court did not just evaluate an old book; it also voided the concept of "obscenity in text and image." Publishers rushed to exploit the ruling. The new flood of explicit works was markedly different than the previous trickle. Artistic, scholarly, and pedagogical features, which had protected "indecent" materials, were irrelevant if "indecent" had no legal valence anyway. Publishers shed all pretense of scholarly or artistic refinement and instead aimed unapologetically to arouse. West German publishers were outdone only by their northern counterparts, as

Denmark legalized pornographic texts in 1967 and images in 1969 and Sweden all porn in 1971. Scandinavians exported prodigiously to West Germany.

The *Fanny Hill* decision and developments to the north transformed the sex wave into a porn wave. Until the mid-1960s, large erotica firms in West Germany had emphasized *consumption as an aid to conjugal sexual pleasure.* Consumption itself was not to be the source of pleasure; rather, it should make relations with one's partner more pleasurable. By 1967, however, erotic novels had overtaken instructional manuals as the most popular book genre,[2] and after the *Fanny Hill* decision, publishers pushed *solo sexual pleasure in consumption.* The very act of consumption was to arouse and satisfy the consumer, no partner necessary. According to one publisher, roughly twenty books qualifying as "pornographic" in the terms of the *Fanny Hill* opinion were on the market on the eve of the decision. Two years later there were at least five hundred, not including the much more heavily illustrated magazines. During those two years some eight million pornographic volumes flooded the market.[3]

The de facto legalization of pornography with *Fanny Hill* dramatically altered the gender and class dynamics of sexual consumption. Erotica firms had always sold arousing texts and images, but in the previous market regime customers had used catalogs and counseling to open up difficult discussions about sex, and they had favored goods that aided conjugal life: contraceptives and educational texts. Meanwhile, economic privilege characterized aboveground access to arousing texts and images. Legal access was at issue, as texts and images acceptable in museums and university libraries were unacceptable in erotica catalogs. Financial access was at issue, as erotic texts and sexual-scientific books on "perversities" were often expensive. And intellectual access was at issue, since scientific apparatus kept nonfiction out of trouble, while complex literary structure did the same for fiction.

The porn wave put male satisfaction front and center, and it highlighted sexual pleasure freed from the constraints of relationships—or even from a second person in the act. Arousing texts and images might improve sex with a partner, but they mainly served the solo activities of voyeurism and masturbation. The prominence of pornography in mixed-sex spaces such as newsstands was a public reminder that real women were an inconvenience to this marketable variety of male pleasure. Sex shops still carried condoms, aids, and instructional books, but, increasingly dominated by porn, they became uncomfortable spaces for women. Obtaining goods in sex shops became men's privilege, as obtaining them in barbershops or men's restrooms had been a generation earlier.

The debates leading to the second reform (passed in 1973) thus occurred in a very different environment than did the debates leading to the first (in 1969). After the *Fanny Hill* decision, only new legislation could quell the legal limbo. Liberals had long battled state censorship based on church-inspired sexual mores, but they were not prepared for the task that awaited them. In past years, they had targeted the Law on Youth-Endangering Texts, which set a much lower threshold than obscenity for limiting an object's circulation, and which restricted some objects without a trial or Panel hearing. Liberals' protests often noted that truly obscene materials were already restricted, which signaled their tacit acceptance of this fact except when obscenity law threatened art. Perhaps most important, reformers had spoken mainly in abstract terms, opposing liberal principles to restrictive policies.

In the meantime, however, events had raced forward: the porn wave was in full swing even without legal reform. Even as liberalizers continued to press for reform, they expressed nagging uncertainty about its consequences. Liberalizers had avoided confronting the prospect of a pornographized environment, while conservatives, who deeply feared this prospect, were unable to defend restrictions within a liberal framework. When pornography was legalized in 1973 (with new rules to go into effect in 1975), no one was very happy except erotica firms and the consuming minority whose desire for convenient access trumped concern for those who might be troubled by pornographized public spaces.

Fanny Hill

In 1962, the same year the government presented its draft revision to the sexual-criminal code, philosopher Ludwig Marcuse published *Obscene: History of an Indignation*. The widely reviewed work attacked decency advocates for imposing a narrow worldview on the entire reading public. It gave equal measure, however, to liberals for protesting only to protect "art," which stood apart from the mass of materials that, liberals implicitly allowed, were rightly condemned. Marcuse exposed not only the obnoxiousness of the attacks but also the hollowness of a defense based on artistic grounds. The problem with obscenity legislation was not that it sometimes targeted objects that should be sacrosanct. Aside from the class bias of the artistic exemption, such a defense actually reinforced the category "obscene" by delineating what stood outside it. In fact, the very concept "obscenity" was morally and legally illegitimate, a rallying point for an "indignation" that was antiliberal, antidemocratic, and bigoted.[4]

The year 1962 was a fitting time to take on indecency in literature, for the key question in obscenity cases was shifting from medicine to art. In the 1950s, physicians had provided the crucial court testimony, as obscenity cases more frequently targeted sex aids than literary texts. Most conflicts within the government regarding obscene goods concerned sex aids and contraceptives; for example, the two highest courts disagreed on whether outdoor vending machines should sell condoms. The only sexual consumable that attracted serious attention in the 1962 draft revision of the sexual-criminal code was contraceptives.

During the 1950s and early 1960s, the Indexing Panel, not the criminal code, had been the locus of debates concerning literature. Opponents of the Law on Youth-Endangering Texts had reminded their audiences of the Nazis' burning of literary masterpieces. Liberals' hope that the 1961 revision would better protect art was frustrated, but there was movement nonetheless. The Constitutional Court declared in 1961 that the standard for evaluating "religious insult" in art was not whether the pious or even generally religious person found a work offensive; rather, one had to consider "the nature of contemporary art, even that which is not easily comprehended."[5] A few months later, the decision was applied to literature in an indexing case: not the tastes of the "average person" but rather the current standards of art must set the guideposts.[6] Yet it remained the Panel's job to discern the current standards of art. When liberals protested indexings, they continued to employ the terms Marcuse deplored and to insist on the artistic exemption.[7]

But West Germany's decisive literary obscenity trial was on the horizon. In 1964, Munich's Kurt Desch Verlag released a translation of John Cleland's 1748–49 novel *Fanny Hill*, in which a village girl describes her adventures as a London prostitute. The Guardians filed a complaint demanding that the work be investigated for obscenity.[8]

Initially, the case appeared to concern the artistic exemption. The lower court determined that art must accommodate other values, such as moral law. It also, however, found the work's artistic claim wanting. It thus overrode affidavits by literary scholars, cultural critics, and sexual scientists, who testified that the work was an important literary-historical document (and thus had scholarly value) and perhaps was art in its own right.[9]

The Constitutional Court, however, determined that the work's artistic qualities did not matter, because it was not obscene. Impressed by the testimony of the sexual and social scientists, the court affirmed that what exceeded society's threshold of tolerance and was thus obscene had shifted with time.[10] The Bundestag, the court noted, had ratified changing sexual mores by abolishing criminal sanctions for adultery, consensual homosexual sex between partners over twenty-one, and sodomy. In short, the court overturned its 1954 decision declaring sexual-moral values to be timeless. *Fanny Hill* may once have been "obscene" but it was no longer, and so it was unnecessary to determine whether it warranted protection as art.

If concepts of obscenity changed with time, then how should courts rule on it? The court explained what now crossed the threshold: works that por-

trayed sex "in an exaggerated, provocative way without meaningful connection to other aspects of life." Works crossing the current threshold were
characterized by an "intrusive, distorting, unrealistic representation of sexual proceedings; the glamorizing of debauchery or perversions; and an obscene manner of expression." Ernst-Walter Hanack, author of the most important legal criticism of the 1962 draft reform of the sexual-criminal code,
was disappointed in this portion of the opinion. Rather than ruling that the
concept "obscene" was unconstitutional by virtue of its indeterminacy (*Un-
bestimmtheit*), the court offered a definition of contemporary obscenity that
differed from earlier definitions but still relied on such vague terms as "sense
of modesty and morality," "average person," "considerable," and "suitable."[11]
The liberal weekly *Die Zeit* noted that although the court declared an evaluation of *Fanny Hill*'s artistic value superfluous, it nevertheless identified a protected class of "art": items that were not "intrusively crude or provocative."[12]

Still, liberals found much to praise. The court had declared that criminal
law was not to "enforce a moral standard in sexual matters upon adult citizens" but rather must "protect the social order of the community from dis-
turbance and crass harassment." The court's definition of "obscenity" echoed
the definition of "pornography" in Hanack's oft-cited article. It thus eliminated the danger that obscenity statutes had so long posed to art, since the
court's definition "at least in the case of literature is so reduced and impov-
erished" that it clearly fell outside modern notions of art. (Hanack still had
concerns about the visual arts.) By bringing the law and social reality into
reasonable correspondence with each other, the decision might ease the way
to comprehensive reform.

The verdict had an immediate impact on the juridical treatment of sexual
representation. It became difficult to get an indictment, much less a conviction, for distributing explicit texts. Only works that fell under the decision's
definition of obscenity could realistically be prosecuted.[13] When prosecutors filed charges, they took pains to explain that the fact that sexual mores
changed over time did not mean there existed no mores at all.[14] Although
this argument convinced some courts, others refused to determine what was
"intrusively coarsening or provocative," declaring this notion just as subjective as the "sensibilities of the average person."[15]

Entrepreneurs became increasingly brazen in their legal strategies. When
publisher Jörg Schröder faced charges of obscenity for the book *Barbara* in
late 1969, he demanded that the book be read aloud in court to determine
whether the sexual scenes displayed meaningful connection with other aspects of life. The trial was cut short after two hours as a result of participants'
exhaustion.[16] Patently ridiculous affidavits mocked the now irrelevant criteria of artistic, social, and pedagogic value.[17]

In 1971 CDU/CSU–governed provinces began a crackdown.[18] But with the *Fanny Hill* decision resting on changed notions of obscenity rather than artistic license, works claiming no artistic qualities whatsoever became standard. "According to common wisdom," wrote journalist Henryk Broder in 1973, "the so-called liberalization in the form of the porn-wave began with the *Fanny Hill* decision."[19]

The Orgasm Trial

Then there was the so-called Orgasm Trial. This 1971 case concerning Beate Uhse's sex aids addressed the issue at the heart of it all: Was sexual pleasure— not sex outside marriage, homosexuality, or representations of sex, but sexual pleasure—indecent? The Orgasm Trial lacked the constitutional significance of the *Fanny Hill* case, but in light of pornography's stress on male pleasure, the trial warrants note for its focus on female pleasure.

The obscenity statutes of 1900 echoed the church teaching that sexual pleasure was sinful and that it shed this character only by the intent of procreation within marriage. In the secular language of the law, "sinful" became "obscene." Battles regarding objects intended for obscene use were rarely about "perversities" such as homosexuality or sadomasochism. Rather, they asked whether the heterosexual sex involving the object was marital, with procreative intent. Thus, for example, condoms were indecent. The fact that condoms could be sold reflected a determination that their benefits to public health outweighed their injury to decency—not that condom use was in fact decent.

It was harder to justify exemptions for sex aids. Objects permitting an impotent man to penetrate and ejaculate enabled conception; so, presumably, did virility formulas.[20] But what about objects that stimulated the woman? Through the 1950s and 1960s, defenders of the objects argued that "frigid" women avoided sex; making it more pleasurable would increase its frequency and make conception more likely.[21] But the objects' proponents also insisted that marital harmony, not just procreation, was an important function of sex, and that for sex to fulfill this function, both partners must reach climax.[22] In a 1951 case, Beate Uhse presented statements from 1,306 physicians regarding various sex aids' capacity to heal endangered marriages.[23] The argument resonated in official circles. In the mid-1950s, the Federal Health Bureau held that the law permitted exemptions not only for prophylactics, but also for objects that might "heal or alleviate illnesses or complaints of the sexual organs," including frigidity.[24]

Yet the grand commission considering the 1962 revision to the sexual-criminal code confirmed that the objects were intended for indecent use.

Frigid women could learn about sex aids from their physicians; marketing of the objects was really directed at healthy women and their partners. With such couples, to quote an earlier court decision, "the normal process of sexual union is artificially manipulated . . . arousal unnaturally heightened or prolonged. Sexual intercourse is stripped of its normal function. The only goal left is the overly increased stimulation of the senses, the excitement of the sexual partner."[25]

The distinction between nature and artifice, and the equation of nature, normalcy, and decency, thus defined the challenge for those seeking greater lenience in the sale of sex aids. The turning point was a case involving sleeves and rings to be slipped over the penis, with texture or protuberances to stimulate the vagina or clitoris. In overturning the lower court's conviction in November 1969, the appeals court drew on the *Fanny Hill* opinion to state that "the legal designation 'indecent' is not a firmly outlined concept; rather, it requires interpretation."[26] The question was not whether their presumed health benefits exempted sex aids from the restrictions on objects intended for indecent use. The question was whether the use of sex aids was indecent in the first place.

With *Fanny Hill*, changing times alone determined that the work was not indecent. Not so with sex aids, which required consideration of nature versus artifice in sex acts. The key affidavit came from physician Reinhard Wille. Orgasm in women, Wille stated, was a natural phenomenon, so reaching orgasm could not be indecent. Drawing on Masters and Johnson's recent work, he continued that "the schema of the unfolding of the orgasm and its intensity are always the same for a single person. An intensification of the orgasm is medically unthinkable." Thus, no object could "cause an unnatural intensification of pleasure over and above orgasm."[27] The Constitutional Court cited Wille's words in upholding the acquittal.

This was a fitting end to the series of High Court cases regarding erotica that preceded the 1973 reform. The *Fanny Hill* decision had stated that the concept "obscene" was relative, but it did not confront the hostility toward sexual pleasure that underlay the legal category "obscenity." Indeed, it declared that only "meaningful connection with other aspects of life" made sexual representation acceptable. The Orgasm Trial went a step further in determining that sexual pleasure itself was not obscene.

Yet the Orgasm Trial had little impact on sexual consumer culture. The objects in question had never sold well. The verdict did cut short court proceedings on the battery-powered vibrator, introduced in 1969. But vibrators as a masturbatory aid for women were different from porn as a masturbatory aid for men. Porn helped men to masturbate as they always had: with their hands. Women, too, could use texts and images in this familiar way. The vibrator introduced a relatively expensive foreign object with a (sometimes noisy) motor into the act. Sales climbed only when books such as Nancy Friday's *My Secret Garden* and popular magazines began, in the 1980s, to discuss masturbation and sex toys for women.[28] Even then, a woman only needed one vibrator. With arousing texts and images, repeat customers were guaranteed. The market was in porn, not sex toys. And while legal approbation of female pleasure declined with the Orgasm Trial, something else was at play in the silence that surrounded sex aids for women. Fear of the "artificial" manipulation of female pleasure was smothered by an absolute panic at the displays of male pleasure that accompanied the porn wave.

Doing Business during the Porn Wave

The post–*Fanny Hill* years were not easy for the industry. Even with the verdict, courts could be lenient one month, aggressive the next. Formal legalization still lay in the future. And publishers pleased by new market opportunities faced a fresh challenge: competition from the north. Denmark legalized pornographic texts in 1967 and images in 1969; Sweden legalized both in 1971. Publishers in both countries were as interested in exporting as they were in their small domestic markets, and West Germany, with its great wealth, large population, geographic proximity, and constraints on domestic publishers, was the prime prize. West Germans ordered directly from Scandinavian firms and crowded into shops right across the Danish border that accepted German currency. Scandinavian presses published materials in German for export and for sale in tourist-oriented shops. Smugglers carried 100,000 magazines across the border every week.[29]

Beating the Scandinavians at their own game was out of the question. Even after the *Fanny Hill* decision, West German law forbade the sort of materials produced to the north. West German firms could only insert references to sexy Scandinavia into their products. Having previously denoted the exotic erotic through visual cues such as dark skin and tropical backdrops, or at least French fashion, publishers now tried to exploit the Nordic cachet—which offered little by way of physical difference—by using Scandinavian names. "Britta" became an overnight star.[30]

The arrival of Scandinavians as exotic erotics reflected an important aspect of race during the sex and porn waves. With so much going on at home, who needed the racial Other? Representations of the sexual practices of "primitive" peoples, in particular, became less interesting. Untouched by history, such people—along with their sexual behavior—presumably remained the same, whereas in the West there was an exciting new story to tell. Reportages like *Sex + Sex = Group Sex: A Report of Partner Swapping in Germany* and contemporary fiction presented the next-door neighbors as the exotics.[31] If racial others had a place in this environment, it was to pound home the challenge to conservative norms, with the Other no less modern than the European (or European American). Portrayals of sex between black and white Americans made the point.[32]

This was a time of harsh domestic as well as international competition. After the *Fanny Hill* decision, entrepreneurs were attracted to what seemed an easy path to wealth, and authors able to write quickly and to order, like those practiced in producing dime-store novels, thrived.[33] The crowding of the erotica market, however, meant tough competition. The new irrelevance of the artistic and scholarly exemptions made it easier to produce sexually explicit material—it took work to create a text that could claim such qual-ities—but works without literary and scholarly apparatus invited custom-ers of modest means, and they sought bargains. The result was pressure on prices. West Germany experienced a simultaneous "race to the bottom," in which some publishers exploited the demand for more explicit material and the declining importance of "quality," and "race to the top," in which others tread carefully, lest overstepping invite troubles at this delicate moment.

Rotermund personified the "race to the top." She continued her careful public relations work, and so journalists learned that a 1972 survey showed that most respondents considered the firm trustworthy, discrete, and a good source of information about sex. They did not learn that the survey showed that women felt sexually harassed in Beate Uhse shops.[34] Grateful for an easy story on a marketable subject, journalists usually spared themselves the trouble of research by relying on Rotermund's press packets and interviews. Since most hastened to deny independent knowledge of the products under discussion, they were hard put to challenge Rotermund's claims regarding the content of her books, magazines, and films.[35]

Beate Uhse continued to highlight not only the respectability of its cus-tomers and products, but also the efficiency and transparency of its business practices. In an era of shaky start-ups, Beate Uhse provided a foil in being such a well-run firm. Already in 1965, computers maintained customer records and processed orders. Earlier in the decade the firm had moved to custom-built quarters on Flensburg's outskirts, and 1969 saw the dedication of a new, ultramodern facility, with hundreds of guests in attendance and a speech by the mayor. Journalists described the vast quantities of mail that moved through the firm and the speed with which orders were processed.

According to the media, Beate Uhse's efficiency served the public good, not just commercial interests. Even as mailing lists swelled above two million, the firm thoroughly checked customers' ages. This sense that Rotermund's business practices, if not all her products, were wholesome led *Der Spiegel* to append the subtitle "Mrs. Clean at the Top" to the same 1971 cover story that revealed the firm's under-the-counter sales of pornographic film.[36]

If Rotermund was the industry's Dr. Jekyll, then newcomer Jörg Schröder was its Mr. Hyde. Schröder, born in 1938, promoted his disreputability as intently as Rotermund promoted her respectability. He also became a flashpoint of 68ers' tensions over politics, consumption, and sexuality.

In 1967, Schröder took over the respected but failing Melzer Verlag and made it profitable by publishing the German translation of the French novel of sadomasochism, *The Story of O*.[37] He founded the leftist publishing house März Verlag and for a time dominated the prelegalization porn market with his directorship of the West German branch of Olympia Press, the Paris-based publisher of English-language erotic literature that could not be published in the United States.

The stream of obscenity charges against Schröder; the meteoric rise of Melzer, Olympia, and März, and the equally dramatic fall of the first two; and Schröder's position as a major New Left publisher ensured frequent press coverage. But Schröder was no Rotermund, exploiting the media to project an image of respectability. His 1972 coauthored autobiography was the polar opposite of Rotermund's 1989 memoir; his self-published sequels and his ongoing blog continue in the same vein.[38] Heavy with descriptions of his "asocial" upbringing (his words), excessive drinking, and sexual activity, they describe a professional who thrived equally from spectacular failure and spectacular success. They also portray sexual promiscuity within the industry, for example detailing Schröder's sexual contacts with the nude female models he employed.[39] (In fifty years of Beate Uhse's public relations, there is essentially no discussion of models' working conditions or life circumstances.) He could be a sloppy businessman. Careless reading of a contract with Olympia nearly bankrupted him. He found the director of his first film in a pot-hazed Berlin commune and lost DM 30,000 when the director turned out to be less than competent. He named a new press over several beers and neglected to ensure that the name was not already taken—which it was, fortunately by a publisher who declined to sue him.[40] And when it came to content, Schröder pushed the envelope hard and fast. But if Rotermund's respectability had attracted the media in the early 1960s, a decade later Schröder's disregard for bourgeois norms proved equally irresistible. In 1971 the weekly *Der Stern* ran a story titled "The Porn King," which featured one photo of Schröder with two nude women in front of his Jaguar and mansion and another of him peering out from among the behinds of a group of nude women.[41]

Schröder positioned himself centrally in New Left politics and alternative cultural production, and März Verlag provided dozens of New Left authors with a platform for their ideas. Yet Schröder was also a businessman. *The Story*

Der spitzbärtige Jörg Schröder hatte vor zwei Jahren noch nicht einmal Geld fürs Briefporto. Heute posiert er stolz vor seinem Barockschloß im Taunus und schätzt sein Privatvermögen auf eine Million Mark. Herrn Schröders Gewerbe: Er produziert Europas schärfste Pornobücher

Der Pornokönig

Wie es der Frankfurter Jörg Schröder mit Lustbüchern und linker Literatur zu einem Luxusleben brachte.

6.1. "The Porn King." *Der Stern*'s 1971 story showed Jörg Schröder posing with two nude models in front of his home and Jaguar. Although the story angered Schröder, he cultivated a "bad boy" reputation that was the polar opposite of Beate Rotermund's.

of O was Melzer's ticket to solvency.[42] Schröder wanted März to thrive, but few New Left tracts were best sellers, and Olympia made up the difference. As he bluntly put it: "As a publisher one needs money! And we made it with porn."[43] Of his presses' DM 11 million in sales in 1970, DM 9 million came from books on sex.[44] But sex, too, could be a platform for leftist politics. Günter Amendt's youth-oriented manual *Sex-Front*, for example, critiqued consumer culture, "morality law," and West German schools; the film *Sexokratie* turned political slogans into burlesque by presenting vulgar sexual depictions of them.[45]

Unlike Rotermund, who claimed that explicit materials strengthened relationships by spicing up couples' sex lives, Schröder frankly propagated masturbation as porn's worthy aim. In doing so, Schröder went considerably farther than defenders of homosexual relations or nonmarital heterosex. Liberalism granted individuals the right to consider homosexual sex disgusting, premarital sex harmful for one's emotional development, or contraceptive use sinful. Those who felt this way simply lacked the right to translate these judgments into the law. But masturbation was not illegal. To celebrate masturbation was to reject liberalism's distancing language: "I may support decriminalization of homosexuality/adultery/contraception, but that says nothing about my own tastes or practices."

At the same time, promoting masturbation helped to take both class snobs and leftist dogmatists down a notch. Upon reading Susan Sontag's essay on

The Story of O, in which she explained how pornography sublimated itself to pure art, Schröder determined to acquire the German rights for the book. "'Pure art' was, however, not the impetus," he recalled. And when he finally read the novel, he knew his instincts had been right: "No need to talk circles around it: I got a hard-on, that's the most infallible test of pornographic literature, the best 'style analysis.'"[46] Sexual revolutionaries justified pleasure on the grounds that it promoted political liberation. "Sexual cripples are more easily controlled," the Berlin journal *Linkeck* explained. "In order that we not become crippled, we consider it indispensable to live out our sexual impulses as satisfactorily and as often as possible."[47] Schröder responded to such claims in his 1972 autobiography: "This country's Left would have been better off if they'd jerked off once in a while to real pornography instead of just to Karl Marx."[48] Sex's function was not to further art or politics. Rather, aesthetics and politics should make sex better.

For Schröder, better technical and aesthetic qualities helped to foster arousal. When Olympia first began to make pornographic films, the standard of comparison was Danish films, which had a reputation of being unimaginative, ugly, and brutal, even when they avoided depiction of violent acts.[49] As Schröder introduced Olympia's first porn films, he promised that they would be better—even as he promised that they, too, would be "hard." Unlike Danish films, Olympia's films would develop porn stars who were memorable, who clearly enjoyed sex, and who didn't look like they were in it just for the money. Danish films, in his view, had "no psychological dimension" and presented "always hard" and "always fuck-ready" men, with women reduced to "bourgeois-patriarchal sex concepts."[50] Danish films' practical consequences were limited to masturbation, yet they were sexually unsatisfying, even to the voyeur. "No less uptight" than Oswalt Kolle's films (which "stopped at the edge of the bed"), Danish porn "first switches on when the sexual act—boring in itself because there's no room for escalation—is already under way."[51]

If this was porn, then Olympia films were "antiporn," with "precisely the opposite purpose: to lead the way out of frustration, to break open the complexes, not to shove the consumer ever more deeply into the [passive] act of consumption, but rather to give him the possibility of finding his own identity, to do without the filmic father images, to do it himself (and to watch films for the joy of play, why not?)"[52] Schröder did not promise that his films would be more sophisticated than Danish films because they took on political themes, although that was in fact the case. Viewers were freed of the patriarch and passive consumerism *in order to* "do it" themselves and experience "the joy of play." And the models looked good. Politics and aesthetics served pleasure.

By declining to legitimize sexually explicit representation by insisting on its political function, Schröder extended Marcuse's critique in *Obscene: His-*

tory of an Indignation. For older liberals, art legitimized sexually explicit representation; for the New Left, politics served this role.[53] Schröder played it both ways: he challenged liberals and radicals by insisting on the legitimacy of pleasure for its own sake, but he also appealed to them by publicizing his pornography's political and aesthetic content.

Liberal outlets emphasized the aesthetic quality. In their reviews of Olympia films, they noted the attractiveness of the models and the fact that they looked like they were having fun.[54] Yet rather than address the films' political content, liberal outlets lambasted the supposed hypocrisy of a prominent leftist for growing wealthy on pornography.[55] New Left detractors, for their part, had long accused Schröder of profiting from leftist publishing generally, never mind from pornography per se.[56] These accusations, from both liberal and radical sides, pointed to a real tension within liberalizing circles. For many of those who supported legalization, the actual production, dissemination, and consumption of pornography remained shameful. This simultaneous support of liberalization and disapproval of the product, its producers, and its consumers characterized even the parliamentary proceedings that led to legalization.

Gender, Education, and Arousal in the Market

The changing balance among edification, health, and arousal altered the gendering of the marketplace. Initially, the relaxed publishing environment transformed some genres in a more egalitarian direction. Courts had long wrangled over which shots of nude women were indecent. Now it was possible to show couples engaged in sex, subjecting sexualized men as well as women to the viewer's gaze. The same was true of the shift in 8-mm film from striptease and nude gymnastics to heterosexual sex. Sometimes emancipatory messages from New Left politics found their way into porn. Yet the most notable feature of the marketplace was the expanded opportunity for male masturbatory fantasy. If the economic miracle had "domesticated" men, sexual consumption now offered a way out.

Images were central to this development. Customers could now buy explicit German texts, but they could buy Scandinavian magazines with photos of sex acts, so West German publishers sought ways to compete without breaking the law. One result was material that could claim social value while tapping the market for explicit images.

Since the Weimar era, marriage manuals had asserted their respectability in part by separating *consumption as an aid to sexual pleasure* from *sexual pleasure in consumption.* Readers were to implement lessons learned to achieve greater satisfaction with their partners. They were not to experience pleasure in the reading. Dense prose, scientific graphs, and Latin passages did not just

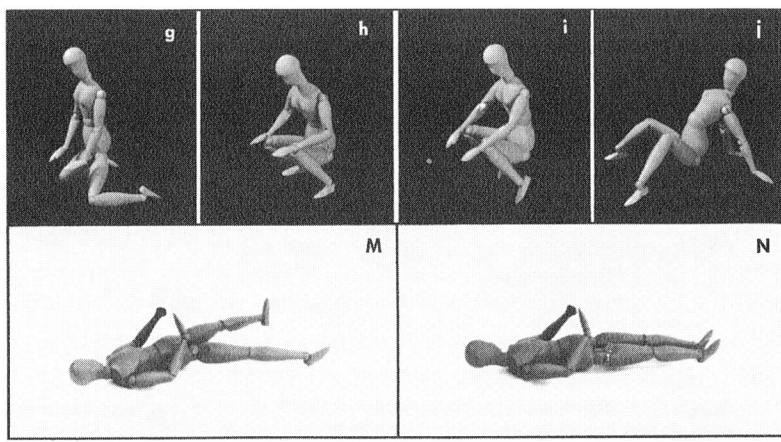

6.2. March through the positions. The speed with which images grew more explicit was disconcerting to many contemporaries, gratifying to others. Even after the *Fanny Hill* decision, however, claims to artistic, scientific, or educational value remained necessary to legitimize sexual imagery. In 1966, Sha Kokken illustrated sexual positions with male and female dolls placed separately; in early 1969, *Helga and Bernd* demonstrated "love positions" together, while dressed in leotards and wearing dispassionate facial expressions; later that year, Schröder's *1 × 1 for 2* featured nude models whose facial expressions suggested pleasure.

reinforce class privilege in access to sexual knowledge and keep the Panel at bay. They also indicated that reading should engage the intellect, not the genitals.[57] The same was true of early "enlightenment" films.

This wall came crashing down in the late 1960s. Illustrated books of positions, sex manuals, reportages, and films combined an education with the

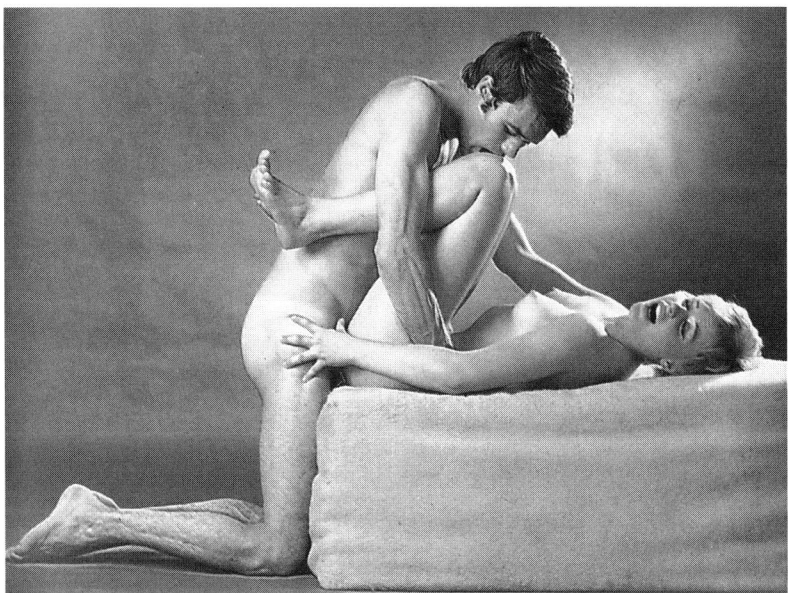

promise of arousal in the reading or viewing. Critics considered educational claims cynical. Yet pleasure in consumption could also tempt those who avoided dry texts to get an education despite themselves.

The revolution began with books of positions. Some older manuals had discussed positions, but it was hard to make more than a few distinctions in words (man on top, woman on top, man from behind). Texts described not sensation but rather which positions improved the chances of conception, which were more stressful, and which were awkward for corpulent or pregnant partners. Yet demand was clear: advertising a chapter on positions greatly increased sales, and books that included positions had the lowest return rate of all sexual texts.[58]

Illustrations provided the breakthrough. First came Sha Kokken's *Sexual Technique in Word and Image*, brought out in German by Beate Uhse in 1966. Aside from a few Japanese characters on the cover, the presentation was anything but orientalizing. The cover showed the physician author in a white lab coat; the book included sketches of genitalia and graphs of the stages of arousal and the fertility cycle similar to what one would find in a Western manual. The text covered familiar subjects like the sexual organs, dysfunction, adolescent sexual development, and contraception. Most readers, however, surely bought the book for its promise of over a hundred pages illustrating positions. Pictured were asexual wooden dolls, with males denoted by their placement against a light background and females against a dark background. Males and females appeared separately, with the text explaining how to combine them, as in: "The combinations Aa, Ab, Da, Db, Ea, Eb, Fb and Gb easily generate strong stimulation, mainly on the forward (upper) wall of the vagina; this also stimulates the forward portion of the head of the penis, while in the combinations Ac, Bc, Cc, Ec, Fc and Gc the rear wall of the vagina and the lower side of the head of the penis are stimulated."[59] Daringly, Sha Kokken applied the same technique to oral sex. The book sold 175,000 copies in its first year, but luckily for bewildered readers, Beate Uhse soon broke the next barrier.[60]

That barrier was the portrayal of men and women in the same picture—albeit wearing full-body leotards and sober facial expressions, and on a bare floor. The text to *Helga and Bernd Demonstrate 100 Love Positions* (1969) was authored not by a physician but by Beate Uhse's director of public relations, who published the book under a pseudonym.[61] A brief introduction recommended good communication and sex education. The remaining two hundred pages were given over to photos of positions. Neither the district attorney nor the Indexing Panel felt the book warranted action.[62] *Helga and Bernd* blanketed the landscape.

Later that year, Schröder slapped together *1 × 1 for 2* in fourteen days. The book mimicked *Helga and Bernd* in nearly every way: dimensions and layout; lighting and props; even, more or less, the order and description of the positions. But there was one big difference: this time the models were nude. The book *1 × 1 for 2*, like its predecessors, was a best seller.[63] In the next couple of years, further imitators offered ever more positions.

Some things truly could be conveyed better with pictures than with words. Both ignorance and shame prevented many couples from venturing beyond the missionary position, and these books normalized a greater variety of positions. They also showed couples having (or simulating) sex at a time when West German publishers otherwise could not do so.

Before the late 1960s, 8-mm filmstrips sold legally had been just a few minutes long, usually featuring striptease or nude female gymnastics.[64] After the *Fanny Hill* decision, films remained short and silent. Rather than focusing on female bodies alone, however, they offered a few minutes of heterosexual sex involving partners who shifted from one position to another in a single setting.[65] These were moving position books. Although consumers may have sought voyeuristic pleasure, they also, perhaps unwittingly, got an education in varieties of positions.

In Beate Uhse's publications, feminism informed the blend of arousal and education. Books like Rüdiger Boschmann's 1968 *Sex Play, Surrender and Ecstasy*, Günter Hunold's *Sexual Atlas for Adults* (1972), and Rotermund's own *Sex in the Partnership* (1974) represented the tail end of the peculiarly feminist sex education Rotermund had provided since the 1950s.[66] Photographs subjected men and women alike to the viewer's gaze and required that the reader take in not just straight sex involving beautiful young bodies, but also pregnancy and childbirth, contraception, older couples' pleasure, and male and female same-sex pairings. (The inclusion of contraception was notable at a time when many books omitted mention of it, as if the pill had made discussion of this aspect of sexuality, so laden with gender politics, conveniently unnecessary.) They distinguished "nontypical behaviors" like homosexuality from "abnormal" or "perverse" practices that indicated a neurosis, and practices involving coercion. Texts not only retained chapters on "unsexy" subjects like reproduction, but underlined the impossibility of true sexual harmony in an unequal relationship. Rotermund's passages on the subject in *Sex in the Partnership* stand up well even today. The book addressed housework (does the man not only put away the groceries but clean the bathroom—after having noticed *himself* that it was dirty?), paid work (is the man unthreatened by a higher-earning wife, and does he take over housework and childcare if her salary is the household's main means of support?), and bed (does the woman feel comfortable enough not only in her relationship but also with the possibility of single status that she can assert herself if sex is unsatisfactory?). Some of Beate Uhse's books won praise from reviewers, readers, and even the Indexing Panel for portraying women not as objects of men's pleasure but rather as equals.[67]

In other ways, too, Beate Uhse pushed greater equality while seeking new markets. The firm introduced lingerie for men in the late 1960s, and photographs of men modeling it revealed penises, pubic hair, and buttocks.[68] Nude photography outside gay male subcultures had long presumed a female subject; now Beate Uhse produced collections like *Sons of the Sun* (featuring Rotermund's sons) and *Young Apollo*.[69] The Munich district attorney suspected that these books served homoerotic purposes (indeed, they became cult objects among gay men), though his proof—that the models' penises were sometimes partially erect—was perplexing: evidently an erect penis would repel a straight female viewer.[70] The legalization of male homosexual acts in 1969 made it possible to openly market such items to men. Beate Uhse's "homophile" list included images, books, lingerie, and LPs of gay-themed songs.[71] Schröder began work on "seducers' guides" for gay men and lesbians.[72]

The new environment also made it possible to embed New Left critiques—including attacks on the commodification of sexuality—in sexually explicit formats. Even as he prioritized pleasure, criticizing bourgeois society was important to Schröder in the early 1970s, just as presenting sex in a respectable manner had been to Rotermund in the 1950s. Günter Amendt's youth-oriented *Sex-Front*, which appeared in 1970 with März Verlag, described the chemical industry as responsible for both the birth control pill

BEATES MEN-SHOP

Sexy Wäsche für Männer, die das Besondere lieben!

Der Slip mit dem schnellen Reißverschluß!

Roxy 100% Polyamid
Wie eine zweite Haut sitzt dieser knappe Slip aus schimmerndem Helanca-Satin. Er ist anatomisch geschnitten. Dadurch bietet er Ihnen markante männliche Form und guten, bequemen Sitz. Der Clou an diesem Modell ist der praktische schwarze Reißverschluß im Vorderteil.
rot
Best.-Nr. 29 003 07
gelb
Best.-Nr. 29 002 07
Jeder Slip DM 12,80

Goldvision
Für Männer mit eigenwilligem Geschmack: Ein extravaganter Slip für die intimen Stunden zu zweit. Der besondere Pfiff an diesem Modell ist die mit Rüschen besetzte Öffnung im Vorderteil. Aus hauchzarter Perlon-Charmeuse mit violetter, durchwirkter Borte.
Best.-Nr. 29 027 07 DM 12,80
100% Polyamid

Sonny
Betonen Sie Ihre Männlichkeit mit diesem Hauch von Helanca-Netz! Sonny ist ganz knapp geschnitten und anschmiegsam wie eine zweite Haut. Dieser kesse Netz-Slip verbirgt kaum etwas! Ein toller Slip für Männer, die das Besondere lieben.
schwarz Best.-Nr. 29 001 07
DM 12,80
100% Polyamid

64   Bitte benutzen Sie den beiliegenden Bestellschein

6.3. In the late 1960s, Beate Uhse took advantage of the more lenient environment to market items that made men into the objects of (presumably female) lust. Yet the promise of "sexy lingerie for men who appreciate something special" addressed a male consumer, leaving open the question of whether such men appreciated lingerie—or the men in it. A year after the publication of this 1968 catalog, the decriminalization of male same-sex relations made it possible to market openly to gay men. *Source: Beate Uhse Informations-Katalog* [1968].

and napalm, and the sexual revolution as too embedded in capitalist society to be anything other than the expansion of consumerism. It included a spoof of an illustrated position book as well as a satirical photo essay of hat salesman Udo and his stay-at-home wife Beate, whose days were peppered by the use of Beate Uhse products.[73]

Likewise combining political critique with humor were Olympia's short films, the most explicit aboveground films of the day. The preproduction treatment of *The Smooth Thief* cited theorists of the sexual revolution on the intersection of sexual repression, class, consumption, fear, fetish, and arousal. This complex was to be illustrated with a shoplifting housewife, a voyeuristic male store manager, a disciplinarian female cashier, and sex involving objects the housewife has stolen.[74] Echoing writings on sexual repression as part of the authoritarian fabric of West German schools, *The Schoolchildren* portrayed a sexually sadistic teacher who becomes the object of her students' aggression.[75] In *The [Female] Boss: Or, the Unstoppable Rise of the Window-Washer Salvatore G*, an Italian window washer demonstrates his superiority over two sexually inept German applicants for a white-collar job. The title plays on Brecht's allegory of the rise of Hitler, *The Stoppable Rise of Arturo Ui*.

Schröder both employed and challenged the conventions of pornography to make his political critique. To be sure, *The Boss* reiterated stereotypes of virile southern Europeans, and none of the action would have startled viewers familiar with the conventions of pornography of the day. In *Sexokratie*, however, the clichés of pornography made the point about political clichés. Most interestingly, in *Amazons: For Valerie Solanas and S.C.U.M.* and in *Colt and Quiver: The Exploitation*, the political message involved tweaking the conventions of porn.[76] The first played with the expectation that lesbian sex is the prelude to straight sex, with men's satisfaction the true aim, while the second incorporated the most taboo theme of straight porn: male homoerotic desire.[77] Yet *Amazons* permitted ample fantasy about dominatrices, male voyeurism of lesbian sex, and threesomes of two women and one man, while *Colt and Quiver* distanced male homoerotism by locating it in the racial other. In other words, Schröder's political critique and play on pornographic convention permitted reiteration of those conventions and the sexual politics that underlay them. Even the film company's name, Super Stag Productions, invoked a tradition of male bonding through heterosexual arousal.

With few exceptions (such as *Sex-Front*), objects that presented a political critique did not sell especially well. Olympia's six films sold a total of 30,000 copies, but German Olympia separated from its parent company in 1972 and soon went bankrupt. For the most part, erotica firms' response to the *Fanny Hill* decision was to exploit the demand for sexualized images of female bodies—and this was as true for Beate Uhse as for anyone else. Already on the eve of *Fanny Hill*, Beate Uhse catalogs had moved in this direction, with nude women on the covers inviting the customer to flip through the pages, which featured more nude women.[78] Self-help books sometimes blended strikingly progressive messages (regarding men's and women's interests, regarding hetero- and homosexual relations) with photos playing on men's fascination with underage girls and other such voyeuristic attractions.[79] Covers of reportages, self-help books, and novels featured women in the throes of sexual ecstasy. The images occasionally presented a couple or a group, but except in gay-themed works never a lone man. Perhaps most indicative of Rotermund's willingness to trade egalitarianism for business was the firm's introduction in 1971 of sex tours to the Far East and Amsterdam, with promises of compliant women at the point of destination. The firm dropped the tours—because they sold poorly, not because of any qualms about sex tourism.[80]

In feature-length films, too, enlightenment gave way to voyeurism. In Kolle's films, expert commentary had interrupted (simulated) sex scenes in order to ensure—in Kolle's words—that male filmgoers did not masturbate in public.[81] The hits of the early 1970s, however, belonged to the "report"

6.4. "Over 430 Attractive Offerings"—plus the one on the cover. The nude woman on the cover of Beate Uhse's 1968 cata-log—with an erect nipple revealed—invites the shopper to look inside for "a trip to the magical land of love." *Source: Beate Uhse Informations-Katalog* [1968].

genre. The fourteen-part *Schoolgirl Report* series set the standard with over a hundred million viewers worldwide by the early 1980s. In the series, teenaged girls dramatized their sexual maturation, which typically involved initiat-ing sex with adult men. Documentary apparatus enhanced the films' pruri-ent qualities rather than neutralizing them: discussions of how equality had brought a new sexual aggression in women (against a teenager's seduction of her middle-aged teacher) or the need for politicians to address race (against white schoolboys' gang rape of a black schoolgirl). The report genre featured not only schoolgirls but also nurses, housewives, female apprentices, host-esses, and girls who visited Munich.[82]

Sex shops, too, shifted from selling *pleasure in companionate sex through consumption* to selling *solo male sexual pleasure in consumption*. Shops moved away from the counseling center/library look and toward a style announcing less therapy, more fun. Flyers advertised not only "the most modern means of birth control" and "the best marriage manuals" but also "the one-of-a-kind 'Beate's Gag Box.'"[83] Redesigned windows, interiors, and advertising materials included brightly colored pop-art graphics.

6.5. "What Parents Really Should Know." In this publicity shot for the fifth installment of the *Schoolgirl Report* series, an adolescent girl seduces a middle-aged man.

The new look, however, also introduced a blunt sexual inequality that Beate Uhse had formerly avoided. Photos of couples in street clothes were replaced in shop windows by pictures of women wearing lingerie or nothing at all. Film screenings in back rooms re-created the environment of the stag film. The several small rooms of earlier layouts were transformed to a single large room, which reduced privacy and made it harder for those interested only in self-help books to avoid gag items and pornography.

With men making up the large majority in the shops—95 percent, according to *Time* magazine—women were intimidated.[84] Men had always dominated erotica firms' mailing lists, but women could browse catalogs alone or with their partners rather than in a room full of male strangers with sex on their minds. A 1972 marketing survey revealed that few women who were not already mail-order customers entered the shops, and few ventured in without male partners. A twenty-five-year old Munich actress gave a typical woman's response to the question "What disadvantages do the shops have?": "There are practically only men inside, as a woman you don't like to go in. You feel like you don't want to provoke the men. You feel like you're being hit on. The men think you're looking for sex and I like to avoid that."[85]

Female customers overwhelmingly sought contraceptives when they visited

6.6. Attracting passersby. The window to Beate Uhse's Cologne shop in 1973 featured a nude woman and promised "spicy books," "hot films," "spicy magazines," "love potions," "sex-film automats," and continuous admission to "sex movies." Courtesy of FZH.

6.7. Beate Uhse shops: the modern look. With a more exposed architectural aesthetic, this Beate Uhse shop in Saar, opened in 1968, allowed customers to observe each other while shopping—whether for informational or titillating books, sex aids, contraceptives, or items from Beate's Gag Box. Courtesy of FZH.

sex shops[86]—but in the meantime contraceptives had become available elsewhere. If sex shops were off-putting, women might pick up condoms in a self-service drug store or order them from Quelle (similar to Sears). They could find a self-help book or an erotic novel at a department store or book shop. Aspects of sexual consumption were thus integrated into nonsexual consumption. The price was the resegregation of sexual consumption per se. Contraceptives and advice books joined mainstream, sexually integrated commerce. Sex aids occupied a separate space in sex shops. Pornography, however, was ubiquitous; it was prominent in sex shops, newsstands, and some bookstores.

Male sexual revolutionaries criticized the commodification of sexuality under capitalism, but they enjoyed male privilege. Schröder's phrase "bourgeois-patriarchal" was principally a generational complaint. At issue was a paternal authority (with mothers playing a subordinate, yet still oppressive, role) from which young people needed to liberate themselves. If young women objected to the new sexual world, this stance showed they were still trapped by their parents' morals, not that they might have a legitimate complaint. Feminist protests against pornography lay in the future.

It was left to conservatives to express fears about a marketplace aimed squarely at male arousal. Earlier regimes of sexual consumption had alarmed conservatives—but now there was so much more of it, and it was so much more explicit.[87] Most conservatives believed women *were* defined by their sexuality, with motherhood their destiny. But procreation, not the satisfaction of lusts, was also the purpose of male sexuality, even if men's missteps were treated more lightly. To package, display, and sell women to satisfy men's lusts separated men's privilege from their responsibilities toward women and children. The same was true of the impersonal sex depicted in pornography.

Those responsibilities not only justified men's privilege; they also provided deeply felt rewards for men who cared about their wives, sisters, and daughters. The social consensus regarding those responsibilities had implied that those women would be treated respectfully even by strangers. Respectable men might exploit prostitutes or women considered promiscuous, but the removal of illicit sexuality into red-light districts had protected respectable women by requiring that men act decently elsewhere. If porn was everywhere, then men were nowhere required to behave decently and women were nowhere protected. Conservatives' anxiety, in the end, was a criticism of the male sexuality that drove the market in pornography. Cultural conservatives disapproved of women who would disrobe before a camera, but they were at least as distressed at what they felt the porn wave revealed about men, including those who consumed passively by seeing porn as they moved through the streets. The fact that they themselves might be those men did not make the implications any less frightening.

The Legalization of Pornography

With the marketplace rapidly changing, lawmakers debated the legalization of pornography. Yet the marketplace did not script the debates; rather, older disputes about liberalism did.[88] The result embedded liberal principles in the law yet struck even supporters as tone-deaf to present-day realities.

The reactionary 1962 draft reform of the sexual-criminal code was the subject of several scholarly conferences in ensuing years. All demanded genuine reform. The 1968 Jurists' Conference recommended that the government consider an "alternative draft" that a group of progressive scholars had recently published. Among other things, the alternative draft proposed the decriminalization of consensual homosexual acts between adults, bestiality, incest, adultery, pimping, and dissemination of indecent writings and images.[89] Liberals noted developments elsewhere in western Europe, such as the report of Great Britain's Wolfenden Departmental Committee on Homosexual Offences and Prostitution in 1957, which emphasized the distinction between morality and law and became the basis for British reforms.[90]

When the government renewed work on the sexual-criminal code, both major parties in the Grand Coalition accepted the primacy of *Rechtsgut:* that protecting individuals and the community from injury, not upholding a moral order, was the law's job. In June 1969, the Bundestag decriminalized noncommercial homosexual acts involving partners aged twenty-one or above with no relationship of dependency, as well as acts of bestiality, and adultery in which the spouse claimed no legal injury.

A year later, Gerhard Jahn, minister of justice of the new SPD-led government, presented a draft for further reform. The draft limited prosecution of procurement to cases involving youth under the age of sixteen and prostitution. It lowered the age of consent for gay male sex to eighteen. And it proposed the legalization of pornography. Making pornography available to minors or displaying and advertising it in ways that disturbed those who wished to avoid it would remain criminal, as would promoting objects intended for sexual use (not "indecent use") in an offensive manner. Pornography involving children or violence would remain illegal.

According to the appended justification, pornography was distinct from literary works, including those that were obscene. Pornography (1) "communicate[d] no intellectual content, however offensive or shocking, but rather [was] intended to stimulate sexually," and in doing so (2) "unequivocally transgress[ed] the borders of sexual decency that [were] in harmony with commonly-held social values."[91]

Thirty-one nationally and internationally known scholars, theologians, and practitioners testified before the Bundestag's committee on the reform of sexual-criminal law in November 1970, and research on sexuality finally made its mark.[92] The primacy of *Rechtsgut* placed high demands on empirical science. Liberals had long insisted there was no evidence that smutty literature led youth to criminality or that gay men disproportionately seduced minors, but evidence had, in a way, been beside the point. If upholding a moral code was the job of the state, then educating youth in contrary standards or pursuing *any* homosexual sex was crime enough. Now, however, the question was: What sexual behaviors actually hurt people? It would be up to science to answer this question.

"Science" was unevenly prepared for this task. Germany had been a pioneer in sexual science, but the field had progressed under less than ideal conditions. Sexology of the early twentieth century had been marginalized from mainstream academia. The National Socialists had promoted sexual science, but racist imperatives had influenced the research agenda. Postwar sexology remained the province of a handful of specialists who were keenly aware of their reliance on decades-old work, their institutional marginalization, and how far U.S. scholars had pulled ahead of them. Only in the mid-1960s did West German sexual scientists begin empirical research based on large groups of subjects.[93] Still, by the time of the hearings, they could cite substantial work on homosexuality, premarital sex, contraception and abortion, and juvenile sexuality.

The availability of research on such subjects made the lack of scholarship on the effects of exposure to explicit materials all the more glaring. Homosexuality and contraception had long been on sexual scientists' agenda; indecent texts and images had not. Even scholars who testified in cases like *Fanny Hill* were not specialists in erotic literature, and their concerns were the text and its literary-historical context, not its effects on readers. "Youth-endangering" items had long worried pedagogues and psychologists, but their research had involved tallying the frequency of young people's exposure to such material, not investigating its effects on them.[94] Until the late 1960s, the research community paid no attention to the effects of explicit texts and images on sexual response, behavior, or attitudes.[95]

By fall 1970, the best that liberalizers could offer was a study by physician Volkmar Sigusch, future director of the German Society for Sexological Research. The author or coauthor of groundbreaking works on such subjects as working-class and youth sexuality, Sigusch also boasted the only data concerning long-term effects of exposure to pornography rather than just immediate responses. "Long-term" observation, however, meant reinterviewing subjects several weeks after their initial exposure in a laboratory setting, and even liberalizers were disappointed by the study's limitations.[96] But if reformers could present little research demonstrating harmlessness, then opponents were even less prepared to demonstrate harm. Of all the debates on the sexual-criminal code, those regarding obscenity in texts and images were singularly ill informed by research.

The most radical proponents of liberalization to testify were Sigusch and psychologist Helmut Kentler, who felt pornography had no effect on sexual attitudes, desires, or behaviors, and who saw no need to limit minors' exposure.[97] Others supported legalization, but with reservations. Physician Wilhelm Hallermann felt that pornography did not harm youth who had received a good sex education from their families, but it could damage those from "repressed" backgrounds.[98] Jurist Ernst-Walter Hanack protested the claim that pornography could aid the sexually repressed, who might otherwise turn to violent crime: "If a citizen is really so repressed, we have other and better ways to help him than with pornography."[99] Psychiatrist Reinhart Lempp warned that by giving young people unrealistic ideas about sex, pornography could hinder their formation of happy partnerships.[100] Almost all distinguished between "soft" and "hard" porn: the latter, involving violence or children, should remain illegal. Some complained that the government tolerated violent and racist representations, which they considered far more damaging than sexual material.[101]

Most liberalizers found pornography obnoxious. They worried about its effects, especially on youth. They doubted that the bill's measures to protect minors could be effective in the current media and market environment. They agreed that the right to move freely without confronting pornography, like the right to consume it, was *Rechtsgut*. They felt that the definition of "pornography" was unclear, just as the definition of "indecent" had been before it. Yet all these concerns ran up against their conviction that the state may not limit rights unless the exercise of those rights caused demonstrable harm, and in their opinion no harm had been demonstrated.

Conservatives' challenge was to redefine their position so it concerned the protection of *Rechtsgut*, not the preservation of a moral order.[102] Whereas liberalizers considered restrictions illegitimate if no harm was demonstrated, opponents believed the burden of proof lay on those who denied harm, as it did for pharmaceutical firms wishing to release new medications. Legalization without knowledge of pornography's impact would constitute a mass experiment, with minors bearing the risk.[103] Law professor Hans-Heinrich Jescheck alone considered possible harm not only to consumers but also to those who appeared, often as a result of economic duress, in pornography.[104]

Opponents argued that the Basic Law protected not only individual *Rechtsgut* but also community *Rechtsgut* like the cultural order. The state should not restrict private activities (they now conceded), but unlike homosexuality and premarital sex, pornography was disseminated in public spaces. There it offended the cultural order.[105] Furthermore, the constitutionally guaranteed "human dignity" must concern the dignity of humanity, not just individuals. In pornography, according to pedagogue Hans Böttcher, "people don't meet, only organs do."[106] For sociologist Erwin Scheuch, pornography transformed a human activity to one of machines and denied individuals' uniqueness.[107] Pornography particularly violated the human dignity of women by degrading them to objects for the satisfaction of men's lusts.[108]

Finally, opponents made an argument regarding democracy. A recent poll showed that 72 percent of West Germans opposed legalization. How could a democracy ignore the desires of the majority?[109]

This assertion, of course, was also a political threat. After the *Fanny Hill* decision, West Germans saw what liberalization looked like, and rather than ratify it, the majority wanted the state to establish and enforce new limits. The Bundestag received mountains of mail opposing legalization and next to none in favor.[110] Newspapers were awash in letters to the editor opposing legalization, and a petition drive collected millions of signatures opposing reform.[111] Protestant and Catholic organizations released documents approving liberalization of homosexual and premarital sex but denouncing the proposed legalization of pornography.[112]

Faced with this uproar, the SPD retrenched.[113] The party roundly attacked its critics. "Human dignity" sounded good in the abstract, but only "Greek colonels or Stalinist functionaries" could enable a state to determine what was "dignified." Those people protesting the "devaluation of all values" had been silent when taboos regarding the portrayal of violence had fallen. And what notion of female sexuality underlay the claim that *women's* dignity was uniquely endangered? Presumably one that denied female desire and considered female sexuality a necessary evil for reproduction.

The party's new positive arguments, by contrast, were striking for their conservative appeal. Rather than aggravate the "flood of porn," the new law would combat it by updating an unenforceable and obsolete system. Its provisions for protecting youth surpassed older measures. Pornography did not create hedonists with weak work and family ethics; rather, people free of sexual repression were better workers and better able to produce children.

Two weeks later, Jahn "clarified" his recommendations. Addressing a common complaint of the Left, Jahn proposed criminalizing the dissemination of violent and racist materials (except historical and contemporary reportage). Further revisions spoke to conservatives' concerns. Dissemination and advertisement of pornography would be banned outside commercial spaces, in movie theaters, and on television and radio. Portrayals of bestiality would remain illegal. The new draft sharpened penalties for crude or obtrusive advertisement and display, forbade advertisement in periodicals and through the mails, and banned mail-order sales without proof of the customer's age.[114]

The revised draft worried publishers and sellers of explicit material. The industry had so far kept a low profile, preferring to arrange for sympathetic academics to make their case for them.[115] But the proposed ban on advertising through the mail and the requirement of proof of age for mail-order sales were alarming.

Yet organizing a response was not easy. The industry faced rifts with "legitimate" mail-order booksellers, who favored liberalization but feared costly measures, like ID checks, aimed at those few firms that gave all of mail-order bookselling a bad name.[116] Even among publishers of explicit materials there were tensions. Some members of the Alliance wished to publicize sales data to challenge opponents' claim that only marginal citizens consumed such materials. Fearing bad press, Rotermund quashed the effort. The Alliance rejected a proposal to solicit customer signatures for a petition to challenge decency advocates' claim that their 400,000 signatures represented the "silent majority." Frustrated, publisher Andreas Zettner sent parliamentarians his calculations showing that eight million pornographic books (and many more magazines) had been sold in the last two years, each with four to six readers. *This*, he said, was the real silent majority.[117] Shortly thereafter, Zettner formed a competing trade group—the first such schism in the industry's history.[118]

The marketplace was awash in pornography, yet the industry's future was uncertain. A post–*Fanny Hill* backlash had brought police raids and confiscations in many regions.[119] Demand for explicit material was matched by revulsion at its ubiquity. Price wars had diminished profits. New firms, inexperienced at negotiating the law and public opinion, made errors that endangered the whole industry at this delicate moment.[120] The optimism that had met the original draft and supportive testimony had given way to doubt regarding the form in which the law would pass, or whether it would pass at all. Perhaps the demand for porn would abate once the novelty wore off.[121] And competition from Scandinavia was fierce. Beate Uhse had long publicized its ever-rising sales and profits, but in the early 1970s it demurred, and for good reason. In 1971, for the first time in the firm's history, earnings declined. A year later, the firm cut back on newspaper subscriptions, phone lines, and Christmas gifts.[122] Other firms, with a less solid base, simply crashed. This troubling situation led the Alliance to emerge from the shadows. The Alliance sent parliament a statement arguing that the requirement of an ID check would cause customers to send their money abroad and testified to the industry's measures for blocking underage customers without ID checks.[123]

Jahn's revisions did nothing to ameliorate conservatives' fears that legalization would worsen the porn wave. At the same time, they irritated liberals by placing new restrictions on adults' ability to read and view what they liked.[124] And the shifting arguments for liberalization created new concerns.

The emphasis on "hard" porn led even some proponents of liberalization to worry that anything not involving violence, minors, or animals was escaping scrutiny. Ridiculing the old codes had such rhetorical effect that reformers often spoke as if the "flood" of obscenity decried by conservatives was "grandpa's porn"—grainy pictures of women in their petticoats, that sort of thing. Liberalizers tended to avoid discussion of what was really bothering people: magazines and films lacking violence, minors, or bestiality but featuring anonymous, promiscuous sex, with close-ups of erect penises and spread labia, and a march through heterosexual positions, masturbation, and lesbian and group scenes. Perhaps "soft" porn *was* harmless. But it was disingenuous to argue this point by mocking those who would censor "girls in miniskirts advertising motor oil," as one expert did before the parliamentary committee.[125] Certainly Kentler's definition of "soft" pornography as "the portrayal of sexuality as it actually is" raised questions about just what liberalizers thought they were liberalizing.[126] Still, the SPD had shifted from what appeared a reckless commitment to liberal principles come what may, to a promise that easing adults' access to most materials would aid the protection of youth, the battle against the worst materials, and the preservation of a porn-free environment for adults who desired it. Doubt remained about how effectively the law could achieve all this. But at least the new draft seemed to take the problem seriously.

The parliamentary commission endorsed Jahn's revised draft but recommended greater limits on advertising, a ban on exports (to avoid tensions with foreign states), and a prohibition on showing pornographic film if customers' payment was solely or mainly for the film. A club might screen porn if its main revenues were from food and drink. The aim was to prevent the creation of pornographic theaters. (The result, instead, was the creation of pornographic theaters that required the purchase of an overpriced drink or magazine to see the show.) Despite these cautions, the commission was reassured by reports from Sweden and Denmark indicating that legalization had not led to an increase in sexual crimes. With most expert witnesses having testified that soft porn was generally harmless, a continued ban was unwarranted.[127] After a bit more tinkering on provisions to protect youth, the Bundestag approved "partial legalization" with a party-line vote on June 7, 1973. The new law went into effect on January 1, 1975.[128]

Conclusion

In 1973, the same year pornography was legalized, the oil crisis brought the economic miracle to an end. And so the porn wave was the last of the many "waves" of consumption that marked West Germans' path from the hunger years through recovery and on to affluence. By the time legalized porn officially appeared in 1975, West Germany—like the rest of western Europe and North America—had become a grittier place, with high unemployment the most obvious marker of the new era. And the economy was not the only thing that had changed. The heady idealism of the early New Left had dissolved into a grim world of mutual recrimination, with police and media campaigns against protesters in the late 1960s, leftist terrorism starting in the early 1970s, and repressive antiradical measures by mid-decade. The Left was bitterly divided about the use of violence, but that was not the only internal schism. Not only could Maoists not get along with Trotskyists, but New Left women accused their male peers of sexism and formed separate feminist organizations. The age of legalized porn coincided with an age of weariness and pessimism, with the state's inability to establish and enforce moral standards appearing as one marker of its helplessness.[129] The recession, the "crisis of governability," and the legalization of porn coincided across the Western world, not just in West Germany.

This outcome should not blind us to the ways that the legalization of pornography could appear as the final frontier in liberalism's long struggle. After all the battles over liberalism in the nineteenth century, after the violence of the first half of the twentieth century, the Federal Republic promulgated a liberal constitution in 1949. But West Germany's Basic Law had limitations—certainly in the implementation. To be sure, jurist Herbert Jäger exaggerated a bit when he called morality law a *unique* exception to the prioritization of individual liberties in the early Federal Republic: feminists who spent the 1950s and 1960s fighting for women's equal rights may have begged to differ. Yet these realms were closely intertwined, as preserving the sexual-moral order justified both male privilege and state regulation of sexuality. For West Germans nostalgic for a Wilhelmine sexual-moral order, maintaining distinct roles for men and women and preserving a strict sexual morality were of a piece. Still, in the third quarter of the twentieth century, the problem took a distinctly modern cast, as those who saw preserving the sexual-moral order as liberalism's task now understood themselves to be battling fascism and communism, even as they also feared a return to an ineffective liberalism such as that of the Weimar Republic. That regime was well remembered as a time of sexual liberation when, coincidentally or not, economic crises increased Communism's appeal and Nazism made its fateful rise.

Legal guarantees of male privilege began to fall in West Germany during the late 1950s, and by the late 1960s adherents of a liberalism prioritizing individual liberties held power in parliament. Whereas opponents of state regulation had earlier sought to protect sexual representation as part of a larger defense of freedom of the press, and whereas proponents of strict standards had defined their concern as the protection of youth, sexual representation now became part of a politicized public discourse about sexuality per se.

West Germany never acted in isolation. Participants in the debates of the 1950s had looked abroad to see how foreign states handled youth endangerment, and reformers of the 1960s and 1970s looked abroad to see how foreign states were liberalizing sexual-criminal law. With the legalization of porn in Scandinavia, foreign law became not just a reference point for lawmakers pondering reform, but also a defining feature of a marketplace awash in illegally smuggled goods. In the short term—until legalization in West Germany—this matter highlighted West Germany's difference from its northern neighbors. But more deeply, it indicated that this was an international, not a national, development.

The battle over pornography continued after legalization. Despite the preponderance of men among porn's customers and women among those portrayed nude and sexually available, those who debated legalization had little to say about gender and liberalism. Conservatives, who expressed concern about pornography's sex-specific meanings, could not cast their argument in liberal terms. Reformers understood liberalism to be gender-neutral. In the 1980s feminists would make pornography a focus of disputes about whether the law must be gender blind or whether it must take gender difference, whether biologically or socially determined, into account.

Although discussion about the politics of feminism, liberalism, and porn lay in the future, the fact that pornography had a mainly male audience was lost on no one. What attracted next to no comment was the fact that until recently, the market in erotica had been gendered very differently. Young adults mocked Beate Uhse's and Oswalt Kolle's emphasis on conjugal harmony, but they missed what lay under the surface of such language: a demand for good communication and equal consideration of both partners' needs. Well into the "sex wave," consumption supported these aims, with items important to cooperating couples the best sellers. Unlike in the Weimar era, this type of sexual consumption did not become part of a politicized public sphere in the 1950s. By contrast, opposition to it did. West Germans who grew up in those years could be acutely aware of moral purity rhetoric while remaining ignorant of the lively commerce in erotica that provoked moral purity advocates to battle. As they came of age, defining themselves against moral purity activism was close at hand; understanding their relationship to the previous generation of sexual consumption was not.

Although sexual consumption helped their parents to overcome the traumas of the war and postwar years, as well as some of the ignorance and shame with which they had grown up, it had not brought sexual equality. Nor had it satisfied all yearnings for sexual excitement. The desire for pleasure outside sex with committed partners remained. Sexual texts and images had always been important masturbatory aids, and the *Fanny Hill* decision enabled dissemination of much more explicit materials in much greater quantities. Women might use the products of the "porn wave," but men, who were privileged both as consumers and as desiring sexual subjects, were the main beneficiaries. After the *Fanny Hill* decision, the marketplace in erotica was most visibly a location for solo male pleasure in consumption.

And how visible it was! With nearly all other aspects of sexual reform, liberalizers could frame their arguments in terms of privacy. If two men or an unwed straight couple wanted to have sex behind closed doors, what business was it of the state? Only abuse of youth and "public" sex warranted intervention. But was "private" dissemination of pornography a possibility in the late twentieth century? Or was commerce inevitably "public," the equivalent of solicitation but with the additional power of mass media and big advertising budgets? And if so, did the dissemination of pornography *inevitably* involve youth in some way? But could a liberal state impose such thorough protections for youth and unwilling consumers that consenting adults could not exercise their liberties? The majority in the SPD-dominated Bundestag determined that porn caused no demonstrable harm to consenting adult consumers. Layer upon layer of revisions to protect youth and push commerce out of "public" spaces, however, indicated great anxiety on these points. Neither liberal philosophy nor empirical research could address this anxiety. Legalization, in the end, was a leap of faith.

7 Postlude   *The Beate Uhse Myth*

From Wife and Mother to Feminist Heroine

After 1973, pornography remained controversial, as debates over hypothetical effects of reform turned into debates over the real postlegalization landscape. Beate Rotermund became the public face of the porn industry, and she was called upon to defend pornography in the media and public hearings. If 87 percent of West Germans recognized the name Beate Uhse in 1972, by 1984 the number had risen to 94 percent.

The Beate Uhse myth continued to evolve, as much that had shaped it changed. The marketplace in erotica completed its transition from one emphasizing education and companionate harmony to one dominated by pornography. Rotermund, who had introduced herself to customers as a young mother and publicized her youthful exploits as a flier, became an old woman. And Germany's relationship to its Nazi-era and postwar history changed. With these developments, not only the content but also the function of the myth were transformed.

From the 1950s through the 1970s, Rotermund told the following story about the origins of her business: In the desperate environment following the war, a male doctor told her about women's fears of unwanted pregnancy and explained the rhythm method to her. His words were a revelation: she had had no idea such a method existed. Rotermund educated herself by reading a book authored by a doctor, and she condensed the lesson into a short pamphlet—her first product. Between 1980 and 1982, the doctors disappeared from the story. Now, according to press packets and interviews, Rotermund had learned about women's problems by talking to them herself. Those conversations had sparked recollections of lessons about the rhythm method provided by her mother, one of Germany's first female physicians. Rotermund had reviewed the details at the library, and after a period of calculating fertile days for women who streamed to her as word spread about her expertise, she published her pamphlet.[1]

A story of womanly self-reliance replaced a story that made male doctors the legitimizing experts.[2] There is no record of why the story was changed, just as there is no record of why the firm began publicizing Rotermund's Luftwaffe history in the early 1960s. Given Rotermund's instinct for savvy deployment of her autobiography, we cannot be sure the change was calculated. But if it was not, then Rotermund's sharp instincts were responding to something real—something demanding a response.

In fact, two things had changed. One was Rotermund's business. Rotermund had made her name in the 1950s with a mail-order business that enhanced companionate harmony, education, and health through instructive books and catalogs. By the mid-1970s, arousing materials were the industry's mainstay, film and video were overtaking print and still photography, and shops enjoyed an advantage over mail-order, which could not sell porn. The effect was exaggerated for Rotermund, as structural changes within Beate Uhse limited her activities to pornography, film, and storefronts in the early 1980s. Rotermund needed new ways to articulate her firm's relevance to women and companionate couples.

At the same time, feminism entered the equation. The feminist movement was a double-edged sword for Rotermund. On the one hand, it honored pioneering female entrepreneurs and those who challenged the sexual double standard. On the other hand, it vilified pornography. By this time Rotermund's position was secure: activist efforts could no longer endanger her firm's survival as had been the case in the 1950s, when moral purity organizations had the firm in their sights. But feminism did pose a public relations challenge.

In the early years, Beate Uhse's wholesome corporate personality had not just been good business. It also had shaped a pleasing self-image for the founder and her employees. There is no reason to doubt that Rotermund continued to strive for an image that served the bottom line *and* was personally satisfying. But in the age of porn, succeeding in business and advancing the interests of companionate couples, in which women's desires were as important as men's, no longer neatly meshed.

There were two possible responses. One was to try to square the circle: to make the current marketplace in erotica a matter of women's interest after all. The other was to adapt personally, so service to women and couples would no longer be necessary for a satisfying self-image and a sympathetic public image. Rotermund never resolved the problem: through the remainder of her career, she vacillated between the two positions.

The effort to square the circle involved claims that porn aided couples and appealed to women and men equally. It also involved schemes to attract more women to shops by moving porn from the front to the back. These contradictory impulses reflected the depth of the problem. So did Rotermund's revised biography. Feminizing the firm's origins made Rotermund a more convincing feminist pioneer, but it also highlighted the contrast between the firm's early contribution to women's reproductive autonomy and its current appeal to men's hunger for autostimulation.

Unable to square the circle, Rotermund simultaneously denied the need to do so. She was not a missionary, she now said: she was a businesswoman. In the 1950s and early 1960s, the firm had claimed a higher social function that was in harmony with good business. Now Rotermund denied that a higher social mission was a necessary part of good business behavior. Beate Uhse was a good firm because it understood its customers, offered quality products, and obeyed the law.

Feminizing the firm's origins and prioritizing good business practices over a social mission: these were changes to the *content* of the Beate Uhse myth. But there was an even more fundamental change to the myth, and that was in its function. Once a vehicle for promoting the firm, the Beate Uhse myth became a vehicle for understanding German history.

Toward the end of the century, history acquired an ambivalent meaning for Beate Uhse. History raised questions about how to evaluate the firm by contrasting its very different functions over the years. Furthermore, the most appealing parts of the history—when the firm had braved hostile courts to aid couples in need—appeared remote from present-day concerns. The firm needed a modern image, one that reflected today's customers' concerns, not those of their grandparents.

At the same time, history became more important to the image of the founder. History ameliorated the notion of Rotermund as having made her fortune in goods that were at best tasteless, at worst harmful. Furthermore, history cemented Rotermund's appeal to the media, which was increasingly concerned with the postwar era as history. In the last decade of her life, one retrospective after another rehearsed Rotermund's life story—to tell a historical tale, not to discuss sexuality at the turn of the millennium.

A Businesswoman, Not a Missionary

A year after the legalization of pornography, Beate Uhse commissioned a study by a well-known market research firm. The findings were dismal.[3] Customers evaluated identical products as valuable when told they came from a general retailer or a scientific institute, undesirable when told they came from Beate Uhse. Better-off Germans avoided the firm, women were put off, and couples felt Beate Uhse had little to say to them. A good many customers were "simply primitive buyers seeking porn." The catalog was a nightmare. Gaudily colored, confusing, and full of screaming superlatives, it left the study's author amazed that the firm sold anything at all. The equally garish shops did an abysmal job of putting customers at ease. Men entered looking guilty and left looking guiltier. Some clung to the exterior wall then sprang inside; departing customers sometimes dashed the first hundred meters out the door before slowing to a normal tempo. All in all, men's comportment resembled that of shoplifters in a recent study by the same institute. The only people whose behavior could be described as "natural" were women who entered the shop, but their numbers were few indeed.

Yet business was booming. After dipping in 1971, sales more than doubled between 1973 and 1977.[4] So management might well ask: should it revamp its image, as the survey suggested? Or was the formula for success to erect tacky shops, publish tackier catalogs, and appeal to "primitive buyers" prowling for porn, even if that meant alienating women, couples, and wealthier consumers?

Beate Uhse's corporate identity hung in the balance. In its founding years, a wholesome image had been good business and provided Rotermund and her employees with a rewarding self-image. During the sex wave and porn wave, as some erotica firms had "raced to the bottom," Beate Uhse had "raced to the top," taking care not to cross legal boundaries or crassly violate popular tastes. With pornography legalized, the relationship among successful business, positive public relations, and self-image had to be renegotiated.

The first task was to adapt to the new market regime. Already in 1971, shop sales exceeded mail-order sales.[5] With pornography legal in shops but not through mail order beginning in 1975, the gap was likely to widen. Furthermore, legalization promised the growth of film and video. In 1972, the firm began offering film screenings in its shops, and it soon introduced booths for private viewing.[6] Shortly after legalization, the firm built dedicated porn theaters and began producing full-length films.[7]

The new market regime coincided with generational change. Rotermund's three sons, born in the 1940s, had grown up with the firm.[8] Rotermund had a trusted circle of managerial employees, but this was a family business, and there was never any question that the sons would inherit it.

In 1981, the firm split down the middle. Rotermund and her youngest son Ulrich retained the shops and the film and video sections, while older sons Klaus and Dirk got the mail-order business and the publishing house, in keeping with the divisions that each son had directed in recent years. For five years each pair was prohibited from competing with the other: Rotermund and Ulrich could not conduct mail-order sales or start a new press, and Klaus and Dirk could not open shops or make films.

In her memoirs, Rotermund described her need to permit her sons to take greater responsibility.[9] When introducing their new firm to customers, Klaus and Dirk attributed the division vaguely to "conceptual differences" within Beate Uhse.[10] The media suggested favoritism among the sons: Ulrich, it seemed, was the Chosen One.[11] Ulrich recalled his concern that if Rotermund should die, each son would inherit a third of the company, leaving him with a minority holding in the face of Klaus and Dirk, who were close.[12] There is little question that Rotermund and Ulrich retained the branches that seemed to have the brightest future, while Dirk and Klaus got the branches whose importance appeared to be declining. Whether making a virtue out of necessity or expressing their preference as it emerged from those "conceptual differences," Dirk and Klaus contrasted their firm's "gentle erotic" with Beate Uhse, which, they said, was "riding the porn wave."[13]

With legalization, pornography would inevitably begin to overshadow other functions Beate Uhse had served, but the division of the firm hardened this trend. For the first half of the 1980s, Rotermund did not engage in those activities that had been most valuable to customers seeking something other than porn. No more mail-order catalogs to get couples talking about sex at home and to enable women to shop in private; no more enlightened books on sex, although the shops could sell books by other presses. Instead, Beate Uhse acquired West Germany's second-largest erotica chain, the S and M–oriented Dr. Müllers.[14] Beate Uhse also opened a production company for pornographic films and launched movie houses.

How did Rotermund respond to those who accused her of serving something other than the common good? "I'm not Jesus; I'm a businesswoman," she told *Die Zeit* in 1985.[15] For decades critics had accused Rotermund of debasing human relationships in favor of profit, but in the past she had embraced the identity of a crusader.[16] Now she described a choice: either do-gooder or businesswoman. This tone was not just a matter of public relations: rather, it described a changing mood within the firm. A longtime employee who fondly recalled the pioneering years said, a bit mournfully, of the post-legalization era: "All that remained was rivalry with the competition."[17]

A Woman Who Emancipated Herself on Women's Backs

In the lead-up to legalization, only conservatives held that pornography posed a special danger for women. Voices farther to the left, from liberal parliamentarians to student radicals, derided this position as prudish.

When parliamentary debates regarding legalization opened in 1969, New Left women were beginning to challenge sexism in their own circles. The years 1968–70 saw a flurry of feminist organizing. Initially, however, the new groups focused on recasting priorities within the New Left, discussing the relationship of Marxism and feminism and how to link proletarian with feminist revolution.

In 1971, feminism entered national politics with a campaign to decriminalize abortion. Following a similar action in France, a cover story in *Der Stern* featured 374 women who publicly acknowledged their illegal abortions. A new organization committed itself to legislative reform.[18] In 1974, parliament decriminalized abortion. Less than a year later, in February 1975, the Constitutional Court invalidated the new law, declaring abortion legal only with a medical, eugenic, social, or ethical justification. Until reunification, West Germany had one of the most restrictive abortion laws in the industrialized world.

As parliament debated the legalization of pornography, organized feminism was just getting onto its feet. Between the passage of the new law (November 1973) and its implementation (January 1, 1975), the movement experienced both its greatest triumph and its most demoralizing defeat with the decriminalization, then the recriminalization, of most abortions. Organized feminism entered the age of legalized pornography in crisis.

Many feminists emerged from the struggle over abortion and their battles with New Left men convinced that there was more to be gained by autonomous organizing than by engaging the male-dominated spheres of politics and government. Consciousness-raising groups, women's centers, and women's bookstores opened in urban areas. And two important magazines began publication. *Courage* (1976–84), published by a West Berlin collective, promoted freewheeling debate and rejected a feminist orthodoxy. By contrast, *Emma* (1977–) was associated with the disciplined editorial opinion of its editor, Alice Schwarzer, who had organized *Der Stern*'s cover article on abortion. Schwarzer became West Germany's best-recognized feminist.

In 1978, *Emma* sued *Der Stern* for routinely featuring nude women on its covers, charging that the practice violated women's human dignity and equal rights.[19] The fact that feminists first targeted a newsweekly reflected an important reality of the era. In eliminating the category "obscenity in text and image," the 1973 reform had removed mainstream publications' last inhibitions regarding the publication of photos that were highly sexual but stopped short of displaying sexual acts. At the same time, pornography could be displayed and sold only in shops that prohibited entry to minors, and it could not be sold at all through the mail. Porn's visibility paled in comparison to objects like *Der Stern* magazine. The court agreed that the proliferation of such images could hinder women's strivings toward equality but found that the law did not provide a vehicle for addressing such complaints. The plaintiff should address legislators, not the courts.[20] And there the matter lay. *Emma* did not appeal the decision, nor did it approach lawmakers.

Only in 1987 did the magazine initiate its *PorNO!* campaign by publishing a draft law modeled after legislation proposed by U.S. antipornography activists Catherine McKinnon and Andrea Dworkin.[21] *Emma*'s draft defined pornography as representations that demeaned women by portraying their rape, their enjoyment of their own debasement, their subjection to violence, or their penetration by objects or animals. But it would not be the state's job to sniff out objectionable items. Any woman or girl could sue; so could organizations representing women and girls.[22] The magazine published summaries of research linking consumption of porn with violence toward women, sought out women in the industry for reports on their experience, critiqued the alternative press's coverage of the controversy, and surveyed its readers on their reactions to porn.[23]

American feminists were sharply divided over pornography. Many opposed the censoring potential of the McKinnon/Dworkin legislation and distrusted the campaign's links to conservatives. A "pro-sex" feminist faction objected to antiporn feminists' portrayal of women as inevitably victimized by pornography, or by male sexuality more generally. Some wondered if the whole business wasn't a side show—whether pornography wasn't at most a symptom rather than a cause of women's oppression.[24] *Emma*'s campaign attracted similar criticism among West German feminists.[25] But these debates were lost on much of the public, for whom Schwarzer was *the* voice of feminism. It was easy for the casual observer in the late 1980s to assume that pornography was the top item on feminism's agenda. *Emma*'s campaign garnered extensive media coverage and prompted the Greens (who joined parliament in 1983) and the SPD to hold hearings on pornography in 1988.[26]

In March 1988, *Emma* published a cover story on Rotermund. Its thesis was well encapsulated in its opening paragraph: "At 25 she flew Stukas to the front. For Hitler's Luftwaffe. At 69 she sells women. For 90 million a year. Sometimes as Poor Little Thing, sometimes as Dominatrix. Just as the gentlemen like it. She is a woman who's one of the guys and always fighting on the front lines. For herself and for her [male] comrades." The magazine acknowledged Rotermund's independence, but with a twist: "Beate Uhse is an emancipated woman. One who emancipated herself on women's backs."[27]

This critique voiced *Emma*'s unambivalent position regarding pornography's impact on women, and its equal conviction that German women had been among Nazism's victims; the article contrasted Rotermund's privileged Nazi-era existence with other women's suffering due to bombing raids and rape by allied soldiers. By linking Rotermund's Nazi-era pursuits with her present-day activity, *Emma* linked most women's victimization during the Nazi era with their victimization by pornography.

The notion that German women were among Nazism's victims was a staple

7.1. "Bomber Pilot and Porn Producer." *Emma*'s 1988 cover story on Beate Rotermund linked her service to the Nazi state with her exploitation of women in the pornography industry.

of early second-wave feminism. Yet by the late 1980s, West German feminists were beginning to recognize that their mothers and grandmothers had often welcomed the opportunities Nazism had offered members of the racial elite.[28] *Emma*, however, rejected this revision of women's history, just as it rejected doubts about women's victimization by pornography.

By making herself into "one of the guys," Rotermund had defeminized herself and so did not disturb *Emma*'s story of women's victimization through time. But *Emma* did place Rotermund in a larger female community. And it did so at a critical juncture: the immediate postwar years. *Emma* relayed the revised story of Beate Uhse's origins. Living as a refugee in a landscape dominated by women, Rotermund saw her neighbors' desperation to avoid pregnancy. She recalled her mother's lessons on the rhythm method, reviewed the details at the library, and calculated the fertile days of her neighbors. Then she published her pamphlet.

Rotermund's story contradicted popular feminist accounts of women's victimization under Nazism. It melded beautifully, however, with tales of women's suffering and heroism at the end of the war. Women had suffered bombing raids, flight, and rape, only to face hunger and homelessness once the war was over. Yet they had performed miraculous feats to ensure their families' survival, and they began Germany's reconstruction by clearing away the rubble from destroyed cities. Rotermund's story of postwar suffering and heroism was a more sympathetic feminist tale than one focusing on her position in the Third Reich.

In 1985 the fortieth anniversary of the defeat brought a flood of popular publications on the end of the war, and women's experience was a favorite theme.[29] As Rotermund's revised biography began to circulate in the mid-1980s, it found an audience drawn to tales of women's struggle and survival after the war. And so Rotermund's story became a feminist morality tale, but not in the way antiporn activists wished it.

Women's sufferings in the postwar years and Rotermund's determination to help had always been central to her story. But early tellings had embedded Rotermund's actions in relationships with men. It was "as a wife and mother of four children" that Rotermund had resolved to assist women in need, according to her breakthrough catalog of 1952, and a male doctor had set her on her path. No longer. Now Rotermund's contact with women had moved her to action, and a new feminist heroine was introduced: Rotermund's mother, one of Germany's first female physicians and the source of Rotermund's enlightened upbringing.

In many ways, this slant reprieved the story the firm had marketed in the 1950s—and it similarly linked the founder's autobiography and the firm's social contribution. But this time around, women were much more active sexual subjects, in keeping with Rotermund's new emphasis on her own initiative after the war. No longer was it up to men to learn how to make love to their wives. Today's woman knew all about sex, and she knew what she wanted. And what she wanted was porn.

A Complex Culinary Culture

At the parliamentary hearings prompted by *Emma*'s petition, Rotermund underlined women's interest in her products. To demonstrate that the current law was too restrictive, she quoted a professional middle-aged woman who complained that she could see harder stuff on TV than on the video she had acquired by mail order. Rotermund explained: The customer assumed she was ordering porn because the source was Beate Uhse, but like most customers, she did not understand that porn could only be sold in shops. Restrictions on mail order didn't protect consumers but simply confused them.[30]

Rotermund expanded upon these arguments in media appearances throughout the next decade. Protests about violent porn or porn involving animals only confirmed the wisdom of the law as it stood. The claim that pornography portrayed women as passive objects to be penetrated by men was false. In Beate Uhse films, women were desiring subjects who experienced joy in sex.[31] Most journalists and lawmakers demonstratively denied firsthand knowledge of the genre and were thus hard put to challenge Rotermund on the matter of content.[32] It was also untrue that only men liked porn while women were disgusted by it, Rotermund said. In a study Beate Uhse had commissioned in 1986, a majority of women confessed to viewing pornographic videos; other research demonstrated women's arousal by porn.[33] Finally, in the age of AIDS, porn helped couples enjoy greater erotic variety without straying from their partners.

Pornography's form, function, and means of consumption were intertwined in Rotermund's claims regarding its role in companionate relationships. It was misguided, Rotermund held, to complain that pornography simply strung together sex scenes, with interchangeable characters and a flimsy plot. The proper comparison for pornography was not the novel but rather the cookbook. Humans could survive on potatoes and a bit of boiled meat, but societies that could afford it took pleasure in a more complex culinary culture. Yet without instruction, few people would know how to cook. A cookbook provided that instruction. A really good cookbook made the reader's mouth water; it made the reader want to try unfamiliar dishes. So it was with pornography. Most people, Rotermund said flatly, had little sexual fantasy. Left to their own devices, they would share nothing but meat and potatoes—the missionary position—year after year, and boredom would set in. They needed to be shown how to enrich their sexual lives. Many people were unmoved by texts, and so pictures, moving and still, were necessary. If the images aroused, so much the better: this would inspire the viewer to try out a new recipe at home.[34]

With her cookbook analogy, Rotermund made the cozy hearth the context for consuming porn. Theaters had been important in the years immediately following legalization, but with the spread of VCRs in the late 1970s, the home became the favored location for viewing porn. Rotermund's emphasis on home as the site of a couple's consumption, as the dinner table was the site of the family meal, complemented her arguments about content (her films showed women as desiring subjects) and reception (both sexes' physiological responses to pornography were similar). She implicitly minimized not only mainstream porn's masturbatory function for men, but also the possible significance of a distinctly feminist pornography.[35] Rotermund's claim in the 1980s and 1990s was her claim from the 1950s: by bringing couples together in an erotically charged home, her products strengthened relationships.

Did the public believe Rotermund's claims? It's hard to tell. There is evidence that couples viewed pornography together. There is also evidence that men were responsible for most of the consumption, and that the women in their lives either failed to see the attraction or felt downright uncomfortable with their partners' habits. Some studies noted the overlap of the categories: women who watched porn with their male partners sometimes did so reluctantly, in order to please the men.[36]

Rotermund had a problem—less with feminists' attacks than with women's persistent underrepresentation among customers. Beate Uhse's first catalog upon reentry to the mail-order market in 1986 protested perhaps too much about its concern for women, with multiple references to research confirming women's interest in erotica.[37] Rotermund noted with relief that the first orders in 1986 showed that about one-third of customers were women.[38] This was not exactly progress: customer cards from the 1950s had shown the same. An unsystematic survey in 1987 found that 60 percent shared their catalogs with partners, supporting claims that the firm served couples. But it also found that men's and women's tastes continued to differ in predictable ways. Men showed particular interest in visual stimulation, whereas women preferred lingerie, vibrators, and other sex aids.[39] Ten years later, the proportion of female customers still hovered between 30 and 33 percent.[40]

Forced to concede that male customers outnumbered female customers by a ratio of two to one, Rotermund underlined her commitment to women by emphasizing that they were "the customers of the future." Hiding behind this flattery was the fact that if the erotica sector were to expand, it would have to be among women, since it had already saturated the male customer base. It had, in short, served men far better than women. In order to attract women, Rotermund said, the firm was adjusting its marketing, for example by placing lingerie in the front of shops so women would not have to walk through pornographic videos in order to reach it. This strategy, of course, simply acknowledged women's discomfort with porn. And as Rotermund announced, year after year, that women were "the customers of the future," one might reasonably wonder when the future was finally going to arrive.[41]

Even those sympathetic to claims regarding Rotermund's service to women and couples could easily see how those claims served her self-interest. No one could imagine any longer that Rotermund was an underdog, braving hostile courts and public opinion to bring desperate couples basic goods and information. Consumers hardly needed Beate Uhse if they wanted porn—or condoms, racy lingerie, or sex aids. To the contrary: even those who were disgusted by erotica could hardly avoid it.

In this environment, Rotermund's holistic story about her biography, her firm, and West Germans' sexual needs served a new function. Rotermund's autobiographical marketing had originated in the 1950s as a savvy (if intuitive) business decision: it attracted customers to an industry they might otherwise have feared. During the sex wave, Rotermund's biography had helped to make her an industry spokesperson, which in turn had made her firm uniquely recognizable as sexual consumption was going public. In the 1980s and beyond, however, emphasizing the firm's challenges to a prudish society would make it appear behind the times, expert at addressing the challenges of a bygone age.

After the late 1980s, the dissemination of Rotermund's biography was no longer really about sexual consumption. The media increasingly profiled Rotermund simply because she was interesting, not because they sought to understand sexuality in Germany.[42] Germans tuned in because they liked her story. And they liked her story because it was *theirs*: that is, it was the story of their country's last century.

The History of Sexual Morals in the Federal Republic

From the 1980s until her death, the barrage of stories about Rotermund never ceased. And so the more feminist version of her biography became the "final word." But the function of media coverage changed. With the big public debates receding (pornography was legalized; the antiporn campaign fizzled), the media had less need to tap Rotermund as a spokesperson for the industry but discovered a growing fascination with her as a historical figure. Major birthdays, the publication of her as-told-to memoir (1989),[43] the opening of the Beate Uhse Museum in Berlin (1996), and round-number anniversaries of the firm's founding: all garnered media retrospectives. Lengthy obituaries (and reruns of old television appearances) followed Rotermund's death in 2001. However significant for the firm, these events attracted press coverage because they allowed journalists to tell stories they wished to tell.

The shift toward using Rotermund's story to tell German history began in the mid-1980s, when Rotermund provided a tale of strong women in Germany's rubble years and the early Federal Republic. Shortly thereafter, the Berlin Wall fell—and postwar history, defined by the division of Europe, came to an end. The day after the opening of the Wall, Beate Uhse vans were in Berlin to distribute catalogs to East Germans, who had enjoyed nudism and greater reproductive liberties than West Germans, but who had had little access to porn. Within months, two million of East Germany's sixteen million citizens were customers.[44] East German feminists saw yet another warning of how women stood to lose by reunification, together with the loss of guaranteed child care, the possible expansion of West Germany's restrictive abortion policies, and the imposition of West German assumptions about the priority of male employment.[45] Some East Germans preferred to open their *own* sex shops, resisting the "colonization" of the East German marketplace by a major West German corporation.[46] Others, perhaps hoping to protect themselves and their neighbors from looming unemployment, invited Rotermund into partnerships, offering their local expertise and networks. In letters to the firm, East German customers criticized their regime's "prudishness" and described their hopes for a more sexually liberated future.[47]

For the firm, the opening of the Wall was clearly a business opportunity. But the drama of 1989–90 also provided another chance for the firm to write itself into German history. In addition to repeating the tale of the firm's presence in Berlin after the Wall's opening, and deploying images of East Germans emptying the shelves of Beate Uhse stores, it published letters by East Germans to the firm—letters that credited Beate Uhse with East Germans' sexual liberation, even as they presented East Germans as ideal (that is, uninhibited) customers. This version of history, in which East Germans gratefully accepted Western rescue, found a receptive audience in West Germany.[48]

Controversies in the 1980s about the relationship between the Nazi state and its West German successor made clear that, even if the issues were far from resolved, West Germans were increasingly tackling Germany's past *as history*.[49] With the end of the Cold War, this trend accelerated.[50] The coincidence of the tenth anniversary of reunification and the turn of the century extended the time frame: now journalists reviewed Germans' journey over the last hundred years, not just since 1945 or 1933, with all but the last ten years part of "history." In this context, not only were Rotermund's wartime and postwar careers important, but so were her Weimar-era upbringing and her mother's activities in the Wilhelmine era.

The media's fascination with Rotermund meant publicity that most firms could only dream of, but it also contained certain dangers. Those dangers were apparent at the latest by 1983, when a marketing survey revealed that people linked the name Beate Uhse to the past. Over one-third of respondents were unsure if the founder was still alive.[51] It was in the company's interest to take advantage of its founder's fame, but simultaneously to loosen the association of the pioneering entrepreneur of the 1950s with the firm of the late twentieth century, lest the public assume that Beate Uhse was old-fashioned. As Ulrich explained, it was important that the firm "not carry around these fifty years of history like a hump on its back."[52]

One strategy was to make sure the firm remained in the news for its cutting-edge work. The firm publicized its pioneering efforts in electronic media, and in 1999 Beate Uhse became the first erotica firm to be traded publicly on the stock exchange.[53] Both developments confirmed Beate Uhse's place at the avant-garde of business practice within the world of erotica. But the entry onto the stock exchange also separated Rotermund's symbolic and PR functions from business decisions and operations, which were now in the hands of a management team involving no family members.[54]

Already in 1997–98, Rotermund and the firm's management discussed ways to maintain Beate Uhse's positive image after Rotermund's death. They determined that employees should take inspiration from Rotermund's personal qualities: hard work, courage, intelligence, creativity, empathy, and so on.[55] The founder's photo and her "golden rules" for good business should hang in employees' rooms—but not in shops, since they ill fit an environment in which, as one advisor noted, 80 percent of profit came from porn and video booths.[56] In other words, rather than presenting the founder and her story directly to customers, Rotermund's example must be "lived and practiced" by employees cognizant of timeless values. Good business practice, not identification with the founder, would bind customers to the firm.

Upon Rotermund's death in 2001, the media noted the passing of a celebrity whose biography had become a shorthand for German history: "Her success story—it is the history of sexual morals in the Federal Republic."[57] The Beate Uhse myth stood in for the passage from Wilhelmine feminism to Weimar reform, to National Socialism through postwar crisis, sexual conservatism, economic recovery, and finally to a liberated sexuality in a consumer society. So neatly did it encapsulate German history that it told inspirational and cautionary tales with equal ease. Sexual revolutionaries saw Rotermund as personifying the corruptions of sexuality under capitalism, and by extension under a fascism that had not been fully overcome. For antiporn feminists, Rotermund showed that both Nazism and the pornography industry profited as a few women liberated themselves at the expense of the many. Popular histories excerpted Rotermund's autobiography to portray women's strength (Rotermund's) and distress (her customers') during the "rubble years."[58] Business writers featured Rotermund as an icon of the economic miracle.[59] Psychoanalytically minded commentators described a perverse fascist sexuality that had infiltrated postwar West Germany on Rotermund's back.[60]

Few elements of the Beate Uhse myth were unique to it. War movies and pulp fiction recalled the excitement of the Luftwaffe; images of the "women of the rubble" portrayed women's strength after the war; the myth of the "zero hour" told of a new world in which West Germans created wealth and built democracy. What was unique about the Beate Uhse myth was that the destination of the trajectory was *sex*. Sexual revolutionaries' theories of sexual liberation required a sharp break with the past. The Beate Uhse myth required only incremental steps to move from the early twentieth century through the Nazi era to sexual liberation: energetic and decisive steps, to be sure, but drawing on the same energy and decisiveness that Germans like Rotermund had exhibited even before 1945. Sexual revolutionaries' dreams had fizzled, but the Beate Uhse myth told of evolution, not revolution. So self-evident has this story become, in popular consciousness, that the firm no longer needs to articulate it. Popular memory has replaced public relations as the main purveyor of the Beate Uhse myth. Today, Beate Rotermund's story is frequently cited in popular tellings of Germany's last century. Visitors to the firm's website, however, will have a hard time finding any reference to its founder or history.[61]

If Rotermund's biography was "the history of sexual morals in the Federal Republic," then how should we evaluate that history? Indeed, was it the history of sexual morals in the Federal Republic—or in the West? The most German parts of Rotermund's story preceded the establishment of the postwar state: her enlightened Weimar-era upbringing, her Luftwaffe service, her activities in the rubble years. The subsequent chapters—fighting hostile courts in the conservative 1950s, participating in a more open sexual marketplace in the 1960s, profiting from the legalization of pornography in the 1970s—paralleled developments elsewhere. Yet Rotermund's celebrity shaped West Germans' interpretation of their experience. A former Luftwaffe pilot who, during the rubble years, penned a manual on the rhythm method—a manual informed by her reformist Weimar upbringing—became the symbol of erotica. How could West Germans not conclude that this was a very German story?

West Germans tended to think less about the ways the postwar story *was* peculiarly German. First, in the early postwar decades, West Germany alone had large, aboveground firms with mailing lists in the millions using modern business practices to sell all items related to sex in the pages of a single catalog. Such firms eased women's access to the marketplace and joint decision-making. And by the mid-1960s, Rotermund was the public face of the industry. This made West Germany unique in a second way: nowhere else was the erotica industry dominated by a female voice that prioritized conjugal harmony and women's equal claim to sexual autonomy and fulfillment.

Did West Germans, as a result, experience a more egalitarian sexuality? There is abundant evidence of West German women's continuing disadvantage in heterosexual relationships. Women's massive resort to illegal abortion signaled not only a repressive abortion regime but also a failed contraception regime. New Left women found their male peers almost aggressively insensitive to demands for equality in sexual relationships. Although entrepreneurs knew that women found erotica shops that were dominated by porn uncomfortable, they did little to rectify the situation.

Yet if we consider expectations as well as experience, there is reason to believe that West Germany's unusual consumer regime and Rotermund's prominence had an impact. Customers praised not only Beate Uhse's products but also the firm's language of mutuality and equality in sexual matters. West German women's resistance to the birth control pill indicated concern about its medical side effects, but also an awareness that there was an easily available alternative in the form of condoms, and the belief that one might reasonably expect men to use them. The early date at which New Left women criticized their male peers' marketing of female bodies—1964, in the case of *Konkret*—suggests that rather than having to create a feminist critique from scratch, they had expectations regarding mutual respect that were now being violated. Even the New Left's mockery of Rotermund and Kolle pointed to a vocabulary of erotically charged conjugal harmony that was broadly enough recognized that satire would be effective, and widely enough accepted that attack was perceived as necessary.

Given the continuing controversies regarding pornography, it is easy to lose sight of the ways the earlier marketplace in erotica succeeded. The market share for informational texts declined because the texts had done their job. By the late 1960s, adults who wanted to inform themselves about sexuality had done so, and youth learned about sex from popular magazines or sex education classes. In part because erotica firms distributed condoms in such large numbers, taboos surrounding them were sufficiently lowered that drug stores, department stores, and mainstream mail-order firms began to carry them.

Still, pornography's share of the market did not increase only as a result of the decline of other products' sales. Rather, sales of pornography took off after the *Fanny Hill* decision, as if a dam had burst. And this raises the question: Were prior sales of pornography kept artificially low by legal restrictions on its dissemination? Or were prior sales low because pornography genuinely had less appeal during the first postwar years than it had a generation later?

Before the porn wave, stimulating texts and images were available in comprehensive mail-order catalogs, even if the items did not qualify as pornography by later standards. Yet well into the 1960s, they sold relatively poorly. Consumers chose informational texts and contraceptives not only in the earliest years, when an expenditure for a nude photo series or a steamy book might have been hard to justify. Objects associated with education and conjugal harmony continued to dominate the marketplace in the early 1960s, when the cost of arousing materials had become trivial. With men the more powerful consumers, even in the heyday of catalog sales, this lesser interest in stimulating materials is striking. If we turn around Freud's classic question and ask, "What do *men* want?" then the answer does not seem to be a timeless: "more sex, fewer responsibilities." For nearly two decades after the disruptions of the war, male as well as female consumers focused on items well suited to creating greater mutuality in heterosexual relationships.

By the late 1960s, however, consumer demand for pornography was clear. A significant if unquantifiable portion of the population considered porn downright harmful to women and mutually respectful relationships, whether from a conservative or a feminist perspective. Even if their claims regarding porn's societywide impact could not be empirically demonstrated, the passion of their critique suggests that, at the very least, the prevalence of porn disturbed *their* sense of sexual safety, health, and autonomy. Even those unconvinced by the broader claims of pornography's opponents did not maintain that pornography aided conjugal harmony or women's interests—unless, like Rotermund, they had a commercial interest in doing so. The claim that pornography was harmless and so the state should not restrict its distribution was, at most, a claim that masturbation was harmless—male masturbation, given the demographics of porn's customers. This was a far cry from backing a consumer regime assertively promoting women's interests and companionate harmony, as the earlier marketplace had done.

In fact, however, debates about pornography were essentially silent on the form of sex most associated with pornography. Few people joined Jörg Schröder in saying what, exactly, porn's function was. And so they could not even engage the questions: Would a more liberal regime of male masturbation aid, hurt, or have a neutral effect on companionate relationships and women's sexual self-determination? Did the precise nature of the trigger matter? For example, was a world in which men masturbated to images of nude women more dangerous than one in which they masturbated to texts? The intense nervousness around pornography, even among proponents of legalization, suggests worry about a consumer regime prioritizing solipsistic male pleasure. But participants in the debate focused almost exclusively on the fear that young people's exposure to porn might harm their development. Even these discussions elided mention of the sex act at the heart of it all, and the possibility that its practice might continue into adulthood. For their part, sexual reformers like Kolle and sexual revolutionaries such as Amendt reassured youth (and their parents) that masturbation was normal but did not discuss the use of porn for this purpose. Protagonists in the debate thus skirted around the questions: Was a society of adult masturbators unhealthy? If not, then was a society in which pornography was a prime impetus to male masturbation unhealthy? Who would be hurt in such a world, and how?

The reform of the sexual-criminal code made clear that the liberal state's task was to protect individuals and the community from harm, not to promote a sexual-moral order. The legalization of pornography, however, left open as many questions as it settled. What was the connection of pornography to sexual activity? Was liberalism gender blind, and if so, was this an asset or a shortcoming? Were theories of rights too abstract to account for the realities of the marketplace? And what, in the end, were the effects of pornography on its viewers and models? These questions—open to this day—are the legacy of the legalization of pornography according to the terms of liberalism.

Interviews

Recordings and transcripts of all interviews except that of Jürgen Weber are held at the Forschungsstelle für Zeitgeschichte in Hamburg.

Jörg Dagies. Dagies is a great-nephew of Walter Schäfer and the present-day CEO of the Walter Schäfer Gruppe. Interviewed with Lore Schumacher on September 4, 2003, in Fellbach.

Irmgard Hill. Hill was a lawyer by training and personal assistant to Beate Rotermund from 1982 until Rotermund's death. Interviewed on February 25, 2003, in Flensburg.

Helmut Kanzler. Kanzler was a district attorney in Flensburg from 1972 to 1994. Interviewed February 27, 2003, in Flensburg.

Bärbel Melzer. Melzer was employed by Beate Uhse during 1960–90; her jobs included leadership of the Organizational Division and the organization of data processing. Interviewed with Hans-Werner Melzer on September 9, 2003, in Flensburg.

Hans-Werner Melzer. Melzer was employed by Beate Uhse during 1961–81; his positions included leadership of the Advertising Division and managing director (*Geschäftsführer*). He was employed by Orion during 1981–89. Interviewed with Bärbel Melzer on September 9, 2003, in Flensburg.

Gesa Münzmaier. Münzmaier was employed at Beate Uhse during 1975–2004; her positions included leadership of the Legal Division. Interviewed June 25, 2003, in Flensburg.

Claus Richter. Richter was a pharmacist from 1956 to 1960 and was then employed by condom conglomerate MAPA, where he worked in sales and purchasing and, from 1990 to 1997, was codirector. He was founder of Deutsche Latex Forschung, the industry group of condom manufacturers. Interviewed June 13, 2003, in Rotenburg.

Dirk Rotermund. Dirk, a stepson of Beate Rotermund, was until 1981 an employee of Beate Uhse; his positions included leadership of the Publishing Division. He then became CEO of Orion, serving first with Klaus Uhse and then, since 1984, alone. Interviewed June 19, 2003, and September 8, 2003, in Flensburg.

Ulrich Rotermund. Ulrich, a son of Beate Rotermund, is an employee of Beate Uhse. His positions have included leadership of the Shops Division, membership on the board of directors, and today the presidency of the Beate Uhse Advisory Board. Interviewed July 17, 2008, in Meggen, Switzerland.

Lore Schumacher. Schumacher is a cousin of Walter Schäfer and was his personal secretary throughout his career. Interviewed with Jörg Dagies on September 4, 2003, in Fellbach.

Eberhard Strohm. Strohm was a Stuttgart-based attorney who represented erotica firms, including Beate Uhse and Walter Schäfer's firms, before the legalization of pornography. Interviewed April 2, 2003, in Stuttgart.

Hans-Dieter Thomsen. Thomsen was an employee of Beate Uhse during 1958–99; his jobs included sex counseling, leadership of the Shops Division, and deputy director (*stellvertretende Direktor*). Interviewed March 26, 2003, and June 17, 2003, in Flensburg.

Jürgen Weber. Weber was son of Alfred Weber, founder of AWF-Gummiwarenfabrik; later he took over the firm. Interviewed September 3, 2003, in Gross-Zimmern.

Reinhard Wille. Wille was a physician and lawyer by training; he was an instructor and then a professor at the Institute for Sexual Medicine, University of Kiel, until 1997. Interviewed March 7, 2003, in Kiel.

Abbreviations

AFJ	Ausschuss für Familie- und Jugendfragen
B Arch	Bundesarchiv
BayHStA	Bayerisches Hauptstaatsarchiv
Bay M Inn	Bayerisches Ministerium des Innern
Bay OLG	Bayerisches Oberlandesgericht
BEH	Bundesverband Erotik Handel
BGBl	Bundesgesetzblatt
BMFJ	Bundesministerium für Familie und Jugend
BMI	Bundesministerium des Innern
BMJ	Bundesministerium für Justiz
BPrSt	Bundesprüfstelle für jugendgefährdende Schriften
BVG	Bundesverwaltungsgericht
B-W M Inn	Baden-Württembergisches Ministerium des Innern
DBT	Deutscher Bundestag
DLA	Deutsches Literatur-Archiv, Marbach
FZH	Forschungsstelle für Zeitgeschichte in Hamburg
GeschlKrG	Gesetz zur Bekämpfung der Geschlechtskranheiten
GewO	Gewerbeordnung
GjS	Gesetz über die Verbreitung jugendgefährdender Schriften und Abbildungen
GStA	Generalstaatsanwalt
HAEK	Historisches Archiv des Erzbistums Köln
HHStA	Hessisches Hauptstaatsarchiv
HWWA	Hamburgisches Welt-Wirtschafts-Archiv
LANRW	Landesarchiv Nordrhein-Westfalen
LASH	Landesarchiv Schleswig-Holstein
LG	Landgericht
LZBujS	Leiter der Zentralstellen zur Bekämpfung unzüchtiger und jugendgefährender Schriften, Abbildungen, und Darstellungen
OLG	Oberlandesgericht
OStA	Oberstaatsanwalt
PA	Parlamentsarchiv
RdSchr	Rundschreiben

StA	Staatsanwalt
StA Fl	Stadtarchiv Flensburg
StAL	Staatsarchiv Ludwigsburg
StGB	Strafgesetzbuch
VDBT	Verhandlungen des deutschen Bundestages
VdV	Verband deutscher Versandunternehmen
VjS	Vertrieb jugendgefährdender Schriften
VWB	Volkswartbund
WSG	Walter Schäfer Gruppe

Notes

Prelude: The Beate Uhse Myth

1. Uta van Steen, *Liebesperlen: Beate Uhse: Eine deutsche Karriere* (Hamburg: Europäische Verlagsanstalt, 2003), 72–73.
2. Good summaries of Rotermund's life appear in her memoir and in a recent biography: Beate Uhse and Ulrich Pramann, *Mit Lust und Liebe: Mein Leben* (Frankfurt am Main: Ullstein, 1989); Beate Uhse and Ulrich Pramann, *Ich will Freiheit für die Liebe* (Munich: List Taschenbuch, 2001); Steen, *Liebesperlen*.
3. Forschungsstelle für Zeitgeschichte in Hamburg (hereafter FZH) 18-9/2.5, Institut für psychologische Markt- und Sozialforschung (Frankfurt am Main), "Beate Uhse: Eine kombinierte Motiv-Image-Studie," 1972.
4. FZH 18-9/2.5, Wickert Institut (Tübingen), Untersuchung, "Bekanntheitsgrad Beate Uhse," 1984.
5. "Vorher gab es bloss Beischlaf, mit Beate Uhse kam der Sex," *Berliner Zeitung*, 19 July 2001, 54.

Chapter 1. Introduction: Sex, Consumption, and German History

1. Axel Schildt and Arnold Sywottek, eds., *Modernisierung im Wiederaufbau* (Bonn: Dietz, 1993); Kaspar Maase, *Grenzenloses Vergnügen: Der Aufstieg der Massenkultur, 1850–1970* (Frankfurt am Main: Fischer, 1997).
2. Ulrich Herbert, "Liberalisierung als Lernprozess: Die Bundesrepublik in der deutschen Geschichte—eine Skizze," in *Wandlungsprozesse in Westdeutschland: Belastung, Integration, Liberalisierung, 1945–1980*, ed. Ulrich Herbert (Göttingen: Wallstein, 2002), 7–49; Konrad Hugo Jarausch, *After Hitler: Recivilizing Germans, 1945–1995* (New York: Oxford University Press), 2006; Habbo Knoch, "'Mündige Bürger,' oder: Der kurze Frühling einer partizipatorischen Vision," in *Bürgersinn mit Weltgefühl*, ed. Habbo Knoch (Göttingen: Wallstein, 2007), 9–53; Gabrielle Metzler, "Der lange Weg zur sozialliberalen Politik," in Knoch, *Bürgersinn mit Weltgefühl*, 157–80.
3. Isabel V. Hull, *Sexuality, State, and Civil Society in Germany, 1700–1815* (Ithaca, NY: Cornell University Press, 1996); Carole Pateman, *The Sexual Contract* (Stanford, CA: Stanford University Press, 1988); Judith Surkis, *Sexing the Citizen: Morality and Masculinity in France, 1870–1920* (Ithaca, NY: Cornell University Press, 2006); Anna Clark, *The Struggle for the Breeches: Gender and the Making of the British Working Class* (Berkeley: University of California Press, 1997); Catherine Hall, Keith McClelland, and Jane Rendall, *Defining*

the Victorian Nation (Cambridge: Cambridge University Press, 2000); Geneviève Fraisse, *Reason's Muse: Sexual Difference and the Birth of Democracy* (Chicago: University of Chicago Press, 1994).

4. Kaspar Maase, "Schundkampf und Demokratie," in *Prädikat wertlos: Der lange Streit um Schmutz und Schund*, ed. Kaspar Maase (Tübingen: Tübinger Vereinigung für Volkskunde, 2001), 8–18.

5. Uta G. Poiger, *Jazz, Rock, and Rebels: Cold War Politics and American Culture in a Divided Germany* (Berkeley: University of California Press, 2000).

6. Herbert Jäger, *Strafgesetzgebung und Rechtsgüterschutz bei Sittlichkeitsdelikten: Eine kriminalsoziologische Untersuchung* (Stuttgart: Enke, 1957); Karl Siegfried Bader, "Gutachtliche Äusserung zur Reform der Paragraphen 175, 175a StGB [Strafgesetzbuch]," *Zeitschrift für Sexualforschung* 1, nos. 3–4 (1950): 215.

7. Jeffrey Weeks, *Sexuality and Its Discontents* (New York: Routledge and Kegan Paul, 1985), 53–56.

8. Thomas W. Laqueur, *Solitary Sex* (New York: Zone, 2003).

9. Robert G. Moeller, *Protecting Motherhood: Women and the Family in the Politics of Postwar West Germany* (Berkeley: University of California Press, 1993); Klaus-Jörg Ruhl, *Verordnete Unterordnung: Berufstätige Frauen zwischen Wirtschaftswachstum und konservativer Ideologie in der Nachkriegszeit (1945–1963)* (Munich: R. Oldenbourg, 1994); see also Elaine Tyler May, *Homeward Bound: American Families in the Cold War Era* (New York: Basic Books, 1988); Claire Duchen, *Women's Rights and Women's Lives in France, 1944–1968* (New York: Routledge, 1994).

10. Lutz Niethammer, "'Normalization' in the West: Traces of Memory Leading Back into the 1950s," in *The Miracle Years*, ed. Hanna Schissler (Princeton, NJ: Princeton University Press, 2001), 237–65.

11. Till van Rahden, "Demokratie und väterliche Autorität. Das Karlsruher 'Stichentscheid'-Urteil von 1959 in der politischen Kultur der frühen Bundesrepublik," *Zeithistorische Forschungen*, no. 2 (2005); Heide Fehrenbach, "Rehabilitating Fatherland: Race and German Remasculinization," *Signs* 24 (1998): 107–27; Axel Schildt, *Moderne Zeiten: Freizeit, Massenmedien und "Zeitgeist" in der Bundesrepublik der 50er Jahre* (Hamburg: Wallstein, 1995); and Michael Wildt, *Am Beginn der "Konsumgesellschaft"* (Hamburg: Ergebnisse Verlag, 1994).

12. William Reddy, *The Navigation of Feeling: A Framework for the History of Emotions* (New York: Cambridge University Press, 2001).

13. Ibid., 129; see also Birgit Aschmann, "Einleitung," in *Gefühl und Kalkül: Der Einfluss von Emotionen auf die Politik des 19. und 20. Jahrhunderts*, ed. Birgit Aschmann (Stuttgart: Steiner, 2005); Frank Biess, "'Everybody Has a Chance': Nuclear Angst, Civil Defence, and the History of Emotions in Postwar West Germany," *German History* 2009 (27): 215–43; Ute Frevert, "Angst vor Gefühlen: Die Geschichtsmächtigkeit von Emotionen im 20. Jahrhundert," in *Perspektiven der Gesellschaftsgeschichte*, ed. Paul Nolte, Manfred Hettling, Frank-Michael Kuhlemann, and Hans-Walter Schmuhl (Munich: Beck, 2000), 95–111.

14. Herbert, "Liberalisierung als Lernprozess," 13.

15. Schildt and Sywottek, *Modernisierung im Wiederaufbau*; Kaspar Maase, "Establishing Cultural Democracy: Youth, 'Americanization,' and the Irresistible Rise of Popular Culture," in Schissler, *Miracle Years*, 428–50; Matthias Frese, Julia Paulus, and Karl Teppe,

eds., *Demokratisierung und gesellschaftlicher Aufbruch: Die sechziger Jahre als Wendezeit der Bundesrepublik* (Paderborn: F. Schöningh, 2003).

16. Victoria de Grazia, introduction to *The Sex of Things: Gender and Consumption in Historical Perspective*, ed. Victoria de Grazia and Ellen Furlough (Berkeley: University of California Press, 1996), 1-10, esp. 8.

17. Dagmar Herzog, *Sex after Fascism: Memory and Morality in Twentieth-Century Germany* (Princeton, NJ: Princeton University Press, 2005).

18. On German uniqueness versus "Europeanness" more generally, see Ute Frevert, "Europeanizing Germany's Twentieth Century," *History and Memory* 17, nos. 1-2 (2005): 87-116.

19. E.g., Walter Schäfer Gruppe (WSG), *Leben und nicht verzichten!* ca. 1951-52, pp. 22, 35, in author's possession; *Intim*, catalog of Metropol-Versand, ca. 1959, p. 17, in author's possession.

20. Literature on "coming to terms" with the Nazi past that highlights gender and sexuality includes Robert G. Moeller, *War Stories: The Search for a Usable Past in the Federal Republic of Germany* (Berkeley: University of California Press, 2001); Frank Biess, *Homecomings: Returning POWs and the Legacies of Defeat in Postwar Germany* (Princeton, NJ: Princeton University Press, 2006); Heide Fehrenbach, *Race after Hitler: Black Occupation Children in Postwar Germany and America* (Princeton, NJ: Princeton University Press, 2005); Elizabeth D. Heineman, "The Hour of the Woman: Memories of Germany's 'Crisis Years' and West German National Identity," *American Historical Review* 101 (1996): 354-95; Elizabeth D. Heineman, "Gender, Sexuality, and Coming to Terms with the Past," *Central European History* 38 (2005): 41-74.

21. Marcus Collins, *Modern Love: An Intimate History of Men and Women in Twentieth-Century Britain* (London: Atlantic, 2003); John D'Emilio and Estelle B. Freedman, *Intimate Matters: A History of Sexuality in America*, 2nd ed. (Chicago: University of Chicago Press, 1997); Duchen, *Women's Rights and Women's Lives in France*. Distinguishing "postwar" from "postfascist" in the German case is Klaus Naumann, "Einleitung," in *Nachkrieg in Deutschland*, ed. Klaus Naumann (Hamburg: Hamburger Edition, 2001), 9-20.

22. Atina Grossmann, *Reforming Sex: The German Movement for Birth Control and Abortion Reform, 1920-1950* (New York: Oxford University Press, 1995); Cornelie Usborne, *The Politics of the Body in Weimar Germany: Women's Reproductive Rights and Duties* (Ann Arbor: University of Michigan Press, 1992); Katharina von Ankum, ed., *Women in the Metropolis: Gender and Modernity in Weimar Culture* (Berkeley: University of California Press, 1997).

23. Christina von Hodenberg and Detlef Siegfried, "Reform und Revolte," in *Wo "1968" liegt: Reform und Revolte in der Geschichte der Bundesrepublik*, ed. Christina von Hodenberg and Detlef Siegfried (Göttingen: Vandenhoeck und Ruprecht, 2006), 7-14.

24. Edward Ross Dickinson, "'A Dark Impenetrable Wall of Complete Incomprehension': The Impossibility of Heterosexual Love in Imperial Germany," *Central European History* 40 (2007): 467-97; Michel Foucault, *The History of Sexuality* (New York: Vintage, 1988-90).

25. On the trajectory from the Wilhelmine era to the late twentieth century, see Edward Ross Dickinson, "Policing Sex in Germany, 1882-1982: A Preliminary Statistical Analysis," *Journal of the History of Sexuality* 16, no. 2 (May 2007): 204-50.

26. Hugh McLeod, *The Religious Crisis of the 1960s* (Oxford: Oxford University Press, 2007).

27. D'Emilio and Freedman, *Intimate Matters*; Franz Eder, *Kultur der Begierde: Eine Geschichte der Sexualität* (Munich: Beck, 2002).

28. James Woycke, *Birth Control in Germany, 1871–1933* (New York: Routledge, 1988).

29. Lisa Z. Sigel, *Governing Pleasures: Pornography and Social Change in England, 1815–1914* (Piscataway, NJ: Rutgers University Press, 2002).

30. Grossmann, *Reforming Sex*; Collins, *Modern Love*.

31. Alon Confino and Rudy Koshar, "Regimes of Consumer Culture: New Narratives in Twentieth-Century German History," *German History* 19 (2001): 135–61; Konrad Hugo Jarausch and Michael Geyer, *Shattered Past: Reconstructing German Histories* (Princeton, NJ: Princeton University Press, 2003).

32. Arne Andersen, *Der Traum vom guten Leben: Alltags- und Konsumgeschichte vom Wirtschaftswunder bis heute* (Frankfurt am Main and New York: Campus, 1997), 93–97.

33. Paul Betts and Greg Eghigian, eds., *Pain and Prosperity: Reconsidering Twentieth-Century German History* (Stanford, CA: Stanford University Press, 2003).

34. Volkswartbund (hereafter VWB), *Die Gefahren des Sexualismus und ihre Überwindung* (Cologne-Klettenberg: VWB, 1952); Günter Amendt, *Sex-Front* (Frankfurt am Main: März Verlag, 1970); Volkmar Sigusch, "Lean Sexuality: On Cultural Transformations of Sexuality and Gender in Recent Decades," *Zeitschrift für Sexualforschung* 15 (2002): 23–56; Alice Schwarzer, ed., *PorNO: Opfer & Täter, Gegenwehr & Backlash, Verantwortung & Gesetz* (Cologne: Kiepenheuer und Witsch, 1994).

35. Adolf Kloeckner, "Kesseltreiben gegen das GjS," *Jugendschutz* 11, no. 1 (1966): 8–13. On the language of "waves," see Andersen, *Der Traum vom guten Leben*.

36. Arthur Marwick, *The Sixties: Cultural Revolution in Britain, France, Italy, and the United States, c. 1958–c. 1974* (New York: Oxford University Press, 1998).

37. Beth Bailey, "Sexual Revolution(s) in the Sixties: From Memory to History," in *The Sixties: From Memory to History*, ed. David Farber (Chapel Hill: University of North Carolina Press, 1994), 235–62.

38. Heike Hengstenberg and Gabriele Sturm, "Sex macht Lust: Das Thema Sexualität in der neuen deutschen Frauenbewegung," in *Liebes- und Lebensverhältnisse: Sexualität in der feministischen Diskussion*, ed. Interdisziplinäre Forschungsgruppe Frauenforschung (Frankfurt am Main: Campus, 1990), 61–82, here 62; Sabine Weissler, "Sexy Sixties," *CheSchahShit: Die sechziger Jahre zwischen Cocktail und Molotow* (Reinbek bei Hamburg: Elefanten, 1989).

39. Jean Baudrillard, *Selected Writings* (Stanford, CA: Stanford University Press, 2001); Arjun Appadurai, ed., *The Social Life of Things: Commodities in Cultural Perspective* (Cambridge: Cambridge University Press, 1986); Michel de Certeau, Luce Giard, and Pierre Mayol, *The Practice of Everyday Life*, trans. Steven Rendall (Berkeley: University of California Press, 1984); Marius Kwint, "Introduction: The Physical Past," in *Material Memories*, ed. Marius Kwint, Christopher Breward, and Jeremy Aynsley (New York: Berg, 1999).

40. Andrea Tone, *Devices and Desires: A History of Contraceptives in America* (New York: Hill and Wang, 2001); H. G. Cocks, "Saucy Stories: Pornography, Sexology and the Marketing of Sexual Knowledge in Britain, c. 1918–1970," *Social History* 29 (2004): 465–84; Jay A. Gertzman, *Bookleggers and Smuthounds: The Trade in Erotica, 1920–1940* (Philadelphia: University of Pennsylvania Press, 1999). The first big comprehensive erotica firm in the United States was Adam and Eve, founded 1970; see Philip D. Harvey, *The Government vs. Erotica: The Siege of Adam and Eve* (Amherst, NY: Prometheus Books, 2001).

41. Clayton J. Whisnant, "Hamburg's Gay Scene in the Era of Family Politics, 1945–1969," Ph.D. dissertation, University of Texas, 2001.

42. H. G. Cocks, "Modernity and the Self in the History of Sexuality," *Historical Journal* 4 (2006): 1211–27. By contrast, see Lauren Berlant and Michael Warner, "Sex in Public," *Critical Inquiry* 24, no. 2 (1998): 547–66.

43. A comparison of the number of households found on erotica firms' mailing lists and the number of households listed in the West German census suggests this figure is plausible. Industry insiders considered it a conservative estimate (they corrected for customers who appeared on more than one firm's mailing list), but it includes those who made only an initial inquiry or order and did not become regular customers. Collection of the Bundesverband Erotik Handel (hereafter BEH) in Hamburg, Dr. med. E.L., "Statistisches Material aus dem Alltag," talk delivered at the conference *Das süsse Leben*, Evangelische Akademie Tutzing, 7 April 1962. The industry group estimated in 1966 that one-third of West German households patronized its firms (which did not include all firms in the industry). "Sex per Post," *DM* 11 (1968): 38–41; here 40.

44. Linda Gordon, *The Moral Property of Women: A History of Birth Control Politics in America* (Urbana: University of Illinois, 2002); Tone, *Devices and Desires*; Grossmann, *Reforming Sex*; Lynn Avery Hunt, ed., *The Invention of Pornography: Obscenity and the Origins of Modernity, 1500–1800* (New York: Zone Books, 1993); Sigel, *Governing Pleasures*; Linda Williams, *Hard Core: Power, Pleasure, and the "Frenzy of the Visible"* (Berkeley: University of California Press, 1999); Rachel P. Maines, *The Technology of Orgasm: "Hysteria," the Vibrator, and Women's Sexual Satisfaction* (Baltimore: Johns Hopkins University Press, 1998).

45. Katherine Helena Pence, "From Rations to Fashions: The Gendered Politics of East and West German Consumption, 1945–1961," Ph.D. dissertation, University of Michigan, 1999; Erica Carter, *How German Is She? Postwar West German Reconstruction and the Consuming Woman* (Ann Arbor: University of Michigan Press, 1997).

46. Private archive of Claus Richter, Rotenburg, "Das Kondom: Geschichte—Daten—Fakten," 16.

47. Bayerisches Hauptstaatsarchiv (BayHStA), Bayerisches Ministerium des Innern (Bay M Inn) 92082, 29.10.1949 Oberfinanzpräsidium München (z 2500–A 63/6).

48. U.S. Commission on Obscenity and Pornography, *Report of the Commission on Obscenity and Pornography* (New York: Random House, 1970).

49. Woycke, *Birth Control in Germany*, 113.

50. Beate Uhse, *Lustvoll in den Markt: Strategien für schwierige Märkte* (Planegg: WRS, 2000), 69–72.

51. E.g., Monika Siedentopf, "Die Lust-Macherin," *Die Zeit*, 20 March 2003, 28; Hannelore Hippe, "Nur Fliegen ist schöner: Die Unternehmerin Beate Uhse," Mitteldeutscher Rundfunk broadcast on Bayerischer Rundfunk, broadcast 25 February 2001; Rupp Doinet, "Grande Dame der niederen Instinkte," *Der Stern* (26 July 2001): 40–44. The autobiography is Uhse, *Mit Lust und Liebe*.

52. FZH 18-9/3.1, passim; collection of Dublosan e.K., Berlin, passim.

53. Parlamentsarchiv (PA) III/296/A/4, Deutscher Bundestag (DBT) 18.1.1960 Ausschuss für Familie- und Jugendfragen (AFJ), Ausschussdrucksache 23, Anlage 6: Auszug aus den Gründen des Urteils der kl. Strafkammer des Landgerichts (LG) Tübingen vom 31.1.58—II Ns 72 u. 252/56; WSG, Dr. Wunderer, 1968–72, passim; Wolf Mein and Lisa Wegen, *Die Pop-Kommune: Ein Report* (Munich: Wilhelm Heyne Verlag, 1971).

54. Jörg Schröder, West Germany's most important aboveground publisher of porn in the

early 1970s, donated the papers of his New Left publishing house März Verlag to the Deutsches Literaturarchiv in Marbach. März Verlag did not specialize in pornography, but the papers include some materials from Olympia Press, which did.

55. W.P. to Beate Uhse, 26 March 1955 and 17 December 1960, in author's possession.

56. Irmgard Hill, interview with the author, 25 February 2003, 44.

57. Staatsarchiv Ludwigsburg (StAL), EL 317 I, Bü 2342, 16.11.1956, Anzeige Kriminalhaupt-stelle Landespolizeidirektion Nordwürttemberg.

58. Hessisches Hauptstaatsarchiv (HHStA) 461/32036, folio 234, 14.9.1951 statement by G.P. to police.

59. Sharon Abbott, "Careers of Actresses and Actors in the Pornography Industry," Ph.D. dissertation, Indiana University, 1999, 291; Sylvia Plachy and James Ridgeway, *Red Light: Inside the Sex Industry* (New York: Powerhouse Books, 1996).

Chapter 2. The Permissive Prudish State

1. Dr. Georg Schückler, "'Schund- und Schmutzgesetz' im Bundestag verabschiedet," *VWB Mitteilungen* (October 1952); Historisches Archiv des Erzbistums Köln (HAEK), Dienstakten Böhler Nr. 172, 9.5.1953 Gesetz über die Verbreitung jugendgefährdender Schriften (GjS) (Bundesgesetzblatt [BGBl] I S 377).

2. E.g., Michael Kienzle, "Logophobie: Zensur und Selbstzensur in der BRD: Ein geschicht-licher Abriß," in *Zensur in der Bundesrepublik*, ed. Michael Kienzle and Dirk Mende (Munich: Heyne, 1981), 14–50; Stephan Buchloh, *"Pervers, jugendgefährdend, staatsfeindlich": Zensur in der Ära Adenauer als Spiegel des gesellschaftlichen Klimas* (Frankfurt am Main and New York: Campus, 2002), 85.

3. Paul Bockelmann, "Zur Reform des Sexualstrafrechts," in *Festschrift für Reinhart Maurach zum 70. Geburtstag*, ed. Friedrich-Christian Schroeder and Heinz Zipf (Karlsruhe: Verlag C. F. Müller, 1972), 391–414; Karl Peters, "Kuppelei bei Verlobten," *Zeitschrift für das gesamte Familienrecht* (1954): 96–99; "Man darf den Souverän nicht reizen," *Der Spiegel* 22, no. 38 (16 September 1968): 59–64.

4. Robert G. Moeller, "The Homosexual Man Is a 'Man,' the Homosexual Woman Is a 'Woman': Sex, Society, and the Law in Postwar West Germany," *Journal of the History of Sexuality* 4 (1994): 395–429.

5. Anselm Doering-Manteuffel, "Die 'Frommen' und die 'Linken' vor der Wiederherstellung des bürgerlichen Staats," in *Christentum und politische Verantwortung: Kirchen im Nachkriegsdeutschland*, ed. Anselm Doering-Manteuffel and Jochen-Christoph Kaiser (Stuttgart/Berlin/Cologne: W. Kohlhammer, 1990), 88–108.

6. Frank Bösch, *Die Adenauer-CDU* (Stuttgart/Munich: Deutsche Verlags-Anstalt, 2001); Maria Mitchell, "'The Esteem of Women and Girls Is in Danger!': Christian Democracy and Sexual Morality in the Postwar Years," paper delivered at the 2008 meeting of the German Studies Association.

7. Bundesarchiv (B Arch), B117/8, 10.3.1953 Schilling to Speidel.

8. Peter Kuhnert and Ute Ackermann, "Jenseits von Lust und Liebe? Jugendsexualität in den 50er Jahren," in *Die Elvis-Tolle, die hatte ich mir unauffällig wachsen lassen: Lebensgeschichte und jugendliche Alltagskultur in den fünfziger Jahren*, ed. Heinz-Hermann Krüger (Opladen: Leske und Budrich, 1985), 43–83; Ulf Preuss-Lausitz, "Vom gepanzerten zum sinnstiftenden Körper," in *Kriegskinder, Konsumkinder, Krisenkinder: Zur Sozialisationsgeschichte seit dem Zweiten Weltkrieg*, ed. Ulf Preuss-Lausitz (Weinheim: Beltz, 1983), 89–

106; Claudia Seifert, *Aus Kindern werden Leute, aus Mädchen werden Bräute: Die 50er und 60er Jahre* (Munich: DTV, 2006).

9. Herzog, *Sex after Fascism*; Reimut Reiche, "Kritik der gegenwärtigen Sexualwissenschaft," in *Tendenzen der Sexualforschung*, ed. Günther Schmidt, Volkmar Sigusch, and Eberhard Schorsch (Stuttgart: Enke, 1970).

10. See also Helen Horwitz, *Rereading Sex: Battles over Sexual Knowledge and Suppression in Nineteenth-Century America* (New York: Knopf, 2002).

11. Maase, "Schundkampf und Demokratie."

12. Herbert, "Liberalisierung als Lernprozess."

13. Richard Bessel, *Germany after the First World War* (Oxford: Oxford University Press, 1993); Gideon Reuveni, *Reading Germany: Literature and Consumer Culture in Germany before 1933* (New York: Berghahn Books, 2006).

14. HAEK, Bestand Dienstakten Lenne, Nr. 329, 02.1944, Michael Calmes, "Kurze Übersicht über unsere augenblickliche Arbeit"; HAEK, Gen. II, 23.30, Nr. 3, Michael Calmes, "Schleichendes Gift," *VWB Mitteilungen* (March 1950): 1–3.

15. HAEK, Gen. II 23.30b, 4./5.1946 VWB Rundbrief.

16. HAEK, Gen. II 23.30b, 3.1946 VWB Rundbrief.

17. HAEK, Gen. II 23.30b, 2./3.1948 VWB Rundbrief; HAEK, Gen. II 23.30b, 15.10.1946 "Aus der Arbeit des VWB," Michael Calmes, Vortrag gehalten bei einer Tagung des Arbeitskreises caritativer Jugendhilfe in Verbindung mit dem Zentralrat des Deutschen Caritatsverbandes (Cologne-Rohenlind).

18. Robert Schilling, *Das Geschäft mit der Erotik auf dem Gebiete des Zeitschriften- und Inseratenwesens* (Cologne-Klettenberg: Volkswartbund, 1951), 3.

19. Landesarchiv Schleswig-Holstein (LASH) 351/1696, Beschlüsse des Amtsgerichtes München, 1950–52.

20. W., *Pornographie Weltgefahr!* (Cologne-Klettenberg: Volkswartbund, 1950); *Im Abwehrkampf gegen den sittlichen Verfall: Ein Jahresbericht* (Cologne-Klettenberg: Volkswartbund, 1953); Robert Schilling, *Das erotisch-sexuelle periodische Schrifttum als Gegenstand der Beurteilung gemäß Par. 184 StGB* (Cologne-Klettenberg: Volkswartbund, 1951).

21. E.g., Robert Schilling, "Das Geschäft mit der Erotik," *Der neue Vertrieb* 4, no. 74 (5 May 1952): 152–60; Robert Schilling, "Das Geschäft mit der Erotik," *Frauenwelt* 16 (June 1952): 6–7; Robert Schilling, *Im Kampf um Sitte und Sittlichkeit: Ein Jahr Volkswartbundarbeit* (Cologne-Klettenberg: Volkswartbund, 1955).

22. Landesarchiv Nordrhein-Westfalen (LANRW), Dü, NW 41, Nr. 276, folios 160–63, 4.7.1950 Deutscher Stadtetag, betr.: VJS. The Bundesbahn negotiated similar conditions for bookshops in train stations: Verband deutscher Bahnhofsbuchhändler, "Schmutz- und Schundliteratur," *Der neue Vertrieb* 2, no. 19 (6 February 1950): 314.

23. Schilling, *Das Geschäft mit der Erotik auf dem Gebiete des Zeitschriften- und Inseratenwesens*, 11.

24. LANRW, Dü, NW 41, Nr. 274, folios 49–50, 17.2.1949, Calmes (VWB) to Oberstaatsanwalt (OStA) Köln (Abschrift).

25. Schilling, *Das erotisch-sexuelle periodische Schrifttum*, 36–40.

26. BayHStA, Bay M Inn 92025, 7.11.1952 Zentralamt für Kriminal-Identifizierung und Polizeistatistik des Landes Bayern (II a-UB Az: 28 s 19.16 Nr. 289/52) an das Bay M Inn; "Errichtung einer Zentralstelle zur Bekämpfung unzüchtiger Schriften und Abbildungen bei dem GStA in München," *Bayerischer Wohlfahrtsdienst* 2, no. 7 (1950): 71; LASH 351/1696, Beschlüsse des Amtgerichtes München, passim.

27. B Arch, B 141/26574, folio 48, 6.6.1952 Verband deutscher Versandunternehmen (VdV) to Bundesministerium für Justiz (BMJ).

28. OStA Dr. Brey, *Erweiterter sittlicher Rechtsschutz für Jugendliche tut not!* (Cologne-Klettenberg: Volkswartbund, 1951).

29. See also Kurt Runge, "Kampf gegen Schund und Schmutz?" *Der neue Vertrieb* 2, no. 19 (6 February 1950): 309–10.

30. Landesgesetz zum Schutze der Jugend vor Schmutz und Schund vom 12. Oktober 1949 (Ges. u. Verordn. Bl. der Landesregierung Rheinland-Pfalz Teil I v. 19, Oktober 1949 S. 505).

31. Verhandlungen des deutschen Bundestages (VDBT) 1. Wahlperiode, 74. Sitzung 13.7.1950, 2664–74, here 2673–74.

32. Fritz Bauer, "Grundgesetz und 'Schmutz- und Schundgesetz,'" *Juristen Zeitung*, no. 2 (15 January 1965): 41–47.

33. Maria Mitchell, "Materialism and Secularism: CDU Politicians and National Socialism, 1945–1949," *Journal of Modern History* 67, no. 2 (June 1995): 278–308.

34. Doering-Manteuffel, "Die 'Frommen' und die 'Linken.'"

35. B Arch, B141/4680, folios 5–13, 19.–20.5.1950, Kurzprotokoll über die Sitzung des Ausschusses für innere Angelegenheiten (DBR); VDBT 74. Sitzung 13.7.1950, 2664–74.

36. BayHStA, Bay M Inn 92084, 9.1.50 J.N. an Herrn Landeskommissar Mr. Bolds; BayHStA, Bay M Inn 92085, 9.3.50 Msgr. Dr. A. L., Domkapitular, an das Bay M Inn; see also other constituent letters in these files.

37. Klaus Ziegler, "Vom Recht und Unrecht der Unterhaltungs- und Schundliteratur," *Die Sammlung* 2 (1947): 565–74.

38. E.g., Carlo Schmid, "Schmutz- und Schund-Gesetz—Endlose Schraube," *Die Welt*, 13 January 1950; "Freiheit und Zensur," *Der neue Vertrieb* 7, no. 140 (20 February 1955): 88–89.

39. PA I/430/A/41, 9.11.1950 DBT Ausschuss für Fragen der Jugendfürsorge (33. Ausschuss) Protokol nr. 27; W. E. Sueskind, "Schmutz und Schund," *Süddeutsche Zeitung* (7 and 8 January 1950); "Achtung, Zensur!" *Deutsche Zeitung und Wirtschaftszeitung*, 28 January 1950, n.p., and others collected in BayHStA, Bay M Inn 92083.

40. B Arch, B141/4680, folios 59–60, 19.6.1950 Bundesministerium des Innerns (BMI) to Bundeskriminalamt (BKA) (Abschrift) (3426: 423–50).

41. PA I/430/A/38, 5.10.1950 Geheimrat Dr. Hagemann, testimony before the DBT Ausschuss für Fragen der Jugendfürsorge, Protokol Nr. 23; PA I/430/A/40, 25.10.1950 Amtsgerichtsrat Dr. Clostermann, testimony before the DBT Ausschuss für Fragen der Jugendfürsorge, Protokol Nr. 26.

42. BayHStA, Bay M Inn 92084, 6.2.1950 Bayerische Akademie der schönen Künste: Niederschrift der am 1.2.1950 abgehaltenen Besprechung über den Entwurf eines "Gesetzes zur Bewahrung der Jugend vor Schmutz und Schund."

43. Alma de L'Aigle, "Was heißt 'sittliche Gefährdung der Jugend'?" *Die Sammlung* 9 (1954): 450–59.

44. Chad Ross, *Naked Germany: Health, Race and the Nation* (New York: Berg, 2005); Michael Andritzky and Thomas Rautenberg, *"Wir sind nackt und nennen uns Du": Von Lichtfreunden und Sonnenkämpfern* (Giessen: Anabas, 1989).

45. B Arch, B 141/4680, folios 50–58, 2.6.1950 Änderungen des Deutschen Bundesrates zum Entwurf eines Gesetzes über den VjS.

46. VDBT 1. Wahlperiode, 74. Sitzung 13.7.1950, 2665, 2668.

47. B Arch, B141/4685, folios 80–116, here 96, 18.2.1960 Sitzung des DBT Ausschusses für Familien- und Jugendfragen, Kurzprotokoll 38.

48. Gerhard Potrykus, "Neue Rechtsprechung des Bundesverfassungsgerichts zum Schrifttumsgesetz," Zentralblatt für Jugendrecht und Jugendwohlfahrt 11 (1971): 330–34.

49. B Arch, B141/4679, folios 48–52, 3.3.1950 BMI Stellungnahme zur Frage der Zuständigkeit des Bundes zum Erlaß eines Gesetzes über jugendgefährdende Schriften.

50. Buchloh, "Pervers, jugendgefährdend, staatsfeindlich," 86–91.

51. B Arch, B141/90246, folio 37 (Anlage), Grosse Strafrechtskommission: Umdruck J 78: Vorschläge und Bemerkungen der Sachbearbeiter des BJM zum Thema Unzucht.

52. Heide Fehrenbach, Cinema in Democratizing Germany: Reconstructing National Identity after Hitler (Chapel Hill: University of North Carolina Press, 1995).

53. The first decision came on 9 July 1954. Hermann Riedel, "Der Kampf gegen das jugendgefährdende Schrifttum," Unsere Jugend 7, no. 6 (1955): 261–66.

54. B Arch, B141/4685, folios 14–30, here 29, 21.1.1960 Auszug aus dem Kurzprotokoll der 35. Sitzung des AFJ des 3. DBT, Anlage 2: Referat Robert Schilling.

55. Hermann Montanus, "Unerfreuliches Zwischenstadium," Der neue Vertrieb 6, no. 122 (20 May 1954): 190–91.

56. "Aktuelle Probleme des GjS," Der neue Vertrieb 9, no. 199 (5 August 1957): 405–16.

57. B Arch, B141/4676, folios 100–102, 23.–24.10.1956 Tagung der Leiter der Zentralstellen zur Bekämpfung unzüchtiger und jugengefährender Schriften, Abbildungen, und Darstellungen (LZBujS); Wilhelm Wolff, "Genutzte Möglichkeiten," Unsere Jugend 6, no. 2 (1954): 72–74.

58. Hans Joachim Lemme, "Die Stellung des Händlers nach dem BGH-Urteil," Der neue Vertrieb 7, no. 158 (20 November 1955): 653–54.

59. "Pressestimmen zum BGH-Urteil vom 14.7.1955," Der neue Vertrieb 7, no. 156 (20 October 1955): 590–93; Robert Schilling, "Die Bundesprüfstelle in der Praxis," Der neue Vertrieb 6, no. 131 (5 October 1954): 412–15.

60. BGH-Urteil v. 14.7.1955—1 StR 172/55 (Oberlandesgericht [OLG] München), Neue juristische Wochenschrift 8, no. 2 (1955): 1257–59.

61. Bruno Schulze, "Zur Frage der Bewährung des GjS," Jugendschutz 9, no. 4 (1964): 105–7; Walter Becker, "Stimme des Herausgebers," Jugendschutz 9, no. 2 (1964): 48–51.

62. BayHStA, Bay M Inn 89681, "Schmutz, Schund und die Mitverantwortung des Staates," Bayerische Staatszeitung (30 January 1959): 3–5.

63. PA III/296/A, Anlage 2 zum Protokoll der 45. Sitzung des 10. Ausschusses, DBT 3. Wahlperiode.

64. Other estimates of circulation were lower, but always in the hundreds of millions, compared to the tens of millions for public libraries. B Arch, B141/4676, folios 71–78, here 76–78, 16.12.1955 Niederschrift, LZBujS; B Arch, B141/4676, folios 18–26, here 18–19, 15.2.1955 betr. LZBujS; B Arch, B141/4676, folios 143–94, here 150, 21.–23.5.1959 Niederschrift, LZBujS; PA III/296/A/20, 6.10.1960 Sitzung des AFJ, Kurzprotokoll, 47.

65. Schilling, Das Geschäft mit der Erotik auf dem Gebiete des Zeitschriften- und Inseratenwesens; B Arch, B141/26578, folios 8–12, here 10, 10.5.1951 Protokoll über die Konferenz des VWB mit Richtern und Staatsanwälte (StA) in Düsseldorf.

66. "Schreiben des BMI an das Justizministerium Baden-Württemberg vom 10. Dezember 1953: 5432, 946/53," Zentralblatt für Jugendrecht u. Jugendwohlfahrt 41, no. 10 (1954): 232–33.

67. B Arch, B117/47, 18.10.1954 BMI (J 1032: 1667/54) to VWB.

68. BGH-Urteil v. 19.7.1955—5 StR 12/55 (LG Flensburg), *Neue juristische Wochenschrift* 8, no. 43 (1955): 1603–4. Related rulings include BGH-Urteil v. 16.3.1956—5 StR 585/55 (LG Hamburg), *Neue juristische Wochenschrift* 9, no. 43 (1956): 1607; B Arch, B106/782, 12.10.1956 Bundesprüfstelle für jugendgefährdende Schriften (BPrSt) Entscheidung Nr. 232; BGH-Urteil v. 14.1.1959—2 StR 265/58 (LG Wiesbaden), *Monatsschrift für deutsches Recht* 13, no. 5 (1959): 408.

69. Uhse, *Lustvoll in den Markt*, 183–84; LASH Abt. 351 Nr. 3310, 4. Große Strafkammer Landgericht Stuttgart, Sitzung 3.5.1960-29.7.1960, Urteil gegen Walter Schäfer und W.F.L. (V KMs 21/58)(V KMs 1/59)(V KMs 8/59) (hereafter Schäfer/W.F.L. Urteil), pp. 61, 83.

70. Schilling, "Jugendgefährdende Schriften als sexualethische Gefahr," 11.

71. BayHStA, Bay M Inn 92080, 4. Strafsenat des Bayerisches Oberlandesgericht (Bay OLG), Urteil vom 9.8.1962 (R Reg. 4 St 207/1962).

72. Walter Becker, "Jugendgefährdung durch Versandhandel," *Jugendschutz* 3, no. 1 (1958): 22–26; B Arch, B141/26579, 7.–9.6.1961 Niederschrift, LZBujS.

73. B Arch, B106/783, passim; HAEK, Gen. II, 23.30b, VWB Tätigkeitsbericht für das Jahr 1958.

74. "Gesetzwidriger Einfluß des 'Volkswartbundes'?" *Der neue Vertrieb* 15, no. 348 (23 October 1963): 1017–19.

75. HAEK, Gen. II, 23.30b, 27.4.1956 Michael Calmes to Bishop Frings (J. Nr. 1169); HAEK, Gen. II, 23.30b, 28.4.1958 Claes, Schückler to Bishop Frings (J. Nr. 900).

76. FZH 554/6/65 Aktion Jugendschutz Landesarbeitsstelle Hamburg, e.V., Jahresbericht 1959–60; Alexandra Kaiser, "Protestantischer Schundkampf in der Nachkriegszeit," in *Prädikat wertlos*, 30–45.

77. B Arch, B106/776, "Leidgeprüfte Bundesprüfer," *Deutsches Institut für Public Affairs* 7, no. 3 (February 1955): 45–46; "Buchhandel lobt Bundesprüfstelle," *Der neue Vertrieb* 12, no. 216 (21 April 1958): 189; PA III/296/A/8, Kurzprotokoll 35. Sitzung des 10. Ausschusses, DBT 3. Wahlperiode, 1957, Anlage 2.

78. LASH 351/4022, folios 1–8, Dokumentation betr. die Panorama-Sendungen des NDR, EFS, am 12.10.1964 und 7.12.1964, Wortlaut der Panorama-Sendung, 1.Fernsehen, am 12.10.1964, 20.15 Uhr über die BPrSt.

79. Erich Stümmer, "Neufassung des Schrifttumsgesetzes," *Recht der Jugend* 9, no. 4 (1961): 56–58.

80. *Der Bundesgerichtshof über die Normen der geschlechtlichen Sittlichkeit* (Cologne-Klettenberg: Volkswartbund, 1954). The case was BGH, Beschl. des Großen Senats für Strafsachen v. 17.2.1954—GSSt 3/53, *Neue juristische Wochenschrift* 20 (1954): 766–68.

81. B Arch, B117/16, 17.8.1954 Walter Becker to Robert Schilling; B Arch, B117/18, 2.7.1959 Walter Becker to Robert Schilling.

82. See correspondence in B Arch, B117/16; B Arch, B106/21214, 19.7.1953 Prof. Lic. H. Kittel to Prof. Dr. Franken (BMI).

83. B Arch, B106/776, "Leidgeprüfte Bundesprüfer."

84. "Bundesprüfstelle—Quo vadis?" *Der neue Vertrieb* 17, no. 392 (20 August 1965): 718–19; LASH 351/4167, BPrSt Beisitzerrundbrief Nr. 31, August 1965; B Arch, B117/3, 10.11.1966 Kurzbericht über die Arbeitstagung aller Beisitzer [der BPrSt] im Bundesministerium für Familie und Jugend (BMFJ).

85. B Arch, B106/776, 1.7.1956 E.L. to Kultusministerium; B Arch, B106/778, 26.7.1956 H.S. to BMI.

86. B Arch, B106/778, 26.10.1959 G.H. to BMI.

87. B Arch, B106/776, 26.11.1955 H.K. to Schilling.

88. Gerhard Schröder, "Das Geschäft mit dem Schmutz," *Evangelische Verantwortung* 7, no. 7/8 (1959): 4–7; B Arch, B106/778, 5.1.1960 BMI to Pfarrer G.H.

89. B Arch, B117/16, 12.–13.5.1952 Niederschrift über die Sitzung des Fachausschusses "Jugendschutz" der Arbeitsgemeinschaft für Jugendpflege und Jugendfürsorge in Bethel; Robert Schilling, "Jugendschutz gegen Schrifttum," *Der neue Vertrieb* 4, no. 74 (20 May 1952): 177–83; B Arch, B141/4685, folios 14–30, 21.1.1960 Auszug aus dem Kurzprotokoll der 35. Sitzung des AFJ des 3. DBT, Anlage 2: Referat Robert Schilling.

90. B Arch, B141/4676, folios 11–38, here 36, 11.2.1955 Tagung der LZBujS.

91. Robert Schilling, "Der Schutz der Kunst im GjS," *Der neue Vertrieb* 7, no. 155 (5 October 1955): 558–60; Ernst Buchholz, "Die Bundesprüfstelle im Lichte der Kritik," *Der neue Vertrieb* 7, no. 144 (20 April 1955): 193.

92. B Arch, B106/777, BMI (J 1066-9-311/58) to Präfekten R.L.; B Arch, B106/778, 11.11.1954 BPrSt Entscheidung Nr. 467; B Arch, B106/779, 27.11.1959 BMI (III 5 35 260-8304/59) to Pfarrer E.S.; B Arch, B106/777, 10.11.1958 BMI to W.V.; B Arch, B117/51, 15.4.1958 NRW Arbeits- und Sozialministerium to BPrSt; B Arch, B141/4676, folios 79–109, 23.–24.10.1956 Tagung der LZBujS in Hamburg; B Arch, B106/778, 11.11.1958 BPrSt Entscheidung Nr. 467; B Arch, B106/782, 12.10.1956 BPrSt Entscheidung Nr. 232.

93. "Gesamtübersicht über die Tätigkeit der Bundesprüfstelle 1954–1959," *Der neue Vertrieb* 12, no. 262 (20 March 1960): 174.

94. Robert Schilling, "Die Tätigkeit der Bundesprüfstelle im Jahre 1967," *Der neue Vertrieb* 20, no. 453 (5 March 1968): 144–50; see also Robert Schilling, "Die Bundesprüfstelle im Jahre 1966," *Der neue Vertrieb* 19, no. 429 (5 March 1967): 151–54.

95. PA III/296/A/8, Kurzprotokoll 35. Sitzung des 10. Ausschusses, DBT 3. Wahlperiode 1957, Anlage 2; Aigle, "Was heißt 'sittliche Gefährdung der Jugend'?"

96. PA III/296/1/12, 10.3.1960 Kurzprotokoll 40. Sitzung des AFJ, DBT 3. Wahlperiode, p. 38.

97. B Arch, B141/4685, folios 8–30, here 15 and 26, 21.1.1960 Auszug aus dem Kurzprotokoll der 35. Sitzung des AFJ des 3. DBT.

98. "Analyse eines Indizierungsirrtums," *Der neue Vertrieb* 15, no. 335 (5 April 1963): 247–50.

99. B Arch, B106/783, 11.10.1957 BPrSt Entscheidung Nr. 413.

100. Gerhard Potrykus, "Bayerische Vollzugsvorschriften zum Schmutz- und Schundgesetz," *Unsere Jugend* 7, no. 12 (1955): 561; Dr. Rothe, "Was müssen Eltern von den Jugendschutzgesetzen wissen?" *Frau und Mutter* 39, no. 7 (July 1956): 7.

101. B Arch, B141/4685, folios 14–30, here 22, 21.1.1960 Auszug aus dem Kurzprotokoll der 35. Sitzung des AFJ des 3. DBT, Anlage 2: Referat Robert Schilling.

102. "Gesamtübersicht über die Tätigkeit der Bundesprüfstelle 1954–1959," 174. NRW's petitions declined precipitously when the CDU lost power there to the SPD in 1957. "Die Tätigkeit der Bundesprüfstelle im Jahre 1962," *Der neue Vertrieb* 15, no. 331 (5 February 1963): 81–82.

103. BayHStA, Bay M Inn 89681, 15.11.1960 Baden-Württemberg Innenministerium (B-W M Inn) to Niedersachsen M Kultur.

104. "Die Richtlinien für Strafverfahren nach §184, 184a StGB, §18 G.ü.d.V.j.S.," *Der neue Vertrieb* 7, no. 139 (5 February 1955): 72–73.

105. B Arch, B141/4675, folios 72–83, 15.12.1953 BMJ Vermerk (4736: 24046/53); B Arch, B141/4675, folios 122–24, 8 July 1954 BMJ to the Landesjustizverwaltungen; B Arch, B141/26581,

22.–24.9.1965 Niederschrift, LZBujS, Anlage Referat GStA Hühnerschulte; B Arch, B141/4675, folios 99–136; BayHStA, Bay M Inn 89684, 15.6.1960 Bay M Inn (II-4-6713 fc 58/60); BayHStA, Bay M Inn 89684, 24.6.1960 B-W M Inn (IX 2550/29); BayHStA, Bay M Inn 89684, 13.6.1960 Hess M Arb, Volkswohlfahrt und Gesundheitswesen (Vb/52n, 12.01).

106. B Arch, B141/4676, folios 177–91, Janzen, "Das Versandhaus Beate Uhse und die Strafjustiz im Spannungsfeld zwischen Recht und Moral," Anlage zur Tagungsnieder-schrift der Zentralstellenleitertagung vom 21.–23.5.1959.

107. LASH 351/1696, passim; OStA Glang, "So geht es leider nicht!" *Monatsschrift für Deutsches Recht* 9, no. 8 (August 1955): 456–57.

108. HAEK, Gen. II, 23.30/7, 13.9.1955 Calmes to Generalvikar Prälat Josef Teusch (J. Nr. 2038).

109. LASH 351/1697, folios 233–35, 4.10.1955 Zentralstelle (47 Sbd.—1.116) to BMJ, S-H.

110. See also David K. Johnson, *The Lavender Scare: The Cold War Persecution of Gays and Lesbi-ans in the Federal Government* (Chicago: University of Chicago Press, 2004).

111. Karl Peters, "Der Begriff des Unzüchtigen in §184 Abs. 1 StGB," *Juristische Rundschau* 4 (1950): 97–99.

112. B Arch, B141/90246, folio 23c, 21.–26.1.1957 Grosse Strafrechtskommission III. Un-terkommission, Niederschrift über die 2. Arbeitstagung der III. Unterkommission.

113. FZH 18-9/1.2 (1), Rechtsurteil 15.–16.7.1952 LG Flensburg (5b Ms 179/51 [IB 107/52]) and Landgericht's rejection of Staatsanwaltschaft's application for appeal.

114. Hans-Werner Melzer and Bärbel Melzer, interview with the author, 9 September 2003, 57.

115. LASH 351/1774, 1.2.1972 StA bei dem LG (15 Js 1183/71) to Schoeffengericht: Antrag im ob-jektiven Verfahren.

116. Becker, "Stimme des Herausgebers," 49.

117. Kurt Halbritter, untitled comic, *Pardon* 3/6 (June 1964): 30; LASH 351/3027, folio 165, *Münchner Föhn* [September–October 1958]; "Galerie Dr. Filzinger, Amtsgerichtsrat," *Linkeck* 2 [March 1968], n.p. See also Friedrich Koch, *Sexuelle Denunziation: Die Sexualität in der politischen Auseinandersetzung* (Frankfurt am Main: Syndikat, 1986).

118. Jost Nolte, "Pornographie und Kunst" *Der neue Vertrieb* 14, no. 327 (5 December 1962): 1030.

119. Christian Gregor, "Pornosophie oder Verlegerfreuden mit *Fanny Hill*," *Pardon* 3, no. 3 (March 1964).

120. *Stimmt in unserer Ehe alles?* (Flensburg: Beate Uhse, 1952), 8.

121. FZH 18-9/1.2 (1), 28.1.1952 Beate Rotermund to GStA Schleswig; FZH 18-9/1.2 (1), 29.2.1952 OStA to Beate Rotermund.

122. According to family tradition, Schäfer was a member of the Labor Service and Wehr-macht from 1943 to 1945. He was wounded in the battle of Monte Casino and, from 19 January to 6 April 1945, was interned in Buchenwald as an alleged participant in the 20 July 1944 plot to assassinate Hitler. Institutions that maintain records of Buchen-wald internees and political persecutees are unable to confirm any portion of this his-tory. Rückführungsstelle für politische Häftlinge Sonderausweis KZ Walter Schäfer, personal photos, courtesy Jörg Dagies; e-mail communication with Stiftung Gedenk-stätten Buchenwald und Mittelbau-Dora, 23 May 2008; e-mail communication with In-ternational Tracing Service, 14 July 2008.

123. Schäfer/W.F.L. Urteil, 6–9; *Unsere Firma und Wir* (Schmiden bei Stuttgart: Firmengruppe Walter Schäfer, 1958). The figure in deutsche marks is for the first months after currency reform.

124. "Das muß man erlebt haben," *Der Spiegel* 12, no. 45 (5 November 1958): 56–57.

125. Lore Schumacher and Jörg Dagies, interview with the author, 4 September 2003.

126. The Alliance changed its name many times and now operates in Hamburg as the Bundesverband Erotik Handel. In the text I refer to the Alliance, in the footnotes to the VdV as the historical organization (regardless of intermittent name changes), and to the BEH as the location of the archive.

127. Private archive of the BEH, 24.6.1966 VdV Protokoll der Vorstandssitzung; BEH, 19.6.1969 VdV Protokoll der Vorstandssitzung; BEH, 7.11.1963 VdV Protokoll der Beirats- und Vorstandssitzung.

128. B Arch, B117/8, "VdV RdSchr. Nr. 8/52," cited in 10.3.1953 Schilling to Speidel; B Arch, B141/4675, folio 82, 15.12.1953 BMJ Vermerk (4736: 24046/53); also LASH 351/3027, 3.4.1958 VdV RdSchr. Nr. 9/58; WSG, VdV (ab 1968), 24.4.1968 Gromex Grosshandel GmbH to VdV.

129. BEH, 1.10.1965 Mitgliederstand; BEH, Vorschlag für Beitragsfestsetzung [1965]; Eberhard Strohm, interview with author, 2 April 2003, 9.

130. B Arch, B117/8, 10.3.1953 Schilling to Speidel.

131. B Arch, B141/26574, 6.6.1952 VdV to BMJ.

132. B Arch, B141/4687, folios 84–96, 21.10.1952 VdV to the members of the Reconciliation Committee; PA III/296B/9, VdV, Denkschrift und verfassungsrechtliche Würdigung [1960].

133. Schilling, *Das Geschäft mit der Erotik auf dem Gebiete des Zeitschriften- und Inseratenwesens*, 5; LASH 351/3519, folios 41–92, here 68, 23.–25.10.1962 Niederschrift, LZBujS.

134. WSG, Dr. E. Strohm Rechtsanwalt, passim; LASH 351/1778, 29.4.1960 Dr. jur. Werner Kutze to OLG Schleswig-Holstein; FZH 18-9/1.3 (1), 31.10.1958 E.S. to Beate Uhse.

135. E.g., FZH 18-9/1.2 (1), 14.11.1958 BPrSt Entscheidung Nr. 539; B Arch, B117/2, 1.12.1959 Statistik der Tätigkeit der BPrSt vom Beginn ihrer Tätigkeit.

136. By 1977, some 3,200 legal complaints had been filed against Beate Uhse and not a single conviction had resulted. Stadtarchiv Flensburg (StA Fl), XIII Pers. "3200 Ermittlungsverfahren gegen Sexfabrikantin Uhse," *Flensburg Avis*, 8 March 1977.

137. Strohm interview; FZH 18-9/2.4, 24.6.1992 Beate Rotermund, "Stories für Beate Uhse-Drehbuch."

138. Urteil des 5. Strafsenats des BGH vom 19.7.1955, 5 StR 12/55, BGH St 8, 125; see also LASH 351/3026.

139. Volkmar Sigusch, *Geschichte der Sexualwissenschaft* (Frankfurt. Campus, 2008).

140. Reichsgesetz zur Bekämpfung der Geschlechtskrankheiten vom 22.2.1927, RGBl 1927 I no. 9; Gesetz zur Bekämpfung der Geschlechtskrankheiten (GeschlKrG) vom 23.7.1953, BGBl I. 700; StGB 184, 3a.

141. B Arch, B142/1913, Niederschrift über die am 12.7.1954 im BGA Koblenz stattgefundene Besprechung des Genehmigungsverfahrens nach §20 des GeschlKrG, p. 2; B Arch, B142/1913, 4.5.1955 Bekanntmachung betr. das Genehmigungsverfahren nach §20 des GeschlKrG, Bundesanzeiger, Nr. 85; B Arch, B142/1913, 10.10.1960 Präsident, Bundesgesundheitsamt (R-4462-L 11-183/60) to BMI.

142. E.g., LASH 351/3026, BGH 5. Strafsenat 19.7.1955 (5 StR 12/55).

143. FZH 18-9/1.2, 15.–16.7.1952 Rechtsurteil LG Flensburg (5b Ms 179/51—Ns [IB 107/52]); FZH 18-9/1.2, 28.6.1951 Rechtsurteil Schöffengericht Flensburg (5b Ms 31/51 [142/51]).

144. For an "all-star" affidavit, see FZH 18-9/2.3, 27.11.1961 Fachwissenschaftliche Gutachten, signed by Bürger-Prinz, Harmsen, Hallermann, Gesenius, Giese, written for Fa. AWF-Gummiwarenfabrik.

145. FZH 18-9/3.1, 14.4.1952 Giese to AWF; Orion, Rechtsabteilung, file H, Volkmar Sigusch to Beate Rotermund, 11.6.74. See also "Petten und betten," *Der Spiegel* 23, no. 49 [15 December 1969]: 65–68.

146. Volkmar Sigusch, *Exzitation und Orgasmus bei der Frau: Physiologie der sexuellen Reaktion* (Stuttgart: Ferdinand Enke, 1970), which referenced Sigusch's legal brief "Fragen zum Orgasmus bei der Frau im Zusammenhang mit sexuellen Hilfsmittel," Sexualwissenschaftlich-medizinisches Gutachten, July 1968, courtesy of Volkmar Sigusch; Hans Giese, *Das obszöne Buch* (Stuttgart: Enke, 1965).

147. Ove Müller-Neff, "Sexuelle Hilfsmittel durch den Versandhandel: Analyse eines modernen Spezialversandhauses," Med. Diss., University of Hamburg, 1967.

148. Melzer and Melzer interview, 77–86; FZH 18-9/1.1, Jahresplan 1977.

149. *Gesunde Ehe—Glückliche Ehe*, Beate Uhse catalog, [1963], 3, 7.

150. B Arch, B117/16, 2.10.1953 Becker to Schilling; BayHStA, Bay M Inn 92079, 19.10.1954 BMI (J 1032 [1796/54]) betr. Mitwirkung der Polizei bei der Durchführung des GjS.

151. B Arch, B141/4688, folios 24–29, BGH 5. Strafsenat 16.2.1954 (5 StR 475/53); LASH 351/4020, folios 6–11, here 7, Auszug aus einem Urteil des LG Hamburg betr. die Firma Haku-Versand in Hamburg, Anlage 2 zum Beisitzerrundbrief Nr. 19 (BPrSt) [1962].

152. Josef Mueller-Marein, "Unbedenklich oder unzüchtig?" *Die Zeit*, 17 July 1964, as cited in "Die 'literarische Jugendgefährdung,'" *Der neue Vertrieb* 16, no. 373 (23 October 1964): 940.

153. BGH 7.5.1954; see also "Verkauf unzüchtiger Postkartenbilder ist strafbar," *Der neue Vertrieb* 11, no. 255 (5 December 1959): 824–25.

154. B Arch, B141/4688, folios 81–87, BGH 2. Strafsenat 7.5.1954 (2 StR 377/53); B Arch, B117/1, OLG Koblenz 2. Strafsenat 23.4.1958 (2 Ss 344/57) (13 Ms 49/56 StA Koblenz); B Arch, B141/4676, folios 195–201, 6.4.1959 BPrSt (Gen. 11/62) an LZBujS.

155. "Wann ist die Darstellung nackter Frauen als unzüchtig im Sinne des §184 StGB anzusehen? Beschluß des OLG Nürnberg v. 5.7.1961—Ws 103/61," *Juristische Rundschau* 12 (1961): 467–68; "Der jugendgefährdende Charakter von Druckschriften (4)," *Der neue Vertrieb* 7, no. 137 (5 January 1955): 8.

156. B Arch, B141/4688, BGH 5. Strafsenat 26.2.1954 (5 StR 481/53); "Wieder einmal die 'offensichtlich' schwere Jugendgefährdung," *Der neue Vertrieb* 9, no. 205 (5 November 1957): 650–51.

157. Peters, "Der Begriff des Unzüchtigen im §184 Abs. 1 StGB"; "OLG Neustadt a.d.W. Urteil vom 17.10.1951 (Ss 144/51)," *Juristische Rundschau* 7 (1952): 287; see also Schilling, "Der Bundesgerichtshof über die Normen der geschlechtlichen Sittlichkeit."

158. HHStA, 461/30079, 21.12.1949 Beschluß LG Ffm 1. Strafkammer (5 Js 3114/49) (5/1 Qs 220/49).

159. Schäfer/W.F.L. Urteil, 296.

160. Schäfer/W.F.L. Urteil, 331–36; LASH 351/1779, folios 69–70, 1.6.1967 StA Flensburg to Beate Rotermund.

161. The claim could also backfire; see LASH 351/3303, 22.4.1959 Hanseatisches OLG Urteil (Ss 3/59/[34] 145/58) (2a Js 243/55 J. Sch) (138 Cs 12/55).

162. LASH 351/1778, 5.1.1960 GStA Bayern to Zentralstelle S-H; B Arch, B141/4688, folios 63–66, 30.6.1953 LG Berlin 5. Grosse Strafkammer; Orion, Rechtsabt., file "Bio-Mensan," correspondence regarding "Bio-Mensan."

163. B Arch, B141/4688, folios 102–5, 3.8.1954 Ferienstrafsenat des BGH (2 StR 441/53).

164. B Arch, B141/4688, folios 137–40, 5.4.1955 BGH 5. Strafsenat (5 StR 542/54).

165. LASH 351/1778, 15.5.1956 OStA Flensburg to GStA Schleswig.

166. B Arch, B117/47, 18.10.1954 BMI (J 1032—1667/54) to VWB; see also LASH 351/3303, 27.8.1958 LG Wiesbaden 4. Strafkammer Berufungsurteil gegen A.E.R. (6 Ns 1/58) (85 Cs 537/57 AG Wiesbaden).

167. "Der 'Normalmensch' und die Sittenhüter," *Der neue Vertrieb* 18, no. 419 (10 October 1966): 916–20; B Arch, B117/47, 29.10.1953 Urteil Schöffengericht Dortmund (12 Ms 122/53; 12—834/53); Fritz J. Raddatz, "Zensurpraxis und Zensurbestrebungen in der Bundesrepublik," *Die Zeit*, 24 June 1966.

168. B Arch, B106/785, 5.5.1958 VdV an BMI. For a list of Schäfer's acquisitions, B Arch, B106/785, folios 80–116, here 108, 18.2.1960 Kurzprotokoll 38. Sitzung des DBT-AFJ.

169. BGH 18.11.1957—GSSt 2/57, *Neue juristische Wochenschrift* (6 February 1958): 228–29; Rudolf Thomsen, *Der erotisch-sexuelle Versandhandel* (Cologne-Klettenberg: Volkswartbund, 1958), 7–10.

170. LASH 351/3027, folios 158–64, 3.4.1958 VdV RdSchr, Nr. 9/58; B Arch, B141/26579, BPrSt Beisitzer-Rundbrief Nr. 17.

171. FZH 18-9/2.3, 1963–65.

172. StAL, EL 317 I/2342, folios 985–89, 11.5.1959 E.S. to the Grosse Strafkammer Landgericht Stuttgart; LASH 351/3310; Schumacher and Dagies interview.

173. Schumacher and Dagies interview, 27–28.

174. Josie McLellan, "State Socialist Bodies: East German Nudism from Ban to Boom," *Journal of Modern History* 79, no. 1 (2007): 48–79.

Chapter 3. The Economic Miracle in the Bedroom

1. WSG, loose papers, *Preisliste Nr. 25*, Gisela [ca. 1950].

2. Wildt, *Am Beginn der "Konsumgesellschaft."*

3. WSG, loose papers, two order forms filled out by H.G. and mailed together; see also FZH 18-9/2.3, Kundenreaktionen, 20.1.1956 Beate Uhse to Herr H.

4. Order forms required customers to declare their date of birth.

5. Roland Marchand, *Creating the Corporate Soul: The Rise of Public Relations and Corporate Imagery in American Big Business* (Berkeley: University of California Press, 1998); S. Jonathan Wiesen, *West German Industry and the Challenge of the Nazi Past, 1945–1955* (Chapel Hill: University of North Carolina Press, 2001).

6. Atina Grossmann, *Jews, Germans, and Allies: Close Encounters in Occupied Germany* (Princeton: Princeton University Press, 2007); Biess, *Homecomings*; Elizabeth D. Heineman, *What Difference Does a Husband Make? Women and Marital Status in Nazi and Postwar Germany* (Berkeley: University of California Press, 1999), 75–136.

7. Uhse, *Mit Lust und Liebe*, 100–103, quote at 100.

8. Rotermund recalls the book as Hans Jakob Gerster, *Die natürliche Geburtenregelung nach Knaus* (Dischingen: Wadi, 1950). Since this book was published after Rotermund's trip to the library, she probably saw an earlier version of the same work, most likely Hans Jakob Gerster, *Die Empfängnisverhütung auf natürlichem Wege nach Knaus* (Basel: Schwabe, 1937).

9. Schäfer/W.F.L. Urteil, 6–7.

10. HAEK, Dienstakten Böhler Nr. 172, Michael Calmes, "Schamlose Geschäfte! Der erotische Versandhandel," *VWB Mitteilungen* (October 1952).

11. Jürgen Weber, interview with the author, 3 September 2003.

12. HHStA 461/32036, 6.6.1951 statement of E.G. to police, Frankfurt am Main.

13. B Arch, B117/45, 19.2.1954 Urteil, Amtsgericht München (6 Ds 414/53); Claus Richter, interview with the author, 13 June 2003; StAL, FL 300/31, I Zugang 22.3.1982 Teil IV, Handelsakt Metropol-Versand.

14. HHStA 461/32036, 4.4.1955 E.G. to Hess MJus.

15. WSG, allg. Korrespondenz V–Z, 8.10.1954 Versand-Wöhler to WS.

16. Angela Delille and Andrea Grohn, "Hauptmann der Aufklärung," in *Wild Women: Furien, Flittchen, Flintenweiber*, ed. Baerbel Becker (Berlin: Elefanten-Press, 1992), 112–18, here 115; Uhse, *Mit Lust und Liebe*, 107.

17. PA III/296/A, Auszug aus den Gründen des Urteils der kl. Strafkammer des LG Tübingen vom 31. Jan. 58, II Ns 72 u. 252/56.

18. Schäfer/W.F.L. Urteil, 7–9; PA III/296/A, 18.2.1960 StA Wekenmann, Vortrag, Ausführungen der Sachverständigung, 10. Ausschuß, DBT 3. Wahlperiode, p. 55.

19. This figure emerged in an oral history and must be considered imprecise. No written records on exports survive. Schumacher and Dagies interview, 14 and 16.

20. Uhse, *Mit Lust und Liebe*, 162.

21. "Neckermann: Kataloge gegen Kartelle," *Der Spiegel* 9, no. 44 (26 October 1955): 18–29.

22. *sie sind glücklich! Rund um die Liebe: Ein Helfer und Führer für das Liebes- und Eheleben* (Flensburg: Beate Uhse, 1958), 10; see also *"Das mußte ich Ihnen einmal schreiben"* (Flensburg: Beate Uhse, 1963), passim.

23. StAL, EL 317 I, Bü 2339, "Alles Ansichtssache," aus einem Vortrag von W.L., VdV [ca. 1957].

24. BEH, Dr. med. E.L., "Statistisches Material aus dem Alltag."

25. Schäfer/W.F.L. Urteil, 52.

26. Emilie Fried and Paul Fried, *Liebes- und Eheleben: Ein praktischer Berater für die gesunde und harmonische Ehe* (Wolfenbüttel: Verlag der Freude, 1929). Beate Uhse's press obtained, revised, and reissued the book in 1957.

27. Ernst-Walter Rotermund grew up in a Flensburg shipping family and was active in Beate Uhse in the early years.

28. Melzer and Melzer interview, 91; Uhse, *Lustvoll in den Markt*, 57. See also FZH 18-9/2.3, "Liebe Mitarbeiter!" *Absender Beate* 2, no. 2 (April 1963): 1.

29. *Durch einen glücklichen Zufall* (Flensburg: Beate Uhse, n.d., ca. 1951), back cover. See also *Stimmt in unserer Ehe alles?* (1951). The 1952 catalog of the same name is a different work.

30. *Stimmt in unserer Ehe alles?* (1952). In contrast to general catalogs, specialty catalogs focusing on a particular sexual problem sometimes employed sex-specific titles. *Frau Müller will sich scheiden lassen? Die Frigidität der Frau: Ursachen und Überwindung* [ca. 1953–55]; *Mit Herrn Krüger stimmt was nicht! Die Impotenz des Mannes: Formen und Abhilfe* [ca. 1953–55]; *Was ist nur mit Renate? Das Notwendigste über zuverlässige Geburtenregelung* [ca. 1953–55].

31. The description in the text draws on the following general product catalogs. All appeared for many years with relatively minor revisions; here I give the probable date of first publication: *Die besten Jahre unseres Lebens: Ein Helfer und Führer für das Liebes-*

und Eheleben (Flensburg: Beate Uhse, 1958); Gesunde Ehe—Glückliche Ehe (1963); Glückliche Ehe, gesunde Ehe (Flensburg: Beate Uhse, 1964); sie sind glücklich! (1958); Stimmt in unserer Ehe alles? (1952). Specialty catalogs usually omitted the framing texts; see, however, Liebe: Uralt und immer wieder jung (Flensburg: Beate Uhse, n.d., ca. 1962), 16–17.

32. On Weimar reform, see Grossmann, Reforming Sex. On memories of women as victims, see Heineman, "Hour of the Woman." On hope for the family in the early FRG, see Moeller, Protecting Motherhood; Ruhl, Verordnete Unterordnung.

33. Stimmt in unserer Ehe alles? (1952) back cover.

34. Hans-Dieter Thomsen, interview with the author, 17 June 2003, 29.

35. FZH 18-9/2.5, Folgerungen aus der Emnid-Untersuchung für die PR-Arbeit 14.4.1964, Folgerungen aus der Emnid-Untersuchung für die Werbung 8.4.1964.

36. Die besten Jahre unseres Lebens.

37. sie sind glücklich! 72; Gesunde Ehe—Glückliche Ehe, 18.

38. sie sind glücklich! 9; Liebe: Uralt und immer weider jung, 16; Liebe, das schönste Wort auf Erden! (Flensburg: Beate Uhse, n.d., ca. 1960); Uhse, Lustvoll in den Markt, photo insert following 96.

39. sie sind glücklich! 5; Marchand, Creating the Corporate Soul.

40. sie sind glücklich! 106.

41. Stimmt in unserer Ehe alles? (1952), 22. On post–World War II discussions of impotence, see Angus McLaren, Impotence: A Cultural History (Chicago: University of Chicago Press, 2007).

42. FZH 18-9/2.5, Folgerungen aus der Emnid-Untersuchung für die Werbung 8.4.1964.

43. BU (Flensburg: Beate Uhse, n.d., ca. 1958); Eros, Glück und Liebe (Flensburg: Beate Uhse, n.d., ca. 1962).

44. Gesunde Ehe—Glückliche Ehe, 6.

45. The firm moved from Stuttgart-Cannstatt to the farming village of Schmiden in 1956.

46. WSG, loose papers, "Was viele Frauen NICHT wußten!" "Fotos und Zeichnungen für Sammler" advertising flyers, Internationales Verandhaus Gisela, ca. 1948.

47. WSG, Leben und nicht verzichten! 34. Trizonia was the unified economic administration of the French, British, and U.S. zones of occupation. "Fräulein" was the term that occupation soldiers used to address German women whom they sought to attract. "Demontage" was the Soviet practice of dismantling German industrial plant for shipment to the USSR.

48. Was wir alle von der Ehe oft nicht wissen (Stuttgart: WSG, 1957); Glück oder Unglück in der Liebe? Unglückliche oder glückliche Ehen? (Fellbach Württemberg: WSG, n.d., ca. 1957); Preisliste Nr. 7 (Stuttgart: WSG, 1957); Wollen wir ein offenes Gespräch unter vier Augen führen? (Stuttgart: WSG, n.d., ca. 1957); StAL, EL 317 I, 2342, Freyja Versand, Wollen wir ein mal offen miteinander reden? (Stuttgart: WSG, n.d., ca. 1957).

49. WSG, Beate Uhse, 14.1.1964 Beate Uhse to Freyja Verlag.

50. Was wir alle von der Ehe oft nicht wissen, 58, 61. See also Der Schlüssel zum Glück (Stuttgart, n.d., ca. 1956), n.p.

51. Preisliste Nr. 7, passim.

52. WSG, Leben und nicht verzichten!

53. Die richtige Wahl [ca. 1957]. Mancher Ehekrach bleibt aus—Hast Du O-Garant im Haus! (O-Garant, suggesting "guaranteed orgasm," was a ring to be slipped over the penis with a protrusion to increase clitoral stimulation.) Number of leaflets from Schäfer/ W.F.L. Urteil, 72.

54. *Glück oder Unglück in der Liebe?* 62.

55. Ibid.; *Wollen wir ein offenes Gespräch unter vier Augen führen?*

56. *Was wir alle von der Ehe oft nicht wissen.*

57. Schäfer/W.F.L. Urteil, 291.

58. *Die besten Jahre unseres Lebens,* 102; *Wollen wir ein offenes Gespräch unter vier Augen führen?* 34; *Glück oder Unglück in der Liebe?* 38; *BU,* n.p.

59. See also B Arch, B106/777, "Eine ernste Frage," Patentex catalog (1958).

60. Biess, *Homecomings;* Fehrenbach, "Rehabilitating Fatherland"; Moeller, *War Stories;* Thomas Kühne, "Zwischen Vernichtungskrieg und Freizeitgesellschaft: Die Veteranenkultur der Bundesrepublik (1945–1995)," in Naumann, *Nachkrieg in Deutschland,* 90–113.

61. Schumacher and Dagies interview; Dirk Rotermund, interview with the author, 8 September 2003.

62. *Die besten Jahre unseres Lebens,* 141–50.

63. FZH 18-9/1.2(1), 28.6.1961 Sitzung Schöffengericht Flensburg (5b Ms. 31/51 [142/51]); BEH, Dr. med. E.L., "Statistisches Material aus dem Alltag." No comparable data for Schäfer's firms have survived.

64. W. Pohl, "Der Bezieherkreis unzüchtiger Schriften und Bilder," *Kriminalstatistik* 8 (1954): 237–39; "Die Jugend ist besser als ihr Ruf!" *Der neue Vertrieb* 7, no. 152 (20 August 1955): 453; StAL, EL 317 I, Bü 2343, folios 1024–35, 26.11.1960 Hans Giese, fachwissenschaftliche Gutachten.

65. StAL, EL 317 I, Bü 2342, folios 332–39, 25.7.1957 Landeskriminalpolizei HildesheimTgb. Nr. 3811/57.

66. Hans-Dieter Thomsen, interview with the author, 5 March 2003. On 1968, see Herbert G. Hegedo, *Die sexuellen Wünsche der Deutschen* (Hamburg: CITA-Bücher, 1969). In 1988, Uhse again claimed a figure of 70 percent; FZH 18-9/2.3, Öffentliche Anhörung der SPD-Bundestagsfraktion zur Problematik der Pornographie am 13. und 14. September 1988, Ausführung von Beate Uhse.

67. Thomsen interviews.

68. FZH 18-9/2.3, "Wir fragen uns," *Absender Beate* 1, no. 1 (February 1962): 2.

69. Pohl, "Der Bezieherkreis." The "married" category included divorced and widowed women.

70. Melzer and Melzer interview, 21–24; Dirk Rotermund, interview with the author, 19 June 2003, 27.

71. Max Kohlhaas, "Keine sittlich schwere Gefährdung der Jugend?" *Unsere Jugend* 8, no. 2 (1956): 82–85.

72. E.g., LASH 786/2421, folios 2–24, here 11, 17.3.1959 OStA (5 Js 1089/58) Strafkammeranklage gegen Beate Rotermund; WSG, Versandbuchhandlung Karl Raab, 23.3.1963 Verlag Karl Raab to Freyja Verlag.

73. Orion, Geschäftsführer, "Beate Uhse: Eine kombinierte Motiv-Image-Studie" (Frankfurt am Main: PMS Institut für psychologische Markt- und Sozialforschung, 1972), 24.

74. FZH 18-9/1.2(1), Landgericht Flensburg denial of Berufung der Staatsanwaltschaft (5b Ms 179/51 [IB 107/52]); WSG, loose papers, 14.9.1952 Ernst Beckman to Walter Schäfer; Melzer and Melzer interview, 21–24; Dirk Rotermund interview, 19 June 2003, 27.

75. Melzer and Melzer interview, 25.

76. Sibylle Meyer and Eva Schulze, *Auswirkungen des II. Weltkrieges auf Familien* (Berlin: Gerhard Weitner, 1989).

77. *Intim: Der interessante Katalog für Eheleute* (Stuttgart-Untertürkheim, n.d., ca. 1959), 43.

78. *"Das mußte ich Ihnen einmal schreiben,"* 26. The only hard data on the subject come from a much later period: a 1996 survey of customers of Beate Uhse showed that 60.7 percent of customers examined their catalogs with their partners. FZH 18-9/2.3, John David Prescott, "Beate Uhse Company Report," 1996. At the time, some 80 percent of customers lived in steady relationships. FZH 18-9/2.3, "The Story of Beate Uhse," PR brochure, August 1992.

79. WSG, loose papers, 7.1.1953 H.W. to Fa. Gisela.

80. *"Das mußte ich Ihnen einmal schreiben,"* 34.

81. The "primers" evolved not only as new information on sex emerged, but also as social concerns changed; the "population bomb" appeared first in 1963 in *Gesunde Ehe—Glückliche Ehe.*

82. FZH 18-9/2.3, Kundenreaktionen, A.L. to Beate Uhse, n.d.

83. Dr. med. M. Rinard, *Unter vier Augen: Die hohe Schule der Gattenliebe* (Heidenheim: Hoffmann, 1949); Richard Wunderer, *Hygiene des Sexuallebens* (Karlsruhe: Moll, 1951).

84. Sander Gilman, "The Struggle of Psychiatry with Psychoanalysis: Who Won?" *Critical Inquiry* 13 (1987): 293–313; Jane F. Gerhard, *Desiring Revolution: Second-Wave Feminism and the Rewriting of American Sexual Thought, 1920 to 1982* (New York: Columbia University Press, 2001), 13–80; McLaren, *Impotence.*

85. *Beiträge zur Sexualforschung,* passim.

86. See also Uli Linke, *German Bodies: Race and Representation after Hitler* (New York: Routledge, 1999).

87. Adolf Tüllmann, *Das Liebesleben der Naturvölker* (Stuttgart: Günther, 1960); Adolf Tüllmann, *Das Liebesleben der Kulturvölker* (Stuttgart: Günther, 1961); Herbert Lewandowski, *Ferne Länder fremde Sitten* (Stuttgart: Günther, 1958).

88. "Edition VITUS," advertising flyer by Beate Uhse [ca. 1957].

89. WSG, *Leben und nicht verzichten!*

90. Beate Uhse, *Ein ernstes Problem glücklich gelöst* (Flensburg: Beate Uhse, n.d., ca. 1953–55).

91. Alon Confino, "Dissonance, Normality and the Historical Method: Why Did Some Germans Think of Tourism after May 8, 1945?" in *Life after Death: Approaches to a Cultural and Social History of Europe during the 1940s and 1950s,* ed. Richard Bessel and Dirk Schumann (Cambridge: Cambridge University Press, 2003), 323–47.

92. Rudy Koshar, *German Travel Cultures* (New York: Berg, 2000).

93. Eustace Chesser, *Die befreite Ehe: Freiheit in der Ehe und durch die Ehe,* trans. Karl Friedrich (Stuttgart: Günther, 1952). On the sense of having fallen behind, see *Stimmt in unserer Ehe alles?* (1951).

94. "Wie die Frauen sind," *Der Spiegel* 4, no. 31 (3 August 1950): 24–27; "Der Kinsey-Bericht," *Herder-Korrespondenz* 8 (1954): 475–82; Dagmar Herzog, "The Reception of the Kinsey Reports in Europe," *Sexuality and Culture* 10, no. 1 (2006).

95. *Die besten Jahre unseres Lebens,* 20. The book by the Christian marriage counselor was Theodor Bovet, *Die Ehe: Das Geheimnis ist groß* (Tübingen: Katzmann, 1958). For Guardians-approved books, see WSG, Schmitz Verlag München ab 1964, passim; Melzer and Melzer interview, 53; Dirk Rotermund interview, 19 June 2003, 39.

96. FZH 18-9/2.3, Kundenreaktionen, 25.2.1995 K.-H.B. to Beate Uhse.

97. *Stimmt in unserer Ehe alles?* (1952), 10; *Gesunde Ehe—Glückliche Ehe,* 81; *Was wir alle von der Ehe oft nicht wissen,* 77.

98. In the first half of 1960, one firm (probably Beate Uhse) received some 225 letters per day requesting advice. Giese, Fachwissenschaftliche Gutachten. See also StA Fl XIII Dr.

25, "Wem interessiert das schon? Wir dachten: zum Beispiel SIE!" PR brochure, Beate Uhse, 1962. See also Müller-Neff, "Sexuelle Hilfsmittel durch den Versandhandel."

99. Schumacher and Dagies interview; WSG, Umsatzmeldungen, Umsatzmeldungen 1958.

100. B Arch, B117/2, Humanistische Union petition to the Bundestag [late 1963]; "Geburten-regelung in Europa (5. Teil)," *Constanze* (1 October 1963): 7–9, 52. In 1961, Pro Familia (Planned Parenthood) had only three counseling centers nationwide. Ralf Dose, "Die Implantation der Antibabypille in den sechziger und siebziger Jahren," *Zeitschrift für Sexualforschung* 3 (1990): 25–39.

101. Criticizing erotica firms for misleading advertisements regarding chemical aids, see B Arch, B142/1439, 21.10.1955 Interessengemeinschaft Heilmittelwerbung eV to BMI. For admissions of ineffectiveness by industry sympathizers, see FZH 18-9/1.2(1), Rechtsurteil 15.–16.7.1952 LG Flensburg (5b Ms 179/51 [IB 107/52]); "Sex per Post," *DM* 12 (1968): 34–37, here 37. On customers' lesser interest in these products, see "Beate Uhse: Eine kombinierte Motiv-Image-Studie," 144.

102. Dirk Rotermund interview, 19 June 2003.

103. Sponges and pessaries sold in very small numbers. WSG, allg. Korrespondenz V–Z, 10.1.1956 WS an die Firma Wulz und Kopp Hygienische Artikel.

104. Thomsen interviews, 5 March 2003, 40–43, and 17 June 2003; Dirk Rotermund inter-view, 19 June 2003, 31, 34, 41; Uhse, *Mit Lust und Liebe*, 131.

105. Ludwig von Friedeburg, *Die Umfrage in der Intimsphäre* (Stuttgart: Enke, 1953), 88.

106. Giese, Fachwissenschaftliche Gutachten; BEH, Dr. med. E.L., "Statistisches Material aus dem Alltag," 7; *Gesunde Ehe—Glückliche Ehe*. E.L.'s data are certainly and Giese's probably from Beate Uhse.

107. B Arch, B141/26581, Niederschrift, LZBuJS vom 22.–24.9.1965, Referat "Vertrieb von Go-demiches," 1. StA Bohm, Zentralstelle Bremen.

108. W.P. letters to Beate Uhse, March 26, 1955, and December 17, 1960, in author's pos-session.

109. "*Das mußte ich Ihnen einmal schreiben*," 18.

110. Cornelia Filter, "Beate Uhse: Bomber Pilotin und Porno Produzentin," *Emma*, no. 3 (March 1988): 26–31; Delille and Grohn, "Hauptmann der Aufklärung."

111. Victoria de Grazia, "Changing Consumption Regimes in Europe, 1930–1970: Compar-ative Perspectives on the Distribution Problem," in *Getting and Spending: European and American Consumer Societies in the Twentieth Century*, ed. Susan Strasser, Charles McGov-ern, and Matthias Judt (Cambridge: Cambridge University Press, 1998), 59–84.

Chapter 4. Interlude: The Beate Uhse Myth

1. *Gesunde Ehe—Glückliche Ehe*, 5.

2. Melzer and Melzer interview; Dirk Rotermund interview, 10 September 2003, 17.

3. Marchand, *Creating the Corporate Soul;* Wiesen, *West German Industry;* Paul Erker, "'A New Business History'? Neuere Ansätze und Entwicklungen in der Unternehmensge-schichte," *Archiv für Sozialgeschichte* 42 (2002): 557–604.

4. Georg Wamhof, ed., *Das Gericht als Tribunal* (Göttingen: Wallstein, 2009); Edward Beren-son, *The Trial of Madame Caillaux* (Berkeley: University of California Press, 1992); George Robb and Nancy Erber, *Disorder in the Court: Trials and Sexual Conflict at the Turn of the Century* (New York: New York University Press, 1999).

5. Judith R. Walkowitz, *City of Dreadful Delight: Narratives of Sexual Danger in Late-Victorian*

London (Chicago: University of Chicago Press, 1992); Vanessa R. Schwartz, *Spectacular Realities: Early Mass Culture in Fin-de-Siècle Paris* (Berkeley: University of California Press, 1998); Gudrun Kruip, *Das "Welt"—"Bild" des Axel Springer Verlags* (Munich: Beck, 1999).

6. *Gesunde Ehe—Glückliche Ehe*, 6.

7. Uhse, *Mit Lust und Liebe*, 180–82; Melzer and Melzer interview, 47. The indictment quoted here was written no earlier than 1966, but in Rotermund's mind it was clearly of a piece with the tennis club story. Earlier indictments (and judgments) employed language similar to the one Rotermund quotes.

8. FZH 18-9/1.2(1), 29.9.1953 LG Flensburg (5b Ms 31/51 [IB 67/53]).

9. Klaus-Detlev Godau-Schüttke, *Die Heyde-Sawade-Affäre: Wie Juristen und Mediziner den NS-Euthanasiprofessor Heyde nach 1945 deckten und straflos blieben* (Baden-Baden: Nomos Verlag, 1998).

10. LASH 786 passim; see also Klaus-Detlev Godau-Schüttke, *Ich habe nur dem Recht gedient: Die "Renazifizierung" der Schleswig-Holsteinischen Justiz nach 1945* (Baden-Baden: Nomos Verlag, 1993).

11. Curt Garner, "Public Service Personnel in West Germany in the 1950s," in *West Germany under Construction: Politics, Society, and Culture in the Adenauer Era*, ed. Robert G. Moeller (Ann Arbor: University of Michigan Press, 1997).

12. Paul Erker and Toni Pierenkemper, *Deutsche Unternehmer zwischen Kriegswirtschaft und Wiederaufbau* (Munich: Oldenbourg, 1999).

13. Volker Berghahn, "Recasting Bourgeois Germany," in Schissler, *Miracle Years*, 326–40; see also Dirk Rotermund interview, 19 June 2003, 48–49.

14. Not all elements of the biography appear in all judgments, but all listed here appear by 1953. One of the most complete is the following: FZH 18-9/1.2(1), 29.9.1953 I. Grosse Strafkammer des Landgerichts in Flensburg (5b Ms 179/51 [IB 66/53]). Hjalmar Schacht, former president of the Reichsbank, was a distant cousin—and offered both advice and start-up funds for her postwar business; this fact does not appear in court documents. Jürgen Hobrecht, *Beate Uhse: Chronik eines Lebens* (Flensburg: Beate Uhse Holding GmbH, 2003), 35.

15. Uhse, *Mit Lust und Liebe*, 120.

16. LASH 351/1778(a), folios 10–15, 27.9.1951, I. Grosse Strafkammer des LG in Flensburg (5b Ms 31/51), here 14–15.

17. FZH 18-9/1.2(1), 28.1.1952 Beate Rotermund to the GStA Schleswig. Rotermund's father moved from Württemberg to East Prussia in 1917.

18. LASH 351/1778(a), folios 1–9, here 9, 28.6.1951 Schöffengericht Flensburg (5b Ms 31/51); LASH 351/1778(a), folios 10–15, here 15, I. Grosse Strafkammer des LG Flensburg (Ms 31/51 [IB 124/51]); FZH 18-9/1.2(1), 28.1.1952 Beate Rotermund to GStA Schleswig.

19. E.g., FZH 18-9/1.2(1), 28.10.1958 Sitzung II. Grosse Strafkammer des LG in Aachen (6 KMs 1/56: II 146/58); see also Uhse, *Lustvoll in den Markt*, 59; Melzer and Melzer interview.

20. E.g., FZH 18-9/1.2(1), 15.–16.7.1952 LG Flensburg (5 Ms 31/51), p. 4.

21. LASH 786/2421, folio 89, "Inhaberin eines Flensburger Versandhauses erneut angeklagt," *Kieler Nachrichten* 29.11.1961.

22. StAL, EL 317 I, Bü 2341, folios 89–92, 20.11.1962 Sitzung I. Strafsenat des Bundesgerichtshofs (1 StR 426/62); LASH 351/4020, folios 6–11, esp. 11, Auszug aus einem Urteil des LG Hamburg betr. die Fa. Haku-Versand (H.K.) in Hamburg, Anlage 2 zum Beisitzerrundbrief nr. 19 (BPrSt) [1962]; Hans W. Müller, "Eindeutige Zweideutigkeiten," *Der neue Vertrieb* 4, no. 67 (5 February 1952): 49–50.

23. Erich Kuby, *Rosemarie* (New York: Knopf, 1960).

24. Uhse, *Lustvoll in den Markt*, 18–40, 57.

25. Clippings in LASH 351/1778 (a).

26. FZH 18-9/2.3, 3.7.2000 Vortrag Marketing Club, Bremen.

27. Wiesen, *West German Industry*.

28. FZH 18-9/1.2, 7.11.1958 Beate Uhse to the BPrSt. The brochure mentioned in this letter, "Wir über uns," does not survive.

29. FZH 18-9/2.3, Edna Nageshkar, "Unser Presse-Referent," *Absender Beate* 5, no. 1 (February 1966): 3. See also FZH 18-9/2.3, "Liebe Mitarbeiter!" 1.

30. "Der 'unbekannte' Nachbar den Millionen kennen," PR brochure, 1961. See also "Wen interessiert das schon? Wir dachten: zum Beispiel SIE!" PR brochure, 1962.

31. Clippings in LASH 786/2421; "Jugendschutzgesetz umstritten," *Stuttgarter Nachrichten*, 30 November 1961.

32. LASH 786/2421, folio 93, Veronika [no last name], "Bundesverfassungsgericht soll entscheiden," *Flensburger Presse*, 14 December 1961.

33. Melzer and Melzer interview; Dirk Rotermund interviews, 19 June 2003, and 10 September 2003, 11; Uhse, *Mit Lust und Liebe*, 166.

34. FZH 18-9/2.5, Folgerungen aus der Emnid-Untersuchung für die PR-Arbeit, 14.4.1964.

35. "Aufklärung für Erwachsene (5.Teil)," *Constanze* (1 October 1963): 6–9, 52; "Par 218: Abtreibung," directed by Peter v. Jahn and Peter Nischk, broadcast 1. Deutsches Fernsehen, 24 October 1966.

36. "Beate Uhse: Dieses und jenes," *Der Spiegel* 19, no. 22 (1965): 92–93; see also "Rapid Turnover on Supermarket for Sex," *German Tribune* [repr. *Süddeutsche Zeitung*], 20 August 1966, 15; Gert Kistenmacher, "Die Geschichte von Beate Uhse," *Der Stern*, no. 10 (1966): 152–59; "Was hält Herr Uhse von Frau Uhse?" *Jasmin* (14 October 1968): 63–76. Foreign coverage of the Luftwaffe episode was often more pointed, e.g., FZH 18-9/2.1, "Länsberg, Ullerstam lärare i kontinentens största kärleksskola," *Norrländska Social-demokraten*, 23 November 1966, 1; FZH 18-9/2.1, "Cette Allemande veut pervertir les français," [unidentified tabloid], 30 May 1966; FZH 18-9/2.1, George Edwards, "Flying Frau Heads a Sex Empire," *News of the World*, 17 April 1966. The U.S. media began to cover the *Playboy* empire in the same way that it covered other businesses in the early 1960s. Frederick S. Lane, *Obscene Profits: The Entrepreneurs of Pornography in the Cyber Age* (New York: Routledge, 2000).

37. Heineman, *What Difference Does a Husband Make?*

38. Moeller, *War Stories*; Biess, *Homecomings*.

39. E.g., the collection of editorials opposing the GjS in BayHStA, Bay M Inn 92083. On the print media's defense of its liberal privileges (despite its social conservatism), see Lutz Hachmeister and Friedemann Siering, eds., *Die Herren Journalisten: Die Elite der deutschen Presse nach 1945* (Munich: Beck, 2002).

40. Maria Höhn, *GIs and Fräuleins: The German-American Encounter in 1950s West Germany* (Chapel Hill: University of North Carolina Press, 2002); Angela Delille and Andrea Grohn, "Von leichten Mädchen, Callgirls, und PKW-Hetären," in Becker, *Wild Women*, 112–18.

41. Poiger, *Jazz, Rock, and Rebels*.

42. E.g., "Anti-Baby Pillen," *Der Spiegel* (26 February 1964): 75–89; see also Gisela Staupe and Lisa Vieth, eds., *Die Pille: von der Lust und von der Liebe* (Berlin: Rowohlt, 1996).

43. Bernhard Rieger, "Fast Couples: Technology, Gender and Modernity in Britain and Ger-

many during the Nineteen-Thirties," *Historical Research* 76 (2003): 364-88; Peter Fritzsche, *A Nation of Fliers: German Aviation and the Popular Imagination* (Cambridge: Harvard University Press, 1992); Guillaume de Syon, *Zeppelin! Germany and the Airship, 1900-1939* (Baltimore: Johns Hopkins University Press, 2002).

44. Dirk Rotermund intervew, 19 June 2003, 57-58.

45. *Gesunde Ehe—Glückliche Ehe*, inside back cover.

46. Dirk Rotermund interview, 10 September 2003, 17; see also Melzer and Melzer interview, 69.

47. "Rangsdorf: Ein Flugfeld wird sechzig," *Fliegerrevue* 7 (1996): 35-38; see also clippings in FZH 18-9/2.4.

Chapter 5. The Sex Wave

1. Kloeckner, "Kesseltreiben gegen das GjS." On the language of "waves," see Andersen, *Der Traum vom guten Leben.*

2. A. J. Nichols, *Freedom with Responsibility* (Oxford: Oxford University Press, 1994).

3. Doering-Manteuffel, "Die 'Frommen' und die 'Linken.'"

4. BayStA, Bay M Inn 92020, Dr. Max Kohlhaas, "Zur Problematik des Verkaufs von Gummischutzmitteln aus Strassenautomaten" [ca. 1959].

5. LASH 351/1779, 20.12.1968 Anmerkung GStA Schleswig-Holstein.

6. Willy Brandt, Regierungserklärung, 28 October 1969, in Willy Brandt, *Berliner Ausgabe*, ed. Helga Grebing, Gregor Schöllgen, and Heinrich August Winkler (Bonn: Dietz, 2001), 7:218-24; Gustav W. Heinemann, "Der mündige Bürger in Staat und Gesellschaft," speech of 11 February 1973, in Gustav W. Heinemann, *Allen Bürgern verpflichtet: Reden des Bundespräsidenten 1968-1974* (Frankfurt am Main: Suhrkamp, 1975), 263-69; see also Metzler, "Der lange Weg zur sozialliberalen Politik," 157-80.

7. Eva-Maria Silies, "Selbst verantwortete Lebensführung: Der Streit um die Pille im katholischen Milieu," in Knoch, *Bürgersinn mit Weltgefühl*, 205-24; Eva-Maria Silies, "Familienplanung und Bevölkerungswachstum als religiöse Herausforderung," *Historical Social Research* 32 (2007): 187-207; Thomas Großbölting, "Als Laien und Genossen das Fragen lernten," in Frese, Paulus, and Teppe, *Demokratisierung und gesellschaftlicher Aufbruch*, 147-80, esp. 153.

8. "Unerschöpfliches Thema für Kritiker: 'Die Illustrierten'" *Der neue Vertrieb* 14, no. 31 (25 April 1962): 296-304, here 302.

9. Ulrich Beer, "Die Sexualisierung der Öffentlichkeit und der jungen Mensch," *Blätter der Wohlfahrtspflege* 110, no. 2 (1963): 35-52.

10. "Unerschöpfliches Thema für Kritiker," 296.

11. B Arch, B117/41, 16.7.1957, StA Schilling to BMI.

12. Fehrenbach, *Cinema in Democratizing Germany.*

13. Woycke, *Birth Control in Germany*, 113.

14. Annette F. Timm, "Sex with a Purpose: Prostitution, Venereal Disease, and Militarized Masculinity in the Third Reich," *Journal of the History of Sexuality* 11, no. 1-2 (2002): 223-55.

15. Pieter Lagrou, *The Legacy of Nazi Occupation: Patriotic Memory and National Recovery in Western Europe, 1945-1965* (New York: Cambridge University Press, 2000).

16. Private archive of Claus Richter, Rotenburg, Dokumentation dlf, "Vertriebswege/Verpackungsgrößen/Die Kondomanbieter," Condomdokumentation; Arthur Neupert,

Gerhard Potrykus, and Max Kohlhaas, "Zum Begriff des 'Feilbietens' in Par. 41a GewO," *Recht der Jugend* 10, no. 5 (August 1962): 225–29.

17. HAEK, Gen. II, 23/30, Nr. 4, 10.2.1951 Erzbischöfliches Ordinariat, Freiburg, an das badische M Inn in Freiburg, Anlage: Westav-Automaten-Kunden.

18. BayHStA, Bay M Inn 92020, 17.9.1958 Prof. Dr. R. M. Bohnstedt, Stellungnahme zum Entwurf des 4. Bundesgesetzes zur Änderung der Gewerbeordnung (betr. Par. 41 Abs. 4); Kohlhaas, "Zur Problematik des Verkaufs von Gummischutzmitteln aus Strassenautomaten"; Eberhard Schätzing, "Psychologie der 'Geburtenregelung,'" *Münchener medizinische Wochenschrift* 104 (1962).

19. Gerhard Potrykus, "Zur Frage des Schutzmittelverkaufs aus Automaten," *Gewerbearchiv* 5, no. 4 (1959).

20. Quickest to join the battle against the machines was the misleadingly named Landesarbeitsgemeinschaft zur Bekämpfung der Geschlechtskrankheiten Nord Rhine-Westfalen (NRW), founded by Guardians head Michael Calmes to battle such public health strategies as prophylaxis. LANRW, Dü, NW 18, Nr. 142, folios 33–36, 25.10.1950 Protokoll über die 6. Mitgliederversammlung der Landesarbeitsgemeinschaft zur Bekämpfung der Geschlechtskrankheiten NRW; LANRW, Dü, NW 18, Nr. 142, folio 8, 14.3.1949 Sozialminister NRW to Kultusministerium NRW.

21. BayHStA, Bay M Inn 92021, 26.7.1961 III. Kleine Strafkammer bei dem LG Nürnberg-Fürth (638 Ns 541/61).

22. "Gemischtautomaten und Jugendschutz," *Jugendwohl* 37, no. 5 (1956): 192–93; Paula Linhard, "Aktion Jugendschutz, Folge 20/21," *Bayerischer Wohlfahrtsdienst* 3/4 (1959): 1–4.

23. B Arch, B142/1913, 21.7.1954 VWB (J. Nr. 1476 Dr. C/D) an das BMI Abt. Gesundheit; LASH 351/3027, 11.2.1959 GStA Baden-Württemberg.

24. Walter Becker, "Jugendschutz und Verwaltungsgericht," *Jugendschutz* 3, no. 2 (1958): 20–22; Potrykus, "Zur Frage des Schutzmittelverkaufs aus Automaten."

25. Gerald Sammet, "Das Kondom," in *Die Galerie der kleinen Dinge*, ed. Heiner Boehncke and Klaus Bergmann (Zurich: Haffmans Verlag, 1988).

26. Lizabeth Cohen, *A Consumer's Republic: The Politics of Mass Consumption in Postwar America* (New York: Knopf, 2003).

27. Bundesverwaltungsgericht (BVG) Beschluß v. 10.3.1958—1 Bv L 42/56 (OLG Hamm), *Neue juristische Wochenschrift* 11, no. 1 (1958): 865–66.

28. PA III/296/A, 18.2.1960 Ausführungen der Sachverständigen in der Sitzung des AFJ, Referat Montanus, 63–65, here 63.

29. B Arch, B141/4685, Gert Dietz, "Grundsätzliches zum Schmutz- und Schundgesetz" (Cologne: VWB, n.d., ca. 1959–60).

30. PA III/296/A/8, Anlage 2 zum Protokoll Nr. 35 des 10. Ausschusses, DBT 3. Wahlperiode 1957.

31. Robert Schilling, "Reform des GjS?" *Der neue Vertrieb* 11, no. 245 (5 July 1959): 377–80.

32. PA III/296/A/12, 10.3.1960 Kurzprotokoll, 40. Sitzung des AFJ, DBT 3. Wahlperiode, 38ff., here 40.

33. Robert Schilling, "Die Novelle zum Gesetz über die Verbreitung jugendgefährdender Schriften (GjS)," *Recht der Jugend* 9, no. 7 (April 1961): 97–101; PA III/296/A/8, Kurzgefasster Erfahrungsbericht des BMI, Anlage 1 zum Protokoll Nr. 35 des 10. Ausschusses.

34. B Arch, B141/26577, 28.11.1961 I. Grosse Strafkammer des LG Flensburg, Beschluß (5 KMs 1/60) (I 2353/59); see also "Um die Verfassungsmässigkeit von Par. 6 Abs. 2 GjS," *Der neue Vertrieb* 13, no. 303 (5 December 1961): 1023–24.

35. B Arch, B141/26578, 20.8.1959 Zentralstelle München; Arthur Neupert, "Präservative aus Automaten?" (Cologne: VWB, 1962); BayHStA, Bay M Inn 92021, 26.7.1961 III. Kleine Strafkammer bei dem LG Nürnberg-Fürth (638 Ns 541/61); BayHStA, Bay M Inn 92021, 17.7.1961 III. Kleine Strafkammer bei dem LG Nürnberg-Fürth (503 Ns 428/61).

36. BayHStA, Bay M Inn 92020, 1.6.1959 Horst Ganske to Bay M Inn.

37. BGH-Urteil v. 17.3.1959—1 StR 562/58 (LG München) *Neue juristische Wochenschrift* 12, no. 1 (1959): 1092–93. The two decisions are summarized in Gerhard Potrykus, "Zur Frage des Schutzmittelverkaufs aus Strassenautomaten," *Monatsschrift für Deutsches Recht* 14, no. 9 (1960): 726–29.

38. BayHStA, Bay M Inn 92020, 15.5.1960 Hanseatische Gummiwarenfabrik, Bremen, "Merkblatt für den Verkauf von Fromms-Erzeugnissen aus Aussenautomaten"; BayHStA, Bay M Inn 92021, 26.7.1961 III. Kleine Strafkammer bei dem LG Nürnberg-Fürth (638 Ns 541/61).

39. BayHStA, Bay M Inn 92021, 23.11.1961 Urteil des Bay OLG (R Reg. 4 St 224/1961).

40. 4. Gesetz zur Änderung der Gewerbeordnung vom 5.2.1960 (BGBl I 61ff.).

41. "Gummischutzmittel in Warenautomaten," *Recht der Jugend* 10, no. 16 (August 1962): 234–35; BayHStA, Bay M Inn 92022, 22.2.1962 Amtsblatt des Bayerischen Staatsministeriums für Wirtschaft und Verkehr (Gewerbeordnung [GewO] Par. 41a), 35; BayHStA, Bay M Wi 26127, 8.6.1961 VG Hamburg (VII VG 263/61) (Auszug). Both phrases translate to "on the street," although *an* implies direct physical contact, whereas *auf* might be used more figuratively, as in "The kids are running around on the streets."

42. B Arch, B141/90246, folios 20–23, 21.–26.1.1957 Grosse Strafrechtskommission, III. Unterkommission, Niederschrift über die 2. Arbeitstagung der III. Unterkommission.

43. B Arch, B141/90246 Grosse Stafrechtskommission: Umdruck J 78: Vorschläge und Bemerkungen der Sachbearbeiter des BMU; B Arch, B141/90246, 29.4.1958 Grosse Strafrechtskommission: Niederschrift über die 83. Sitzung.

44. Fritz Bauer, Hans Bürger-Prinz, Hans Giese, and Herbert Jäger, "Vorwort," in *Sexualität und Verbrechen: Beiträge zur Strafrechtsreform*, ed. F. Bauer, H. Bürger-Prinz, H. Giese, and H. Jäger (Frankfurt am Main: Fischer Bücherei, 1963), 9.

45. E.g., Hans Harmsen, "Mittel zur Geburtenregelung in der Gesetzgebung des Staates," in Bauer et al., *Sexualität und Verbrechen*; Ernst Buchholz, "Wann ist Kunst unzüchtig?" in Bauer et al., *Sexualität und Verbrechen*.

46. BEH, 16.2.1967 Protokoll der Vorstandssitzung vom 14.2.1967.

47. FZH 18-9/1.1, "Jahresplan für Beate Uhse-Läden 1974"; "Thema eins," *Der Spiegel* 32 (3 August 1970): 32–46, here 34; Hegedo, *Die sexuellen Wünsche der Deutschen*.

48. Ruth Weinkopf, "Beate Uhse betreibt ihr Geschäft mit Liebe," *Mannheimer Morgen*, 29 July 1984, 7.

49. Thomsen interview, 5 March 2003.

50. FZH 18-9/2.3, "Information für die Presse" [February 1965].

51. StA Fl, XIII Pers., "Beate Uhse eröffnete Fachgeschäft in Berlin," *Südschleswigsche Heimat-Zeitung*, 3 August 1966.

52. Uhse, *Lustvoll in den Markt*, 184–85.

53. WSG, loose papers, 7.2.1963 memo.

54. WSG, loose papers, First-Class flyer [1967].

55. "Porno-Markt: Frau Saubermann an der Spitze," *Der Spiegel* 25, no. 45 (1 November 1971): 78–97.

56. LASH 351/1778, 20.6.1967 OStA Flensburg to GStA, Zentralstelle des Landes Baden-Württemberg; FZH 18-9/2.3, "Information für die Presse," [February 1965].

57. Kistenmacher, "Die Geschichte der Beate Uhse."

58. FZH 18-9/2.3, "Das Huhn oder das Ei," 2.–4.5.1973 talk delivered by Beate Rotermund to the Luzern Mail Order Symposium; FZH 18-9/1.1, "Jahresplan 1970."

59. FZH 18-9/2.3, notes for opening of Hamburg shop [1965].

60. "Porno-Markt," 97.

61. WSG, 8.2.1971, Erwin Hagen (Freilassing), Franz Decker Verlag Nachf. to Firma Erwin Hagen.

62. StAL, EL 317 I, Bü 2339, 26.6.1962 Urteil, V. Grosse Strafkammer des LG Stuttgart.

63. WSG, loose papers, 6.2.1963 memo.

64. WSG, loose papers, 9.1.1969 memo.

65. WSG, loose papers, 6.8.1969 memo.

66. WSG, Umsatzmeldungen, 1969.

67. FZH 18-9/2.3, "Ärztebesuch in der Gutenbergstraße," *Absender Beate* 6, no. 4 (December 1967): 3; FZH 18-9/2.1, "Schulische Sex-Aufklärung durch Versandhaus," *Südschleswig-sche Heimat-Zeitung* , 21 June 1968; FZH 18-9/2.3, "Man schreibt über uns—Man informiert sich über uns—Man filmt bei uns," and "Wie wären wir ohne 'unsere Studenten' fertig geworden?" both in *Absender Beate* 8, no. 1 (March 1969).

68. Clippings in FZH 18-9/2.1.

69. Gisela Staupe and Lisa Vieth, "'Man gibt mir zu sehr Recht: Wir liegen nicht mehr gut': Ein Gespräch mit Oswalt Kolle," in Staupe and Vieth, *Die Pille*, 193–204, here 195.

70. Oswalt Kolle, *Deine Frau, das unbekannte Wesen* (Munich: Südwest Verlag, 1967); Oswalt Kolle, *Dein Mann, das unbekannte Wesen* (Munich: Südwest Verlag, 1967); Oswalt Kolle, *Dein Kind, das unbekannte Wesen* (Munich: Südwest Verlag, 1964); Oswalt Kolle, *Das Wunder der Liebe* (Gütersloh: Bertelsmann, 1968).

71. Rolf Thissen, *Sex verklärt: Der deutsche Aufklärungsfilm* (Munich: Wilhelm Heyne Verlag, 1995); Annette Miersch, *Schulmädchen-Report: Der deutsche Sexfilm der 70er Jahre* (Berlin: Bertz Verlag, 2003).

72. Kolle, *Deine Frau*, 67, 117.

73. "Was hält Herr Uhse von Frau Uhse?"; see also "Die Frau, die Sex verkauft," *Freundin*, 30 July 1968, 62–63.

74. Uhse, *Mit Lust und Liebe*, 216.

75. "Beate Uhse: Eine kombinierte Motiv-Image-Studie."

76. FZH 18-9/2.5, Wickert Institute (Tübingen), Untersuchung "Bekanntheitsgrad 'Beate Uhse,'" (1984).

77. FZH 18-9/2.5, untitled document, notes on Emnid Untersuchung [1964].

78. *Söhne der Sonne* (Flensburg: Stephenson Verlag, n.d., ca. 1971).

79. Kristina Schulz, "1968: Lesarten der 'sexuellen Revolution,'" in Frese, Paulus, and Teppe, *Demokratisierung und gesellschaftlicher Aufbruch*, 121–33.

80. *Beate-Uhse Informations-Katalog* [1968], 60.

81. Mein and Wegen: *Die Pop-Kommune*; Torsten Gass-Bolm, *Das Gymnasium 1945–1980* (Göttingen: Wallstein, 2005); Hans Giese and Gunter Schmidt, *Studenten-Sexualität* (Hamburg: Rowohlt, 1968).

82. Sabine von Dirke, *All Power to the Imagination* (Lincoln: University of Nebraska Press, 1997); Schulz, "1968: Lesarten der 'sexuellen Revolution.'"

83. Key texts included Max Horkheimer, ed., *Studien über Autorität und Familie* (Paris: Felix Alcan, 1936); Wilhelm Reich, *Die Funktionen des Orgasmus: Sexualökonomische Grundprobleme der biologischen Energie* (1927; reprint, Cologne: Kiepenheuer und Witsch, 1969);

Theodor Adorno, E. Frenkel-Brunswik, D. J. Levinson, and R. N. Sanford, *The Authoritarian Personality* (New York: Harper and Bros., 1950); Herbert Marcuse, *Eros and Civilization* (Boston: Beacon Press, 1955).

84. Reimut Reiche, *Sexualität und Klassenkampf: Zur Abwehr repressiver Entsublimierung* (Frankfurt: Verlag Neue Kritik, 1968).

85. Detlef Siegfried, "Superkultur: Authentizität und politische Moral in linken Subkulturen der frühen siebziger Jahre," in Knoch, *Bürgersinn mit Weltgefühl*, 251–68.

86. Detlef Siegfried, *Time Is on My Side* (Göttingen: Wallstein, 2006).

87. See also *Konkret*, passim; "Konkret," *Linkeck* 6 [1968], n.p.; also *Linkeck*'s use of similar images, passim.

88. Christoph Kleßmann, "1968—Studentenrevolte oder Kulturrevolution?" in *Revolution in Deutschland? 1789–1989*, ed. Manfred Hettling (Göttingen: Vandenhoeck und Ruprecht, 1991), 90–105.

Chapter 6. The Porn Wave

1. Gesetz zur Reform des Strafrechts vom 25.6.1969, BGBl I S. 645.

2. FZH 18-9/2.3, Informationsmitteilung für alle Teilnehmer der "Auswärtigen Presse," Hamburg, und der Betriebsbesichtigung am 25. März 1968.

3. PA VI/1075/B/31, 28.10.1971 Andreas Zettner, Verleger, an DBT-SA für die Strafrechtsreform.

4. Ludwig Marcuse, *Obszön: Geschichte einer Entrüstung* (Munich: List, 1962).

5. BGH-Urteil vom 23.6.1961, *Goltdammers Archiv für Strafrecht* 1961, 240.

6. Robert Schilling, "Zum 'Kunstvorbehalt' im Gesetz über jugendgefährdende Schriften," *Recht der Jugend* 10, no. 4 (February 1962): 55–56.

7. H. M. Hieronimi, "Erwachsenenzensur via Jugendschutz," *Der neue Vertrieb* 14, no. 327 (5 December 1962): 1028–30; F. A. Herbig Verlages, "Vom Jugendschutz zur allgemeinen Zensur ist in der Praxis nur ein Schritt," *Der neue Vertrieb* 14, no. 324 (20 October 1962): 914; Hermann Montanus, "Eine bedenkliche Stellungnahme," *Der neue Vertrieb* 14, no. 326 (20 November 1962): 996–1001.

8. "*Fanny Hill*: Etwas dazwischen," *Der Spiegel* 18, no. 16 (15 April 1964): 120–23; LASH 351/1778, folios 106ff., here 112, StA bei dem LG (7 Js 1537/64) Anklage: Die Ehefrau Beate Rotermund.

9. LASH 351/1778, folios 59–77, 16.12.1966 Beschluss, OLG Munich.

10. BGH Urteil v. 22.7.1969—1 StR 456/68 (LG München 1), *Neue juristische Wochenschrift* 22, no. 13 (1969): 1818–20. See also affidavits in LASH 351/1779.

11. Ernst-Walter Hanack, "Zur verfassungsmäßigen Bestimmtheit und strafrechtlichen Auslegung des Begriffs 'unzüchtige Schrift' (Par. 184 Abs. 1 Nr. 1 StGB, Art. 103 Abs. 2 GG)," *Juristenzeitung*, no. 2 (1970): 43–48. The criticism of the 1962 draft is Ernst-Walter Hanack, "Die Straftaten gegen die Sittlichkeit im Entwurf 1962," *Zeitschrift für die gesamte Strafrechtswissenschaft* 77 (1965): 398–469.

12. Dieter E. Zimmer, "Agonie eines Paragraphen," *Die Zeit*, 26 December 1969–2 January 1970, 16.

13. Rudolf Stefen, "Pornographie und Jugendschutz," *Die Mitarbeiterin* 22, no. 4 (1971): 105–7.

14. LASH 354/12943, folios 52–57, 15.3.1972, StA (15 Js 1243/71) Anklage.

15. Henryk M. Broder, "Wie an allen Schamhaaren herbeigezogen," *Frankfurter Rundschau*, 16 June 1973, n.p.; Zimmer, "Agonie eines Paragraphen."

16. "Dumpfe Hämmer," *Der Spiegel* 23, no. 51 (15 December 1969): 171; Frank Newman [Sam Abrams pseud.], *Barbara* (Darmstadt: Olympia Press, 1969).

17. LASH 351/1773, 1.4.1971, L.M., "Psychologische Begutachtung des Filmes nr. III mit dem Arbeitstitel 'Der Fernsehnarr' oder 'Der Fussballidiot'"; Jörg Schröder und Barbara Kalendar blog accessed 7 October 2008 (hereafter Schröder/Kalendar blog), http://blogs.taz .de/schroederkalendar/2006/10/.

18. PA VI/1075/B/31, 28.10.1971, A. Zettner, Verleger, an DBT-SA für die Strafrechtsreform.

19. Broder, "Wie an allen Schamhaaren herbeigezogen."

20. "Gold und Silber," *Der Spiegel* 21, no. 16 (10 April 1967): 96; Martin Morlock, "Verhaustierung," *Der Spiegel* 19, no. 11 (10 March 1965): 171.

21. StAL, EL 317 I, Bü 2340, flyer enclosed with advertising packet for Maison-Versand, "Ein Hinweis an unsere Kunden."

22. Fried and Fried, *Liebes- und Eheleben* (1957 ed.), 93, 123; W. Feyerabend, *Liebestechnik* (Stuttgart: Verlag für Sexualliteratur, 1954), 78.

23. LASH 351/1778, I. Grosse Strafkammer des LG Flensburg (Ms 31/51—Ns [IB 124/51]).

24. B Arch, B141/4676, folios 100–109, here 102, Niederschrift über die Tagung der LZBujS in Hamburg am 23. und 24. Oktober 1956; Bekanntmachung betr. das Genehmigungsverfahren nach Par. 20 des GeschlKrG vom 2. Mai 1955, *Bundesanzeiger* 85, 4.5.1955.

25. Schäfer-W.L. Urteil, folio 309. See also Bay OLG, Urteil vom 6.5.1953, Rev. Reg. 1 St 60/53, *Goltdammers Archiv für Strafrecht* (1953), 179f., as quoted in Sigusch, *Exzitation und Orgasmus bei der Frau*, 49.

26. LASH 351/1760, 11.11.1969, LG Flensburg Urteil (7 Ms 90/68—Ns [I B 45/69]).

27. Ibid.; "Finger drauf," *Der Spiegel* 23, no. 47 (17 November 1969): 74; Reinhard Wille, interview with the author, 7 March 2003, 1–3, 50–51.

28. Nancy Friday, *Die sexuellen Phantasien der Frauen*, trans. Antonia Rühl (Bern, Munich: Scherz, 1978); Ulrich Rotermund, interview with the author, 17 July 2008.

29. "Für deutsche Münzen," *Der Spiegel* 23, no. 5 (27 January 1969): 100; Orion, Rechtsabteilung, file "Bio-6," 14.4.1971 VdV Rdschr. 9/71; "Porno-Markt"; "Müdes Lächeln," *Der Spiegel* 23, no. 50 (8 December 1969): 82–101.

30. E.g., Peter Fleming, *Britta: Liebe in Schweden* (Flensburg: Stephenson Verlag, 1971); Bengt Anderberg, ed., *Liebe in Schweden* (Hamburg: Gala Verlag, 1968); *Britta und Marcel*, 8-mm film advertised in *Glücklich—ein Leben lang* (Flensburg: Beate Uhse, n.d., ca. 1971).

31. Rüdiger Boschmann, *Sex + Sex = Gruppensex: Report über Partnertausch in Deutschland* (Flensburg: Stephenson Verlag, 1970).

32. Michael Gantry, *Schwarze Frau, weißer Mann*, trans. Brigitte Konopath (Munich: Moewig, 1969); *Schwarze Haut auf weißen Schenkeln* (Flensburg: Stephenson Verlag, 1972).

33. WSG, Dr. Wunderer, 1968–72, passim.

34. FZH 18-9/1.1, PR-Plan für das Jahr 1973, Jahresplan 1973.

35. For a rare exception, see "Porno-Markt." On commentators' lack of familiarity with the genre, see also Ernst Herhaus and Jörg Schröder, *Siegfried* (Frankfurt am Main: März Verlag, 1972), 220, 226.

36. "Porno-Markt."

37. Dominique Aury, *Die Geschichte der O*, trans. Simone Saint Honore (Darmstadt: Melzer, 1967).

38. Herhaus and Schröder, *Siegfried*; Jörg Schröder and Barbara Kalendar, *Schröder erzählt* (Berlin: self-published, 1990–2000); Schröder/Kalendar blog.

39. Herhaus and Schröder, *Siegfried*, 283–84; Schröder/Kalendar blog, 2006/09/14; 2006/09/20/making-of-pornography-12; 2006/09/14.

40. Schröder/Kalendar blog, 2006/11/28/making-of-pornography-24; 2006/08/24/making-of-pornography-7; 2006/08/28/making-of-pornography-8; 2006/08/16/making-of-pornography-6. Deutsches Literatur-Archiv, Marbach (DLA), März Verlag, 21/4, 27.11.1969 Girodias to Schröder.

41. Jürgen Petschull, "Der Pornokönig," *Der Stern*, no. 17 (13–19 April 1971): 60–66; see also "Nie viel gehabt," *Der Spiegel*, no. 33 (1971): 99–101.

42. Schröder/Kalender blog, 2006/07/22/the-making-of-pornography-1.

43. Schröder/Kalendar blog, 2007/08/17/vom-mythos-leben-2.

44. "Na, Leute? Pornofilme gucken," *Pardon* 10, no. 1 (January 1971): n.p.

45. Amendt, *Sex-Front*; "Sexokratie: Ein Subkurs in Gesellschaftskunde," [1970–71]; Schröder/Kalendar blog, 2006/09/20/making-of-pornography-12; 2007/08/07/sexfront-1.

46. Schröder/Kalendar blog, 2006/07/22/the-making-of-pornography-1; see also WSG, Dr. Wunderer, 1968–72, 24.4.1970, Spethmann to Wunderer.

47. "Happy Coitus to You," *Linkeck* 6 (1968), n.p.

48. Herhaus and Schröder, *Siegfried*, 281.

49. E.g., Ole Ege, director, *Pornografi* (Gemini Film, 1971); Ole Ege, director, *Bordellet* (Gemini Film, 1972); Ole Ege, director, *Bodil Joensen—en sommerdag juli* (Gemini Film, 1970). See also HHStA 461/32188-2.

50. DLA, März Verlag, 24/5, "Sex als Markenartikel: Marketing Überlegungen zum 'Pornofilm'" [ca. 1970].

51. Schröder/Kalendar blog, 2006/08/28.

52. Ibid.

53. Ibid.

54. HHStA 461/32084, order form for "Die Schüler," Olympia Film; "Na, Leute? Pornofilme gucken."

55. Petschull, "Der Pornokönig."

56. Henryk M. Broder and Rolf-Ulrich Kaiser, "Wie man eine goldene Kuh melkt und sagt, es ginge um Sozialismus," *Buchmarkt* 4 (1969): 75–76.

57. FZH 18-9/2.5, Aktennotiz 9.3.1964 betr.: Besprechung mit dem Gutachter-Gremium für Versandhandels-Publikationen, Hannover.

58. WSG, Hans-Heinrich Jörgensen, 4.2.1964 Freyja Verlag to Hans-Heinrich Jörgensen.

59. Sha Kokken, *Sexuelle Technik in Wort und Bild*, trans. Abraham Mitteldorf (Flensburg: Stephenson Verlag, 1966), 90–91.

60. *Beate Uhse Informations-Katalog* [1968], 5.

61. Holger Benson, *Helga und Bernd zeigen 100 Liebespositionen* (Flensburg: Stephenson Verlag, 1969); Ulrich Rotermund interview.

62. LASH 351/1780, 6.3.1970, BPrSt Entscheidung Nr. 2222; LASH 351/1780, 11.6.1969, GStA S-H memo.

63. Istvan Schwenda and Thomas Leuchner, *Einmaleins für Zwei: 108 Liebesvariationen* (Darmstadt: Porta Verlag, 1969).

64. *Die besten Jahre unseres Lebens*, 143–44.

65. E.g., FZH 18-9/2.8, "Magic Movies" marketed by Beate Uhse [early 1970s].

66. "Sex per Post," *DM* (1969): 1; see also LASH 351/1779, 20.12.1968, GStA S-H memo; Günther Hunold, *Sexual-Atlas für Erwachsene* (Flensburg: Stephenson Verlag, 1972);

Rüdiger Boschmann, *Sex-Spiel, Hingabe und Ekstase* (Flensburg: Stephenson Verlag, 1968); Beate Uhse, *Sex in der Partnerschaft* (Flensburg: Stephenson Verlag, 1974).

67. FZH 18-9/1.3 (3), Helmut Kentler, 5.1.1973, gutachtliche Stellungnahme; LASH 351/1781, 27.5.1971, StA Duisburg Verfügung; LASH 351/1780, 6.3.1970, BPrSt Entscheidung 2222.

68. *Beate Uhse Katalog* [1973], 65.

69. *Junger Apoll* (Flensburg: Stephenson Verlag, n.d.); *Söhne der Sonne.*

70. LASH 351/1779, 30.8.1968, GStA Munich to GStA Schleswig.

71. Notice of catalog "Spezial-Angebot H1," in *Glücklich—ein Leben lang*, 28; FZH 18-9/1.1, Jahresplan 1970; FZH 18-9/1.1, Jahresplan 1971.

72. DLA, März Verlag, 21/5, 3.2.1969 Schröder to Girodias; DLA, März Verlag, 21/4, 27.1.1970 Schröder to Girodias.

73. Amendt, *Sex-Front.*

74. "Die glatte Diebin: Oder, Konsumzwang" [1970–71]; DLA, März Verlag, Diverses, 27/2, notes for "Die glatte Diebin."

75. "Die Schüler," [1970–71]; HHStA 461/32084, folios 25–40, 5.9.1970 Hans Peter Kochenrath Gutachten betr. "Die Schüler"; Wolfgang Fritz Haug, "Zur Strategie der Triebunterdrückung und Triebmodellierung in Gymnasien," in *Warenästhetik, Sexualität und Herrschaft: Gesammelte Aufsätze*, ed. Wolfgang Fritz Haug (Frankfurt am Main: Fischer, 1972).

76. "Colt und Köcher: Oder, Die Ausbeutung," Super-Stag Production [1970–71]; "Die Amazonen: Für Valerie Solanas und die S.C.U.M." [1970–71]. On these conventions, see Williams, *Hard Core.*

77. Elizabeth Heineman, "Jörg Schröder: Linkes Verlagswesen und Pornografie," in *Das alternative Milieu: Antibürgerlicher Lebensstil und linke Politik in der Bundesrepublik Deutschland und Europa 1968-1983*, ed. Detlef Siegfried and Sven Reichelt (Göttingen: Wallstein Verlag, 2010).

78. *Beate Uhse Informations-Katalog* [1968].

79. Hunold, *Sexual-Atlas für Erwachsene.*

80. *Glücklich—ein Leben lang*; Ulrich Rotermund interview; Uhse, *Lustvoll in den Markt*, 96; Günter Dahl, "Ach, wärst Du doch in Düsseldorf geblieben," *Der Stern*, no. 52 (1974): 52–54; Horst Zimmermann, "Sexreisen zum Sozialtarif," *Stuttgarter Nachrichten*, 1 October 1974.

81. FZH 18-9/2.8, Video 112 ARD Oswalt Kolle zum 70. Geburtstag 2.10.1998.

82. Miersch, *Schulmädchen-Report*, esp. 176–81, as well as the filmography.

83. FZH 18-9/2.3, flyer for Ludwigshafen shop (1968).

84. "Supermarket for Eros," *Time*, 2 May 1969, 59.

85. "Beate Uhse: Eine kombinierte Motiv-Image-Studie."

86. Ulf Lasa, "An der Sex-Front," *Konkret*, 1 March 1968.

87. Beer, "Die Sexualisierung der Öffentlichkeit und der junge Mensch."

88. See also Christina von Hodenberg, "Konkurrierende Konzepte von 'Öffentlichkeit' in der Orientierungskrise der 60er Jahre," in Frese, Paulus, and Teppe, *Demokratisierung und gesellschaftlicher Aufbruch*, 205–26.

89. The 1962 draft and the alternative draft appear in Friedrich-Christian Schroeder, ed., *Reform des Sexualstrafrechts* (Berlin and New York: De Gruyter, 1971).

90. Jeffrey Weeks, *Sex, Politics, and Society* (New York: Longman, 1981), 239–44.

91. "Begründung zu dem Regierungsentwurf eines 4. StRG," reprinted in Schroeder, *Reform des Sexualstrafrechts*, 83–149, here 38–39.

92. PA VI/1075/A/2, lfd. nr. 73, 1.9.1971 Stellungnahmen der in der öffentlichen Anhörung zum Entwurf eines 4. StrRG angehörten Sachverständigen zum Thema: Pornographie, Sonderausschuß für die Strafrechtsreform Ausschußdrucksache VI/36 [hereafter Stellungnahmen]; "31 Sachverständige äußern ihre Ansicht: Freigabe der Pornographie?" *Das Parlament* 20, no. 49 (5 December 1970): 1-3.

93. Sigusch, *Geschichte der Sexualwissenschaft.*

94. E.g., H. Schmidt, *Das lesende Mädchen* (Vienna, Munich: Bundesverlag, 1959).

95. See also the discussion of this problem in U.S. Commission on Obscenity and Pornography, *Report.*

96. Stellungnahmen, 78, 12-14. Sigusch and his collaborators published results of their research in Gunter Schmidt, Volkmar Sigusch, and Ulrich Meyberg, "Psychosexual Stimulation in Men: Emotional Reactions, Changes of Sex Behavior, and Measures of Conservative Attitudes," *Journal of Sex Research* 5 (1969): 199-217; Gunter Schmidt and Volkmar Sigusch, "Sex Differences in Response to Psychosexual Stimlation by Films and Slides," *Journal of Sex Research* 6 (1970): 268-83; Volkmar Sigusch, Gunter Schmidt, Antje Reinfeld, and Ingeborg Wiedemann-Sutor, "Psychosexual Stimulation: Sex Differences," *Journal of Sex Research* 6 (1970): 10-24; Gunter Schmidt, Volkmar Sigusch, and Sigrid Schäfer, "Responses to Reading Erotic Stories: Male-Female Differences," *Archives of Sexual Behavior* 2 (1973): 181-99.

97. Stellungnahmen, 3, 43, 44.

98. Ibid., 37.

99. Ibid., 78.

100. Ibid., 14.

101. Ibid., 30, 35, 77.

102. Walter Becker, "Strafbarkeit der Pornographie?" *Film und Recht* 2 (1970): 41-51; Gustav Ermecke, "Warum Pornographie-Verbot?" *Concepte* 2 (1971): 17-19.

103. Stellungnahmen, 21, 52, 63.

104. Ibid., 75.

105. "Freigabe der Pornographie?" 3. See also Walter Becker, "Zum Problem der Pornographie-Freigabe," *Monatsschrift für Deutsches Recht* 24, no. 10 (1970): 798-804.

106. Stellungnahmen, 50.

107. Ibid., 9.

108. Ibid., 51, 56, 57, 61, 74, 75, 85.

109. Siegfried Ernst, "Mobilmachung der Bürger gegen Pornographie," *Deutsche Tagespost*, 2-3 October 1970, 11.

110. PA VII/79/B passim.

111. Ernst, "Mobilmachung der Bürger gegen Pornographie," 11; Lisolette Weber, "Millionenfaches Veto zum Streit um Par. 184 StGB," *Eltern Forum* (March-April 1972): 3-4; see also PA VI/1075/B/8, 25.1.1971 Bundesärztekammer/Deutscher Ärztetag Stellungnahme.

112. Several of these documents are reprinted in Schroeder, *Reform des Sexualstrafrechts.*

113. PA VI/1075/A/4/3, 8.2.1971 Martin Hirsch an alle Mitglieder der SPD-Fraktion im DBT.

114. Sog. "Präzisierung des Bundesministeriums der Justiz" zum Pornographieproblem (Presseerklärung vom 25. Februar 1971); Schroeder, *Reform des Sexualstrafrechts*, 220-25.

115. BEH, 7.4.1970 Protokoll der Vorstandssitzung.

116. PA VI/1075/B/16, 26.3.1971 Fackelverlag to H. M. Hieronimi.

117. BEH, 20.10.1971 Protokoll der 20. Generalversammlung; PA VI/1075/B/31, 28.10.1971 Andreas Zettner, Verleger, an den DBT-SA für die Strafrechtsreform.

118. The schism was short-lived. PA VII/79/B/6/339, 21.8.1972 Verlag Andreas Zettner; BEH, 2.5.1974 Protokoll der gemeinsamen Vorstandssitzung des VdV und des Verbandes Erotik in Presse und Buch e.V.

119. BEH, 20.10.1971 Protokoll der 20. Generalversammlung.

120. FZH 18-9/1.1, Jahresplan 1970.

121. "Porno-Markt."

122. FZH 18-9/1.1, 28.10.1971 Aktennotiz, Jahresplan 1972; FZH 18-9/1.1, 29.10.1971 Besprechungszusammenfassung, Jahresplan 1972; FZH 18-9/1.1, 10.11.1972 Besprechungszusammenfassung, Jahresplan 1973.

123. BEH, 15.4.1971 Protokoll der Vorstandssitzung; PA VII/79/A/11, 2.3.1973 Holzmüller, VdV an Herrn Vorsitzenden des Strafrechts-SA Dr. Müller-Emmert; PA VII/79/B/I, 15.11.1972 Prof. Dr. jur. Walter Sax Gutachten über die rechtliche Zulässigkeit und Notwendigkeit einer zeitgemäßen Anwendung von Par. 184 Abs. 1 Nr. 1, 1a, 2 StGB; PA VI/1075/B/16, 6.4.1971 Hieronimi, Verleger-Schutzgemeinschaft, an das BMJ, Herrn Staatssekretär Müller-Emmert.

124. Claus Weiss, "Ist Pornographie staatsgefährdend?" *Gewerkschaftliche Monatshefte* 5 (1971): 274–83; PA VI/1075/A/4/3, Werner Birkenmaier, "Pornographisches," *Stuttgarter Zeitung*, 5 March 1971.

125. PA VI/1075/A/6/32, BT-SA-57. Sitzung, Edgar Mertner and Herbert Mainusch, "Was ist Pornographie?" *Die Zeit*, 23 April 1971.

126. Stellungnahmen, 47.

127. PA VI/1075/A/3/99, Schriftlicher Bericht des SA für die Strafrechtsreform über den von der B Reg eingebrachten Entwurf eines 4.StrRG (DBT Drucksache VI/3521); PA VI/1075/A/2/70, 2.7.1971, DBT 6. Wahlperiode, 48. Sitzung des Sonderausschusses für die Strafrechtsreform.

128. Viertes Gesetz zur Reform des Strafrechts (4. StrRG) vom 23 November 1973 (BGBl I: 1725–35).

129. Gabriele Metzler, "Staatsversagen und Unregierbarkeit in den siebziger Jahren?" in *Das Ende der Zuversicht? Die siebziger Jahre als Geschichte*, ed. Konrad H. Jarausch (Göttingen: Vandenhoeck und Ruprecht, 2008), 243–60.

Chapter 7. Postlude: The Beate Uhse Myth

1. "Die Geschichte der Beate Uhse"; FZH 18-9/2.3, "Beate Uhse Story" (typescript), 1980; FZH 18-9/2.3, "Die Firma Beate Uhse" (typescript), 1982; "Frau Beate Uhse: Konzern-Chefin mit Lust und Liebe," *Bild am Sonntag*, 24 October 1982: 46; Uhse, *Mit Lust und Liebe*, 100; FZH 18-9/2.8, Nachcafe Neue Treue: Neue Zärtlichkeit SDR/SWF 3 8.6.87.

2. On male doctors legitimizing female voices, see also Lutz Sauerteig, "Die Herstellung des sexuellen und erotischen Körpers in der *Bravo*," *Medizinhistorisches Journal* 42 (2007).

3. Orion, Geschäftsführer, file "Gottwald," 24.5.1976 Psychologisches Beratungsgespräch mit Herrn E. von der Gesellschaft für rationale Psychologie, München.

4. FZH 18-9/2.9, line graph of sales.

5. FZH 18-9/1.1, Jahresplan 1971, Jahresplan 1970.

6. FZH 18-9/1.1, Planung, Beate Uhse-Läden 1972, p. 2, Jahresplan 1972; FZH 18-9/1.1, Verlagsziele 1973, Jahresplan 1973; FZH 18-9/1.1, Brutto-Umsatzplan 1974, Jahresplan 1974; FZH 18-9/1.1, Jahresplan für die Beate Uhse-Läden, Blue Movie Studiokinos und Peggy Mae 1976, Jahresplan 1976.

7. Uhse, *Mit Lust und Liebe*, 228–30.

8. Klaus Uhse was born in 1943 and Ulrich Rotermund in 1949. Rotermund's second husband, Ewe Rotermund, brought Dirk, born 1944, into the marriage. His daughter from his first marriage, six years older than Dirk, did not become part of Beate Uhse. Klaus died of cancer in 1984. Dirk runs Orion—Germany's second-largest erotica firm—today. Ulrich serves as president of Beate Uhse's supervisory board (*Aufsichtsrat*).

9. Uhse, *Mit Lust und Liebe*, 243–45.

10. StA Fl, XIII. Dr. 25, Pressemappe Orion, "Flensburger Versand mit neuem Namen und neuer Collection: Orion bietet Erotik von Kopf bis Fuß" [ca. 1984].

11. "Stramme Pflicht," *Der Spiegel*, 4 June 1979.

12. Ulrich Rotermund interview.

13. "Flensburger Versand mit neuem Namen und neuer Collection"; StA Fl, XIII. Dr. 25, "Liebe Leserin, Lieber Leser!" *Für mehr Spaß zu Zweit*, Orion catalog [ca. 1984].

14. FZH 18-9/2.3, Firmengeschichte 1976–81, 29.1.1979 "Dr. Muellers landet bei der Sex-Versenderin Nr. 1," *Düsseldorfer Handelsblatt*.

15. Claudia Pai, "Als Novität ein Gummi-Mann," *Die Zeit*, 15 March 1985; see also Hamburgisches Welt-Wirtschafts-Archiv (HWWA), Mathes Rehder, "Amors clevere Kauffrau," *Financial Times* [German], 10 August 1996; HWWA, Barbara Königs, "Mit Erotik mache ich Geschäft, aber keine Kreuzzug," *Frankfurter Allgemeine Zeitung*, 7 October 1991; FZH 18-9/2.8, 7.11.1989 RTL Stippvisite Beate Uhse.

16. Hobrecht, *Beate Uhse*, 165.

17. Thomsen interview, 5 March 2003.

18. Kristina Schulz, *Der lange Atem der Provokation: Die Frauenbewegung in der Bundesrepublik und in Frankreich 1968–1976* (Frankfurt and New York: Campus Verlag, 2002).

19. *Emma*, no. 8 (August 1978) and no. 9 (September 1978).

20. See also Manfred Engelschall, "Stellungnahme aus richterlicher Sicht zum Gesetzentwurf von *Emma*," in *Frauen und Männer und Pornographie*, ed. Eva Dane and Renate Schmidt (Frankfurt am Main: Fischer, 1990).

21. Articles from *Emma*'s *Der Stern* and PorNO campaigns are collected in Schwarzer, *PorNO*.

22. This was not the only feminist draft law on porn; see also Susanne Baer and Vera Slupik, "Entwurf eines Gesetzes gegen Pornographie," *Kritische Justiz* 2 (1988): 171ff.

23. See the essays collected in Schwarzer, *PorNO*.

24. Ann Barr Snitow, Christine Stansell, and Sharon Thompson, eds., *Powers of Desire: The Politics of Sexuality* (New York: Monthly Review Press, 1983).

25. Irene Stoehr, "Porno Kampagne und Frauenbewegung," *Zeitschrift für Sexualforschung* 2, no. 3 (1989): 199–206; Dane and Schmidt, *Frauen und Männer und Pornographie*.

26. E.g., Hellmuth Karasek, "Ist die sexuelle Freiheit am Ende?" *Der Spiegel* 42, no. 1 (4 January 1988): 122–31.

27. In the German, "comrades" is explicitly masculine. Filter, "Beate Uhse: Bomber Pilotin und Porno Produzentin."

28. E.g., Christina Thürmer-Rohr, "Der Chor der Opfer ist verstummt," *Beiträge zur feministischen Theorie und Praxis* 11 (1984); Lerke Gravenhorst and Carmen Tatschmurat, eds., *TöchterFragen: NS-Frauen-Geschichte* (Freiberg i. Br.: Kore, 1990); Karin Windaus-Walser, "Gnade der weiblichen Geburt? Zum Umgang der Frauenforschung mit Nationalsozialismus und Antisemitismus," *Feministische Studien* 6 (1988).

29. Trude Unruh, ed., *Trümmerfrauen: Biografien einer betrogenen Generation* (Essen: Klartext, 1987); Gerda Szepansky, *"Blitzmädel" "Heldenmutter" "Kriegerwitwe": Frauenleben im*

zweiten Weltkrieg (Frankfurt am Main: Fischer, 1986); Sybille Meyer and Eva Schulze, *Wie wir das alles geschafft haben: Alleinstehende Frauen berichten über ihr Leben nach 1945* (Munich: Beck, 1984); Sibylle Meyer and Eva Schulze, *Von Liebe sprach damals keiner: Familienalltag in der Nachkriegszeit* (Munich: Beck, 1985).

30. Beate Uhse, "Bedarf, Bedürfnis, Befriedigung," in Dane and Schmidt, *Frauen und Männer und Pornographie*, 94–102; Alice Schwarzer, "Auch Experten wollen ein Gesetz: Was beim Anti-Porno-Hearing in Bonn herauskam," in Schwarzer, *PorNO: Opfer und Täter, Gegenwehr und Backlash, Verantwortung und Gesetz*, 53–58; FZH 18-9/2.5, 13.–14.9.1988 Öffentliche Anhörung der SPD-Bundestagsfraktion zur Problematik der Pornographie; Uhse, *Mit Lust und Liebe*, 253. Typically, the reliance on Beate Uhse as representative of the industry resulted in an overly "clean" image. Eva Dane, "Über Sexualität und Gewalt, Macht und Ignoranz und die Angemessenheit von Gesetzen im Verhältnis der Geschlechter," in Dane and Schmidt, *Frauen und Männer und Pornographie*, 268–85, esp. 271; Biggy Mondi, "(K)Ein Job wie jeder Andere: Bericht aus der Praxis einer Pornodarstellerin," in Dane and Schmidt, *Frauen und Männer und Pornographie*, 103–9.

31. On contemporary scholars' differing interpretation of pornographic film, see Werner Faulstich, *Die Kultur der Pornographie: Kleine Einführung in Geschichte, Medien, Ästhetik, Markt und Bedeutung* (Bardowick: Wissenschaftler Verlag, 1994), 209–11; Rüdiger Lautmann, "Ein anderes Verhältnis zur Sexualität," in Dane and Schmidt, *Frauen und Männer und Pornographie*, 263–67.

32. FZH 18-9/2.8, "Das sind wir," Wohnzimmergespräch, N3 1984; FZH 18-9/2.8, "Norddeutsche Profile" N3 15.2.1989; FZH 18-9/2.8, "Stippvisite Beate Uhse" 7.11.1989 RTL.

33. FZH 18-9/2.5, Gesellschaft für rationale Psychologie, *Erotikmarkt-Studie '86*; FZH 18-9/2.8, Nachtcafe Neue Treue: Neue Zärtlichkeit SDR/SWF 3 8.6.87; FZH 18-9/2.8, "Norddeutsche Profile" N3 15.2.89; Henner Ertel, *Erotika und Pornographie* (Munich: Psychologie Verlags-Union, 1990); FZH 18-9/2.3, Pressemitteilung: Erotik-Studie 1986 von Beate Uhse, attached post-it note.

34. FZH 18-9/2.8, Nachtcafe Neue Treue: Neue Zärtlichkeit SDR/SWF 3 8.6.87; FZH 18-9/2.8, "Norddeutsche Profile" 15.2.1989 (N3); FZH 18-9/2.8, "Stippvisite Beate Uhse" 7.11.1989 RTL; "Wir leben heute in einer erotischen Luxusgesellschaft," *Wochenende*, 25 January 1996, 12–13.

35. Claudia Gehrke, "Anregungen zu einer Politik erotischer Kultur von Frauen," in Dane and Schmidt, *Frauen und Männer und Pornographie*, 237–49.

36. Ertel, *Erotika und Pornographie*.

37. *Beate Uhse Journal*, product catalog, 1986.

38. FZH 18-9/2.3, 1.10.1986 Rotermund to Hannes Baiko. Approximately 25 percent of customers of Klaus and Dirk's firm were women. StA Fl, XIII. Dr. 25, Pressemappe Orion, "Wer sind die ORION-Kunden?" [ca. 1984].

39. FZH 18-9/2.3, Auswertung vom 2.238 Fragebögen des Versandhauses Beate Uhse von Januar 1987; FZH 18-9/2.3, 20.2.1987 Hannes Baiko to Rotermund.

40. FZH 18-9/2.3, John David Prescott, Beate Uhse Company Report, May–July 1996; FZH 18-9/2.5, "Erfolg ist wiederholbar," Beate Uhse Referat, GDW Konferenz Hamburg September 1993.

41. "Beate Uhse," *Stag* (September 1981): 33–36; Mark Stephens, "Sex Biz Wizard," *Fort Myers News-Press*, 31 October 1981, 1D–2D; FZH 18-9/2.8, Douglas Chirnside Productions, *Sex and Shopping*, episode 4, "The Queen Mother of Porn," broadcast 9.9.98; Uhse, *Mit Lust und Liebe*, 239; Uhse, *Lustvoll in den Markt*, 153.

42. FZH 18-9/2.3, 19.1.1998 Hans-Dieter Thomsen, "Beate Uhse Image."

43. Uhse, *Mit Lust und Liebe*; a portion of the autobiography was published as a twelve-part series in the tabloid *Berliner Zeitung*.

44. Ibid., 271.

45. Brigitte Young, *Triumph of the Fatherland: German Unification and the Marginalization of Women* (Ann Arbor: University of Michigan Press, 1999).

46. Gabriele Goettle, *Deutsche Bräuche: Ermittlungen in Ost und West* (Frankfurt am Main: Fischer, 1996), 112–19.

47. Dorothee Wierling, "Vereinigungen: Ostdeutsche Briefe an Beate Uhse," *BIOS* 20 (2007).

48. Ina Merkel, "Sex and Gender in the Divided Germany," in *Divided Past: Rewriting Postwar German History*, ed. Christoph Kleßmann (New York: Berg, 2001), 91–104.

49. Rudolf Augstein, ed., *Historikerstreit: Die Dokumentation der Kontroverse um die Einzigartigkeit der nationalsozialistischen Judenvernichtung* (Munich: Piper, 1987).

50. Klaus Naumann, *Der Krieg als Text: Das Jahr 1945 im kulturellen Gedächtnis der Presse* (Hamburg: Hamburger Edition, 1998); Robert G. Moeller, "Germans as Victims?" *History and Memory* 17, no. 1/2 (2005): 147–94.

51. Orion, Geschäftsführer, file "Gottwald," Prof. Dr. Leo Baumann, "Uhse-Versand im Wandel: Teil B. Zu Konzept und Massnahmen-Programm. Erotikversand und öffentliche Meinung," November 1983.

52. Hobrecht, *Beate Uhse*, 142.

53. "Find mich, klick mich, mach mich reich," *Der Stern* (3 February 2000): 64; Uhse, *Lustvoll in den Markt*, 156–66; Cornelia Bolesch, "Beate Uhse: Porno-Händlerin mit Drang zur Börse," *Süddeutsche Zeitung*, 21 May 1999, n.p.

54. FZH 18-9/2.8, "Ein Leben für die Liebe: Die Beate Uhse Story," ca. 2000.

55. FZH 18-9/2.3, 8.10.1997 Jens Jensen "Beate-Uhse-Image"; see also Hobrecht, *Beate Uhse*, 181.

56. FZH 18-9/2.3, 19.1.1998 Hans-Dieter Thomsen; FZH 18-9/2.3, 13.10.1997 Rotermund, "Erhalt des Beate-Uhse-Images in der Zukunft."

57. "Vorher gab es bloss Beischlaf, mit Beate Uhse kam der Sex," *Berliner Zeitung*, 19 July 2001, 54.

58. Till Bastian, *Niemandszeit: Deutsche Portraits zwischen Kriegsende und Neubeginn* (Munich: C. H. Beck, 1999); Delille and Grohn, "Hauptmann der Aufklärung"; Dagmar Deckstein, "Die Aufklärerin: Beate Uhse," in *Jahrhundertfrauen: Ikonen—Idole—Mythen*, ed. Cathrin Kahlweit (Munich: C. H. Beck, 1999).

59. Siedentopf, "Die Lust-Macherin"; Hans Otto Eglau, *Die Kasse muss stimmen: So hatten sie Erfolg im Handel* (Dusseldorf: Econ, 1972).

60. Laurence A. Rickels, *Nazi Psychoanalysis*, 3 vols. (Minneapolis: University of Minnesota Press, 2002), 3:164.

61. With the Beate Uhse Web site undergoing frequent redesign, this has been more true during some periods than others, but the tendency has been toward shunting company history into increasingly obscure spots on the Web site. At this writing (15 June 2010), there is no mention of the firm's history or founder on the site designed for shoppers (http://www.beate-uhse.com or http://www.beate-uhse.de), only on the site designed for the media and business interests (http://www.beate-uhse.ag).

Index